The Foodways of Hawai'i

Offering diverse perspectives on Hawai'i's food system, this book addresses themes of place and identity across time. From early Western contact to the present day, the way in which people in Hawai'i grow, import, and consume their food has shifted in response to the pressures of colonialism, migration, new technologies, and globalization. Because of Hawai'i's history of agricultural abundance, its geographic isolation in the Pacific Ocean, and its heavy reliance on imported foods today, it offers a rich case study for understanding how food systems develop in-place. In so doing, the contributors implicitly and explicitly complicate the narrative of the "local," which has until recently dominated much of the existing scholarship on Hawai'i's foodways. With topics spanning GMO activism, agricultural land use trends, customary access and fishing rights, poi production, and the dairy industry, this volume reveals how "local food" is emplaced through dynamic and complex articulations of history, politics, and economic change.

This book was originally published as a special issue of *Food, Culture & Society*.

Hiʻilei Julia Hobart is a Postdoctoral Fellow in Native American and Indigenous Studies at Northwestern University, USA. Her work looks at the points of intersection between foodscapes and indigeneity. She is especially interested in the history of commodity ice and refrigeration in the Pacific, the development of new technology in the nineteenth century, the affective registers of comfort and home-making, and indigenous embodiment and environmental knowledge.

The Foodways of Hawai'i
Past and Present

Edited by
Hi'ilei Julia Hobart

LONDON AND NEW YORK

First published 2018
by Routledge
2 Park Square, Milton Park, Abingdon, Oxon, OX14 4RN, UK

and by Routledge
711 Third Avenue, New York, NY 10017, USA

Routledge is an imprint of the Taylor & Francis Group, an informa business

© 2018 Association for the Study of Food and Society

All rights reserved. No part of this book may be reprinted or reproduced or utilised in any form or by any electronic, mechanical, or other means, now known or hereafter invented, including photocopying and recording, or in any information storage or retrieval system, without permission in writing from the publishers.

Trademark notice: Product or corporate names may be trademarks or registered trademarks, and are used only for identification and explanation without intent to infringe.

British Library Cataloguing in Publication Data
A catalogue record for this book is available from the British Library

ISBN 13: 978-1-138-57411-3

Typeset in FeniceStd
by RefineCatch Limited, Bungay, Suffolk

Publisher's Note
The publisher accepts responsibility for any inconsistencies that may have arisen during the conversion of this book from journal articles to book chapters, namely the possible inclusion of journal terminology.

Disclaimer
Every effort has been made to contact copyright holders for their permission to reprint material in this book. The publishers would be grateful to hear from any copyright holder who is not here acknowledged and will undertake to rectify any errors or omissions in future editions of this book.

Contents

Citation Information vii
Notes on Contributors ix

Introduction—'Local': Contextualizing Hawai'i's Foodways 1
Hi'ilei Julia Hobart

1. Homegrown Cuisines or Naturalized Cuisines? The History of Food in Hawaii and Hawaii's Place in Food History 11
Rachel Laudan

2. Snowy Mountaineers and Soda Waters: Honolulu and Its Age of Ice Importation 35
Hi'ilei Julia Hobart

3. Dairy's Decline and the Politics of "Local" Milk in Hawai'i 59
Clare Gupta

4. Customary Access: Sustaining Local Control of Fishing and Food on Kaua'i's North Shore 91
Mehana Blaich Vaughan and Adam L. Ayers

5. Cultural Traditions and Food: Kānaka Maoli and the Production of Poi in the He'e'ia Wetland 113
Hōkūlani K. Aikau and Donna Ann Kameha'ikū Camvel

6. Farmer Typology in South Kona, Hawai'i: Who's Farming, How, and Why? 137
Noa Kekuewa Lincoln and Nicole Ardoin

7. From the Sugar Oligarchy to the Agrochemical Oligopoly: Situating Monsanto and Gang's Occupation of Hawai'i 161
Andrea Brower

Index 189

Citation Information

The chapters in this book were originally published in *Food, Culture & Society*, volume 19, issue 3 (September 2016). When citing this material, please use the original page numbering for each article, as follows:

Introduction
'Local': Contextualizing Hawai'i's Foodways
Hi'ilei Julia Hobart
Food, Culture & Society, volume 19, issue 3 (September 2016), pp. 427–436

Chapter 1
Homegrown Cuisines or Naturalized Cuisines? The History of Food in Hawaii and Hawaii's Place in Food History
Rachel Laudan
Food, Culture & Society, volume 19, issue 3 (September 2016), pp. 437–460

Chapter 2
Snowy Mountaineers and Soda Waters: Honolulu and Its Age of Ice Importation
Hi'ilei Julia Hobart
Food, Culture & Society, volume 19, issue 3 (September 2016), pp. 461–484

Chapter 3
Dairy's Decline and the Politics of "Local" Milk in Hawai'i
Clare Gupta
Food, Culture & Society, volume 19, issue 3 (September 2016), pp. 485–516

CITATION INFORMATION

Chapter 4
Customary Access: Sustaining Local Control of Fishing and Food on Kaua'i's North Shore
Mehana Blaich Vaughan and Adam L. Ayers
Food, Culture & Society, volume 19, issue 3 (September 2016), pp. 517–538

Chapter 5
Cultural Traditions and Food: Kānaka Maoli and the Production of Poi in the He'e'ia Wetland
Hōkūlani K. Aikau and Donna Ann Kameha'ikū Camvel
Food, Culture & Society, volume 19, issue 3 (September 2016), pp. 539–562

Chapter 6
Farmer Typology in South Kona, Hawai'i: Who's Farming, How, and Why?
Noa Kekuewa Lincoln and Nicole Ardoin
Food, Culture & Society, volume 19, issue 3 (September 2016), pp. 563–586

Chapter 7
From the Sugar Oligarchy to the Agrochemical Oligopoly: Situating Monsanto and Gang's Occupation of Hawai'i
Andrea Brower
Food, Culture & Society, volume 19, issue 3 (September 2016), pp. 587–614

For any permission-related enquiries please visit:
http://www.tandfonline.com/page/help/permissions

Notes on Contributors

Hōkūlani K. Aikau is an Associate Professor of Native Hawaiian and Indigenous Politics in the Department of Political Science at the University of Hawaiʻi at Mānoa. She currently serves as Director of the General Education Office at UHM. She is the author of *A Chosen People, a Promised Land: Mormonism and Race in Hawaiʻi* (2012) and is currently working on an ethnography of the wetland restoration project described in this volume.

Nicole Ardoin is an Assistant Professor with a joint appointment in the Graduate School of Education and the Woods Institute for the Environment at Stanford University, USA. Professor Ardoin's research focuses on environmental behavior as influenced by environmental learning and motivated by place-based connections.

Adam L. Ayers is a PhD candidate in the Department of Urban and Regional Planning at the University of Hawaiʻi at Mānoa. He is also a Social Scientist for the Joint Institute of Marine and Atmospheric Research (JIMAR) in the Socioeconomics Program at the NOAA Pacific Islands Fisheries Science Center.

Andrea Brower is an activist from Hawaiʻi and a PhD candidate at the University of Auckland, Aotearoa/New Zealand.

Donna Ann Kamehaʻikū Camvel is working on a PhD in the Department of Political Science with a specialization in Indigenous politics at the University of Hawaiʻi at Mānoa.

Clare Gupta is an Assistant Cooperative Extension specialist in the Department of Human Ecology at UC Davis, USA. She specializes in community food systems.

Hiʻilei Julia Hobart is a Postdoctoral Fellow in Native American and Indigenous Studies at Northwestern University, USA. Her work looks at the points of intersection between foodscapes and indigeneity. She is especially interested in the history of commodity ice and refrigeration in the Pacific, the development of new technology in the

NOTES ON CONTRIBUTORS

nineteenth century, the affective registers of comfort and home-making, and indigenous embodiment and environmental knowledge.

Rachel Laudan is a Senior Research Fellow in the Institute for Historical Studies at the University of Texas at Austin, USA. She is the author of many articles on food history and two prize-winning books.

Noa Kekuewa Lincoln is an Assistant Professor in Tropical Plant and Soil Sciences at the University of Hawai'i at Mānoa, with a specialty in Indigenous Crops and Cropping Systems. His main research is on biogeochemical cycles of traditional farming methods.

Mehana Blaich Vaughan is an Assistant Professor in the Department of Natural Resource and Environmental Management at the University of Hawai'i at Mānoa. She holds a joint appointment with Hui 'Āina Momona, and The UH Seagrant College Program, working to enhance the capacity of rural Hawai'i communities to care for and govern natural resources.

'Local': Contextualizing Hawai'i's Foodways

Hi'ilei Julia Hobart

Abstract
Within contemporary concerns about the overall health of the US food system, the "local" has emerged as a key concept for strengthening sustainability, community, and access to affordable and fresh foods. For Hawai'i, the local is more than a geographic category; it is also a core identity by which its residents mark their relationship to place. This double use of localism thereby underlines the personal—and political—stakes of "eating local" in an increasingly globalized food system. This introductory essay for a special journal issue on Hawai'i's Food Systems offers the island archipelago as a case study for understanding how these systems-in-place interact with, respond to, and reinforce histories of colonialism, migration and settlement, monocropping, and importation. By attending to critical discourses about localism through the geographic and social particularities of Hawai'i, themes of place are highlighted as a central concern to the field of Food Studies today.

What does it mean to eat "local"? As the flaws and functions of the US food system come into ever sharper focus for its eating public, the local has become a key word for thinking through community health, economic resiliency, diversified employment, affordable and fresh food, and inequality across class, race, and gender differences.[1] For many, improving the local food system works capaciously to address these complex, overlapping issues.[2] By increasing access to meats, fruits, and vegetables that are produced nearby (however that is determined), the benefits ripple across the micro and the macro, from individual health to the global economy.[3] But whether such logic holds true has been the subject of much academic debate, with arguments against the promotion of local food as being elitist, "white," or inescapably capitalist.[4] This important discussion finds a rich case study in Hawai'i, which is often understood as one of the most ethnically diverse, geographically remote, and economically dependent places within the territorial boundaries of the United States.[5] The archipelago, once a self-sustaining and independent nation, is now disproportionately reliant on the continental United States for its food, economy, and governance.[6] Despite long being hailed as "paradise"—a veritable tropical Eden with a year-round growing season—the State of Hawai'i imports an estimated 85–90 percent of its food, thereby driving up its cost of living to make Honolulu rival New York City and creating vulnerability to global food markets.[7] Not only are Hawai'i residents challenged to feed themselves affordably, but many struggle for access to fresh, healthy foods.[8] This profound contradiction between abundance and scarcity is the product of a deeper social and political history, which witnessed a self-contained ahupua'a system superseded by global capitalism, an indigenous population overtaken by an international labor force, and a Hawaiian monarchy overthrown by the American government at the turn of the twentieth century.[9]

The literature on Hawai'i and its foodways often parallels its economic development. Over the course of the nineteenth century, its culinary landscape expanded to accommodate new ethnic groups who emigrated and made the Islands their home.[10] These groups comprised, by and large, folks who identify as "Local." As such, a term that is elsewhere defined as spatial (the geographically local) is thereby iterated in a way that also encompasses ideology and identity (the culturally Local).[11] The multi-ethnic groups that have come to understand Hawai'i as home over the last several hundred years share a common Creole dialect as well as a shared history of oppression by white elites in the Islands.[12] Thus to be local in Hawai'i is more than just a bodily location: it is a process of placemaking. The term has also attached to the foods that Local people eat—an elaborated cuisine that draws its flavors from multiple immigration waves, Native Hawaiian traditions, and American industrialization.[13] At the same time, however, works that emphasize how Hawai'i's food illustrates its social history can sometimes overlook examples of resistance and cultural survival that—as many works contained herein show—continue to abound. While the project of US settlement across the nineteenth and twentieth centuries certainly produced a framework by which one can understand the cultural and ethnic hierarchies of Hawai'i, scholarship must also account for the complexity with which its residents understand (and perform) their relationship to the Islands through food in ways that are intersectional, at times contradictory, and always historically grounded.[14]

These tensions were at the forefront of my mind when, in March 2014, I organized a panel for the Asian/Pacific/American Center at New York University entitled "System+Taste: Food in Postcolonial Hawai'i." It took inspiration from a keynote lecture given by Amy Bentley a year prior for *Food: The Conference*, hosted by the CUNY Graduate Center. In it, she considered the undertheorized role of "deliciousness" in studies of the food system.[15] Its inherent incalculability and subjective nature, she argued, troubled the data-driven field of public health. Her project to re-center taste within a discourse largely about hunger reminded the audience of the many scholars who have shown how culinary desires index not only biology, but also personal and genealogical histories: that food choices perform identity.[16] With this in mind, then, how does one account for emotionally based senses of taste when trying to determine how a community eats best? How does taste and identity help to shed light on the unevenly deployed benefits of the American food system? The question, with no clear answer, continued to trouble me as I worked my way through literature on settler colonialism and indigenous foodways.

I invited two scholars working on food and Hawai'i to New York in order to join Bentley in an extended discussion that, I hoped, might tease out some of these contradictions by applying the idea to Hawai'i specifically. Kaori O'Connor, a Kanaka Maoli raised in Waikīkī and now Senior Research Fellow at University College London in the Department of Anthropology, gave a paper discussing the anthropological and historical context for the development of taste and cuisine in Hawai'i; Ashley Lukens, Director of the Hawai'i Center for Food Safety, theorized tactical community food activism as a tool for food system development within a settler state. My colleague in Food Studies at NYU, Kelila Jaffee, prepared food tastings that underscored the content of the talks: pa'i'ai from O'ahu, limu from Hawai'i Island, commercially produced Hawaiian Sun Lilikoi Passion juice that allowed the audience sensory engagements with Hawai'i as the last gasps of a New York winter lingered outside on the Washington Mews. The rich discussion that followed made clear that there was a larger project at hand deserving of a special journal issue.

From traditional to contemporary contexts, Hawai'i offers a fruitful site from which we can locate emergent and critical themes around placemaking, local food economies, and identity construction that are of central concern to the field of Food Studies today.[17] Because of the diverse communities that view the Islands as either home or homeland, solutions for improving its food system variously grapple with indigenous erasure and resurgence, histories of land privatization, natural resource conservation, culturally appropriate foodways, affordability, and corporatized agricultural practices. Just as Hawai'i's complex history scaffolds social relations in the Islands today, it also shapes the food system's ship-to-table system. As a critical discourse builds around the alternative food movement, the "local" thereby articulates food justice, and the geographic and social particularities of Hawai'i amplify (and, I argue, clarify) questions about *whom* local food serves best in both material and ideological ways.

FOOD, CULTURE & SOCIETY

This shared sense of "Local" belonging—undoubtedly fraught—also underscores debates both public and academic that have sought solutions for ameliorating the fragility of Hawai'i's food supply.[18] To that end, the increasingly popular rhetoric of aloha 'āina, or caring for the land, draws productively upon native orientations toward sustainability, even though it is at times operationalized in a way that elides the material realities of indigenous displacement.[19]

3

As such, specific visions of the Islands loom large: as a vacationer's paradise, as an ancestral homeland, and as a cultural melting pot. These different ideas of Hawai'i are often celebrated and symbolized through its food (think, for example, about the complex meanings of some of its icons like the tourist's luau, the kalo plant, and the SPAM musubi). Indeed, if this special issue had been written ten years ago, its content might have stayed focused on the symbolic cultural importance of each dish and the multicultural groups who enjoy them. However, as important as these symbols are to understanding the culture of Hawai'i, they become ever more significant when one considers the political and economic infrastructures from which they emerge (or which they resist), including American empire, settler colonialism, and the monocropping of sugar and pineapple for export.[20] It continues to be a great irony that a place with such ecological abundance no longer grows its own food.

The essays included in this issue are linked by a common focus on Hawai'i, but from there take on a full scope of disciplinary perspectives, theoretical frameworks, and subject matter in order to grapple with ideas of what local food has, might, or could look like in the Islands (or anywhere else for that matter). As a reflection of the multiple subjectivities that define Hawai'i's community today—insider and outsider, settler and native, and everything between that upsets these binaries—this collection features scholars writing from various geographic and genealogic vantage points. For a place whose written history has been long dominated by non-native voices, delineating what perspectives are represented here constitutes a necessary part of the collection's introduction. The authors of these articles are both indigenous and haole, local and non-local, and writing from within and outside the geographical boundaries of Hawai'i. All have a relationship to the place they study that is at once intimate and academic, but by no means uniform. Readers will see these multiple identities reflected in both content and form: Hawaiian-language words are employed throughout the essays and, depending on the author's orientation toward Hawai'i, will be variously roman or italicized or shown with or without diacritical marks. These editorial choices were left to authors as a matter of personal politics (for example, Native Hawaiians might not italicize because the language is not foreign to them or their subject matter, though their meanings have been glossed for readability). As a result, the works presented here can be used as standalone pieces. However, together they might also serve as a model for what an intensive, collective study of a single place might look like when different relationships to place are honored and acknowledged as part of, rather than incidental to, scholarly practice.

The intended result is a broad collection of works that explore the multiple historical, cultural, and political registers of Hawai'i's foodscape. Arguing for why Hawai'i is a model for understanding global food history, Rachel Laudan revisits the authoring of her James Beard Award-winning *The Food of Paradise*, which has long served as a primer for the complex grammars of "Local" cuisine. In this issue she contextualizes her landmark work against challenges of legitimization—for local food in Hawai'i, which had not always been viewed as a "legitimate" cuisine, for studying food, which had not always been a "legitimate" field of research, and for being a University of Hawai'i visiting faculty outsider allowed to "legitimately" write about the history of food in Hawai'i. Laudan's assertions that Hawai'i's food is worth scholarly study paved the way for studies like my own, which examines the naturalization of ice and a taste for coldness within Hawai'i's foodscape. Focusing on the earliest importation of ice to Hawai'i by ship in the 1850s and 1860s, I show how culinary engagements with the very cold by Honolulu residents performed an ambivalent relationship with the United States as its economic relationship with Hawai'i strengthened in the midcentury. The arrival and naturalization of foreign foodways to Hawai'i is also illustrated in Clare Gupta's study of the historical legacies of the dairy industry—once "local" to Hawai'i, later imported, and now (once again) re-localized. As values of freshness and sustainability gain greater importance for consumers, milk articulates the different "agrarian imaginaries" used within the local food movement. Indeed, as she shows, the local food system is fraught with differing ideas of where and how local *production* should exist; and that a desire for Hawai'i dairy does not always dovetail harmoniously with the material realities of living near a dairy farm.

While concepts of the "local" shift across time, community, class, we find in Mehana Blaich-Vaughan and Adam Ayers' study of customary fishing practices in Halele'a, Kaua'i, that other facets of localism are timeless. Fisherman who employ ancestral knowledge and foundational concepts of reciprocity with natural resources display cultural resiliency despite land privatization and legal restrictions to traditional hukilau (surround-net fishing). Similar strains can be found also in Hokulani Aikau and Donna Kameha'ikū Camvel's richly narrated analysis of contemporary wetland kalo cultivation and poi production in He'e'ia Uli. Attending closely to the pleasures and challenges of embodied cultural practice, they draw through lines between ways of doing and ways of knowing; struggle and resiliency; the restoration of hāloa and the Kanaka body. For both of these pieces, native epistemologies are linchpins in Hawai'i's sustainability efforts, where indigenous core values comprise the foundation upon which a politics of the local can be equitably built.

Traditional food practices are often and resolutely constrained by the capitalist economies in which they are embroiled, and the final two articles address two poles of Hawai'i's current agricultural economy: the small-scale farm and the biotech industry's GE (genetically engineered) seed and crop research and development fields. Developing a typology for farmers in the South Kona area of Hawai'i Island, Noa Kekuewa Lincoln and Nicole Ardoin articulate the personal and economic drivers behind small-scale operations in order to assess the potential for strengthening the self-sufficiency of Hawai'i's food system. Their metric importantly shows that rising popularity in "leisure and hobby farming" by groups seeking residential space (a significant portion of which are relatively new to the Islands) emerges as one particular factor threatening the development of robust and diverse agricultural production in Hawai'i. From small-scale to large, Andrea Brower draws a historical through-line between the sugar oligarchy that once dominated Hawai'i's economy and the agrochemical oligopoly that has "taken seed" in the Islands today. Reading deeply into histories of indigenous dispossession, Brower suggests that the local/global binary may no longer be a sufficient axis for thinking through the colonial present. Rather, alternative futures for Hawai'i's food system must account for the systemic inequalities that have long characterized both its agriculture and society-at-large.

As food issues articulate locality—people, politics, and geography—they also make visible the potential for transformation. Inflected by its particular brand of "Local," Hawai'i's food system represents the myriad issues that challenge communities in the continental United States and beyond, from the GMO debate, to land-use, to commodity exchange. The seven works presented here offer fresh perspectives on localism that are both deeply emplaced and critical of its construction, showing Hawai'i as more than an idea(l) of paradise, agricultural bounty, and racial harmony. Instead, they map its complex social landscapes in order to offer nodes for thinking through resistance and change. Returning, then, to the original question animating this issue about the place of identity (or the identity of place) in mitigating food system inequality, I introduce a collection committed to seeking answers by engaging diverse theoretical frames and intellectual traditions. By drawing upon the specificity of Hawai'i, these works are brought to bear on the central concern of place within Food Studies today.

Disclosure statement

No potential conflict of interest was reported by the author.

Notes

1. Robert Feagan, "The Place of Food: Mapping out the "Local" in Local Food Systems," *Progress in Human Geography*, vol. 31, no. 1 (2007): 23-42, Steven M. Schnell, "Deliberate Identities: Becoming Local in America in a Global Age," *Journal of Cultural Geography*, vol. 30, no. 1 (2013): 55-89, Amy Trubek, *The Taste of Place: A Cultural Journey into Terroir* (Berkeley: University of California Press, 2008), and David Bell and Gill Valentine, *Consuming Geographies: We Are Where We Eat* (London and New York: Routledge, 1997).
2. Some landmark work that catalyzed this thinking within popular American culture are Michael Pollan's *Omnivore's Dilemma: A Natural History of Four Meals* (New York: Penguin Press, 2006) and Barbara Kingsolver's *Animal, Vegetable, Miracle: A Year of Food Life* (New York: HarperCollins, 2007). Also see C. Clare Hinrichs and Thomas A. Lyon, eds., *Remaking the North American Food System: Strategies*

for Sustainability (Lincoln and London: University of Nebraska Press, 2007), Gary Nabhan, *Coming Home to Eat: The Pleasures and Politics of Local Food* (New York: Norton, 2001), Francis Moore Lappé, *Diet For a Small Planet* (New York: Ballantine Books, 1972) and Joan Dye Gusso, *The Feeding Web: Issues in Nutritional Ecology* (New York: Hawthorn Books, 1978).

3. Safania Normann Eriksen, "Defining Local Food: Constructing a New Taxonomy: Three Domains of Proximity," *Acta Agriculturae Scandinavica*, Special Issue: Local Food—A Step Towards Better and More Environmentally Friendly Products, vol. 63, supp. 1 (2013): 47-55.

4. Laura B. Delind, "Of Bodies, Place, and Culture: Re-Situating Local Food," *Journal of Agricultural and Environmental Ethics*, vol. 19 (2006): 121-146, Teresa M. Mares and Devon G. Peña, "Environmental and Food Justice: Toward Local, Slow, and Deep Food Systems," in *Cultivating Food Justice: Race, Class, and Sustainability*, eds. Alison Hope Alkon and Julian Agyeman (Cambridge, MA: MIT Press, 2011), 197-219, Rachel Slocum, "Whiteness, Space, and Alternative Food Practice," *Geoforum*, vol. 38, no. 3 (2007): 520-533, Julie Guthman, "Bringing Good Food to Others: Investigating the Subjects of Alternative Food Practice," *Cultural Geographies*, vol. 15, no. 4 (2008): 431-447.

5. The conflation of these factors (which are not without their caveats) are often used to identify Hawai'i's particular vulnerability to a globalized food system. See Todd Woody, "Food Independence Could be a Matter of Survival for the U.S." Most Isolated State," *TakePart.com*, 29 June 2015, accessed 3 May 2016, http://www.takepart.com/article/2015/06/29/hawaii-local-food.

6. This overarching idea is more carefully articulated in Davianna McGregor, *Nā Kua'āina: Living Hawaiian Culture* (Honolulu: University of Hawai'i Press, 2007), Noelani Goodyear-Ka'ōpua, *The Seeds We Planted: Portraits of a Native Hawaiian Charter School* (Minneapolis: University of Minnesota Press, 2013) and Manulani Aluli Meyer, "Hoea Ea: Land Education and Food Sovereignty in Hawai'i," *Environmental Education Research*, vol. 20, no. 1 (2014): 98-101.

7. Matthew K. Loke and PingSun Leung, "Hawai'i's Food Consumption and Supply Sources: Benchmark Estimates and Measurement Issues," *Agricultural and Food Economics*, vol. 10, no. 1 (2013), accessed 3 May 2016, doi: 10.1186/2193-7532-1-10. Importantly, high cost-of-living indexes push Hawai'i to the top of their lists in part because they factor in the cost of groceries. Anita Hofschneider, "Is Hilo the 5th Most Expensive City in the Nation?," *Civil Beat*, 14 October 2014, accessed 3 May 2016, http://www.civilbeat.com/2014/10/is-hilo-the-5th-most-expensive-city-in-the-nation/. For more on the ideological creation of Hawai'i as a paradise, see Janeen Arnold Costa, "Paradisical Discourse: A Critical Analysis of Marketing and Consuming Hawai'i," *Consumption Markets & Culture*, vol. 1, no. 4 (1998): 303-346.

8. Stephanie Lee, Melissa Oshiro, Laura Hsu, Opal Vanessa Buchthal, and Tetine Sentell, "Neighborhoods and Health in Hawai'i: Considering Food Accessibility and Affordability," *Hawai'i Journal of Medicine and Public Health*, vol. 71, no. 8 (2012): 232-237. The concept of "food miles" has not been without critique, but is used here as a useful gloss for the distance the majority of Hawai'i's food travels from the U.S. continent. Steven Schnell, "Food Miles, Local Eating, and Community Supported Agriculture: Putting Local Food in its Place," *Agriculture and Human Values*, vol. 30, no. 4 (2013): 615-628.

9. This history is incredibly complex and has been chronicled by many. Here I draw particularly on Noenoe Silva, *Aloha Betrayed: Native Hawaiian Resistance to American Colonialism* (Durham: Duke University Press, 2004), Jonathan Kamakawiwoʻole Osorio, *Dismembering Lāhui: A History of the Hawaiian Nation to 1887* (Honolulu: Univeristy of Hawaii Press, 2002), and Lilikalā Kameʻelehiwa, *Native Land and Foreign Desires* (Honolulu: Bishop Museum Press, 1992).
10. Arnold Hiura, *Kau Kau: Cuisine and Culture in the Hawaiian Islands* (Honolulu: Watermark Publishing, 2009), Kaori O'Connor, "The Hawaiian Luau: Food as Tradition, Trasngression, Transformation, and Travel," *Food, Culture & Society*, vol. 11, no. 2 (2008): 149-172, Judith Midgley Kirkendall, "Hawaiian Ethnograstronomy: The Development of a Pidgin-Creole Cuisine," (PhD Dissertation, University of Hawaiʻi, 1985).
11. This tension is elegantly illustrated in Judy Rohrer, *Staking Claim: Settler Colonialism and Racism in Hawaiʻi* (Tucson: University of Arizona Press, 2016). Also see Dean Itsuji Saranillio, "The Kēpaniwai (Damming of the Water) Heritage Gardens," in *Formations of United States Colonialism*, ed. Alyosha Goldstein (Durham: Duke University Press, 2014).
12. John P. Rosa, "Local Story: The Massie Case Narrative and the Cultural Production of Local Identity in Hawaiʻi," *Amerasia Journal*, vol. 26, no. 2 (2000): 94. Scholarship on local identity has stemmed largely from a University of Hawaiʻi undergraduate student's senior thesis, Eric Yamamoto. "From "Japanee" to Local: Community Change and the Redefinition of Sansei Identity in Hawaiʻi," (Senior thesis for Liberal Studies Program, University of Hawaiʻi, 1974). Also see Jonathan Y. Okamura, "Aloha Kanaka Me Ke Aloha "Aina: Local Culture and Society in Hawaiʻi," *Amerasia Journal*, vol. 7 (1980): 119-137.
13. Rachel Laudan, *The Food of Paradise: Exploring Hawaiʻi's Culinary Heritage* (Honolulu: University of Hawaiʻi Press, 1996), 18.
14. As exemplified by the sharing of multiethnic foods by Hawaiʻi's 19th century plantation workers. Hiura, *Kau Kau*, 57.
15. Amy Bentley, "The Poetics and Pragmatics of Deliciousness," (keynote presentation, Food: The Conference, CUNY Graduate Center, New York, NY, March 5, 2012).
16. To begin, see Diner, *Hungering for America* (1991), Amy Bentley, *Eating for Victory: Food Rationing and the Politics of Domesticity* (Champain, IL: University of Illinois Press, 1998), Pilcher, *Que Vivan los Tamales* (1998).
17. It is important to note here distinctions between "local" and "place," which have been described as sympathetic, but not equivalent terms. Clare Hinrichs, "Fixing Food with Ideas of "Local" and "Place," *Journal of Environmental Studies and Sciences* (2015): 1-6, accessed 3 May 2016, doi: 10.1007/s13412-015-0266-4.
18. Ashley Lukens, "Theorizing Food Justice: Critical Positionality and the Political Economy of Community Food Systems," (Phd dissertation, University of Hawaiʻi, 2013), Margo Machida, "Devouring Hawaiʻi: Food, Consumption, and Contemporary Art," in *Eating Asian America: A Food Studies Reader*, eds. Robert Ji-Song Ju, Martin F. Manalansan, and Anita Mannur (New York: New York University, 2013), Amy Reddinger, "Eating "Local': The Politics of Post-Statehood Hawaiian Cookbooks," *Nordic Journal of English Studies*, vol. 9, no. 3 (2010): 67-87, and LeeRay Costa and Kathryn Besio, "Eating Hawaiʻi: Local Foods and Placemaking in Hawaiʻi Regional Cuisine," *Social and Cultural Geography*, vol. 12, no. 8 (2011): 839-854.

19. For statistics on health, nutrition, and racial disparity in Hawai'i, see K. Kromer Baker, J.P. Derrickson, and S.A.K. Derrickson, *Hunger and Food Insecurity in Hawai'i: Baseline Estimates. Hawai'i Health Survey, 1999-2000* (Honolulu: State Department of Health, Office of Health Status Monitoring, October 2011). For a discussion of Aloha 'Āina activism, see Clare Gupta, "Return to Freedom: Anti-GMO Aloha "Āina Activism on Molokai as an Expression of Place-Based Food Sovereignty," *Globalizations*, vol. 12, no. 4 (2015): 529-544, and for how the concept can be taken up in ways that does not account for indigenous struggles, see Costa and Besio's section on *Terroir, 'Āina*, and Local foods in "Eating Hawai'i," 844-845.
20. Krisnawati Suryanata, "Diversified Agriculture, Land Use, and Agrofood Networks in Hawai'i," *Economic Geography*, vol. 78, no. 1 (2002): 71-86.

Homegrown Cuisines or Naturalized Cuisines? The History of Food in Hawaii and Hawaii's Place in Food History

Rachel Laudan

Abstract

When the author arrived in Hawaii in the mid-1980s, the homegrown model of culinary evolution was widely, if tacitly, accepted. It assumes that cuisines develop in place, evolving from simple peasant cooking of local ingredients to refined high cuisine in cities. Hawaii, where successive waves of migrants had introduced and naturalized cuisines from distant places, was a striking exception to the model. The alternative naturalized model provided the key to writing a global food history, which, in turn, shed new light on Hawaii's place in food history.

Prologue

Islands, particularly isolated islands that are not mere appendages to continental masses, are ideal places to observe changes in species, in societies, in languages, and, not least, in cuisines (styles of preparing and consuming food). Largely cut off from all but episodic outside influences, the changes can be dated and delineated much more easily than in the more fluid circumstances found on continental landmasses. I had no idea this was so when I arrived in the Hawaiian Islands to teach at the University of Hawaii in the mid-1980s. I was sure the charms of this self-described paradise—sun, sand, coconut palms, and luaus—would pale within days, leaving me twiddling my thumbs. Instead I found a diverse, evolving environment, a perplexing multi-ethnic society with its own developing creole language (Hawaii Creole English, locally known as pidgin), and the most baffling food I had ever encountered.

"Local Food," the principle public food, was not local in the usual senses. It was neither biologically local (prepared from foodstuffs indigenous to the place) nor agriculturally local (prepared from foodstuffs grown in the place). Rather it was culturally local, a cuisine that could only have been created by the specific combination of cultural groups that had settled in Hawaii. In the first part of this essay, I describe how I moved from open-mouthed bewilderment at Local Food to writing *The Food of Paradise: Exploring Hawaii's Culinary Heritage* (1996), a series of essays that described Local Food and how it had come about.[1]

Hawaii's culinary heritage suggested that the "homegrown" model of culinary evolution that I had always accepted without thinking was badly flawed. According to the homegrown theory (a name I am offering for the first time in this paper), food systems are shaped by the local natural bounty, created in the countryside, and gradually refined to a high cuisine in the cities. Yet not one of the cuisines in Hawaii was homegrown. Local Food was an invented cuisine that patched together elements from the cuisines of three successive diasporas that had settled the Islands: the Hawaiian from the South Pacific, the Anglo from Britain and the United States, and the Asian, mainly from China, Japan, and Korea. Each group imported and adapted their entire food system (cuisine). This package included ideas about what food was good, techniques and implements for making that food, and the plants and animals preferred as raw materials. Thus Hawaii's culinary history consisted of three periods of rapid change when a new food system was introduced and "naturalized," longer periods of slow evolution in between, and then in the mid-twentieth century the rapid creation of Local Food.

For understanding the global history of food, I thought that the naturalized model of cuisines, which had been carried over long distances by migrants, naturalized in places far from their origin, and often layered on older, established cuisines seemed to me to offer promise. It seemed to fit the food history of many parts of the world better than the homegrown model, which assumed that distinct cuisines evolved in parallel in different regions, with occasional intrusions of plants, techniques, or dishes from elsewhere. In the second part of this article I describe how Hawaii inspired me to write a global history, *Cuisine and Empire: Cooking in World History* (2013).[2] In writing it, I had to expand the ideas I had come up with in Hawaii in a number of ways, particularly in order to emphasize how important ideas were in shaping cuisines, particularly ideas about the social and economic, the moral and religious, and the health and environmental goals of eating.

My more considered understanding of culinary history shed new light on where Hawaii's cuisines fitted into world food history. In part three, I outline Hawaii's culinary history in terms of broad global forces and naturalized and invented cuisines. A brief epilogue offers some thoughts about what the future holds for the cuisines of Hawaii.

Creating Hawaii's Local Food

To say that I did not want to move to Hawaii would be an understatement. Being so far from the US mainland might well be death to my academic career, a foreboding heightened by my colleagues' chortles as they predicted that I would idle away my time on the beach. Having already published quite a bit in history and philosophy of science and technology, I worried whether I would be able to complete my research on the history of ideas of scientific and technological progress. The University of Hawaii offered jobs, however, and since jobs for academic couples were few and far between in the days before spousal hires, my husband and I accepted.

I was as ignorant as I was unenthusiastic. If, in the rush of organizing a move from the East Coast to the middle of the Pacific, I thought about it at all, I assumed that as on the mainland most of my students would be white, in this case with an admixture of Native Hawaiians. It immediately became clear that they were neither white nor Native Hawaiian. My confusion compounded my fear of "rock fever" on an island 30 miles by 50 miles, our struggle to cope with the astronomical cost of living, and the shock of discovering mainlanders were not welcome, notwithstanding the famed "aloha spirit" or attitude of friendly acceptance.[3] I was not the only new faculty member who wondered how to come to terms with the Islands.

As it happened, as soon as the semester started, the answer was, quite literally, handed to me on a plate. "Try these," said Barbara Hoshida, the department secretary, offering golf-ball sized deep-fried objects, adding "they're Okinawan andagi, just like Portuguese malasadas," as if that made everything clear. Shortly after, Barbara led the cross-questioning of one of the student helpers who had been to an academic award ceremony downtown. The all-important question in these Islands, where I was coming to understand that food spoke volumes, was "What had been served for lunch?" "Oh, it was Hawaiian food," replied the student. "Ah," said all the listeners as if that explained something. It did not explain anything to me. Wasn't all food in Hawaii Hawaiian food, just as food in California was Californian food? Apparently not. As an adjective, Hawaiian always referred to Native Hawaiian, so Hawaiian food meant specifically the food of the Native Hawaiians.

Day after day, Barbara, the student helpers and the students in class brought in food to share, not for my benefit, but because that was the custom. Day after day, they explained the different combinations of rice, seaweed, fresh and dried fish, canned meat, and salty dried fruit to an ignorant mainlander more familiar with sandwiches, cake, cookies, potato chips, and candies. I prided myself on my knowledge of food garnered from a farming childhood and years poring over cookbooks and working in the kitchen. As Barbara had spotted, I was not nearly as knowledgeable as I thought. "You don't know much about food, do you?" said Barbara. "Well, we'll just have to teach you."

Barbara and my students, I gradually learned, were drawn from one of the three main demographic groups in the Islands: the group of largely Asian descent. Asians, already present in the Islands from the early nineteenth century, had begun arriving in force from the 1870s on, when the Hawaiian royalty and the plantation owners embarked on a search for contract workers for the cane (and later) pineapple fields.[4] Chinese, Korean, Japanese, Okinawan, and Filipinos (as well as a scattering of others such as Portuguese from the Azores and Puerto Ricans) fleeing hunger and political turmoil in their homelands had entered the Islands in overlapping sequence. Many intended to return once their contracts were up.[5] In fact, a high proportion stayed, setting up small farms or seeking a living in Honolulu and smaller cities. As time went on, they intermarried amongst themselves and to some extent with Native Hawaiians and whites as well.

My students all described themselves as Locals. A Local was someone born and raised in the Islands and usually of color. Native Hawaiians also counted as Local, while whites, known as "haoles" were in an ambiguous position, even if born in the Islands. Together these three groups made up almost equal parts of the population although distinctions blurred, everyone delighting in reeling off complicated ancestries that included all three groups. Since as a general rule few local haoles or Native Hawaiians attended the University of Hawaii, my students as well as the university staff were descended from that subset of Locals who had come to work the plantations.

The university provided Local Asian students and staff their first extended dealings with mainland haoles since the military were tucked away on their bases and the tourists on Waikiki or resort beaches. Locals had good reason to fear that mainland haoles might condescend to them for speaking their first language, pidgin (Hawaii Creole English) and for enjoying Local Food, including the highly regarded Local treat, SPAM. As the importance of Local Food became evident, it occurred to me that one way to break through our mutual lack of understanding and suspicion would be to take my students' Local Food seriously instead of dismissing it as a joke. What were these dishes called butter mochi, bitsu-bitsu, fried fish bones, kau yuk, and kulolo? Why was the plate lunch ubiquitous? Which dishes came from which ethnic group? Why had some entered the canon of Local Food and others not? And why did it matter so much to Locals to eat Local Food?

On weekends I drove out to the center and south west of Oahu to plantation villages of small frame houses surrounded by red dirt and pineapples stretching off to the horizon. In the mornings I walked the length of Liliha Street, a prime hunting ground for mom and pop stores, shave ice stands, crack seed shops, and "plate lunch" places. Saturday mornings saw me at the farmers' markets that popped up for an hour or so in a local park, sold greens and squashes I had never seen, and then just as quickly shut down and moved on to the next location. Saturday nights my husband and I rode his scooter through the warm scented air to Zippy's, a popular local fast-food chain owned by Okinawans. The signature meal, the Zip Pac, comprised teriyaki beef, Spam, mahimahi, and fried chicken on rice with furikake and daikon. And on Sunday mornings I strolled through the empty streets to the bustle of Chinatown to eat noodle soup with skewers of duck. Under the spreading trees in the courtyard of the State Library, surely one of the most beautiful places to read in the United States, I worked my way through histories of the different ethnic groups in the Islands, home economics texts on island diets, and botanical works on foodstuffs such as breadfruit, taro, marungay, and seaweed. I pored over spiral-bound cookbooks published by the Maui Home Demonstration Council, the Hawaii Electric Industries, Japanese Women's Associations, and Buddhist temples. Their authors took for granted that Local readers would be able to follow the sketchy recipes and understand their context. As an outsider, I began by trying to map the recipes on to Japanese or Chinese recipes in cookbooks published on the mainland. This failed dismally. Those who had come to work the plantations ate very differently from those authors who came from much wealthier circumstances and who used their books to show off the most glamorous aspects of their cuisines.

To my effort to understand Local Food, I also brought a background in history of technology, which addressed the transfer of people, organisms, and things from one place to another. History of technology, which I saw as part of the wider project of history and philosophy of science, was directly applicable because cooking, and processing more generally, were the technologies that turned raw materials into food. I taught a course in food history as part of the history of technology, thanks to special permission from the Dean of Natural Sciences since food history was not yet a respectable academic subject. Armed with an electric wok and a food processor, my students and I tried out basic culinary techniques in different cultures: the grinding, cooking, curdling, and fermenting of beans in East Asia; the churning, fermenting, and evaporating of milk in South Asia; the threshing, grinding, and fermenting of wheat and barley in the Middle East and Europe, for example. We talked about relations between the techniques, the available plant resources, the society's religious, political, and nutritional goals, and how techniques were diffused beyond the region of origin.

FOOD,
CULTURE
SOCIETY

Food processing, we concluded, was part and parcel of a wider system of dealing with the world, and an understanding of the world just like other technologies, bearing out the truism of historians of technology that technology was more than just "nuts and bolts."[6] Individual discoveries and inventions were embedded in systems that included goals, know-how, and artifacts. Just as the light bulb was part of a system for providing light with the resources of generating stations, electrical wires, and switches, so soy sauce was part of a system for creating taste with readily available and inexpensive soybeans. Sometimes these systems could change dramatically as when electrical systems replaced gas lighting or soy condiments replaced simple salt. Transferring technological systems from one place to another was never straightforward but was eased when an individual familiar with the system was at hand to help. Adopting and adapting systems from elsewhere stimulated the economy and enriched lives. In short, when Asian immigrants brought their methods of processing to Hawaii, they created new businesses and wider culinary choices.

Also invaluable to my project were conversations with my colleagues at the university. Stimulated by the multicultural society they found themselves in, my colleagues also deemed contact between cultures, variously characterized as encounters or exchanges, as central to the evolution of societies. Sociologists pondered the Islands as a laboratory for race relations. Linguists studied "pidgin" as an incipient Creole language. Philosophers and religion professors traced the expansion of Buddhism, Confucianism and Shintoism. Area studies professors teased out the intertwined histories and cultures of China, Japan, Korea, and Southeast Asia.[7] Above all, the History Department pioneered courses in world history.

Of less help were academics specializing in food culture. Although there were more of them than retrospective accounts might lead one to believe, they were still few and far between whether in Hawaii or on the mainland. Anthropologists formed the largest group, most of them concentrating on food in simple societies. Although K.C. Chang's anthology *Food in Chinese Culture*, with contributions from leading Asianists, had appeared in 1977, E.N. (Gene) Anderson's *The Food of China* was not published until 1988.[8] Historians focused on the history of diet and nutrition, pioneered by the French *Annales School*, and were further fueled by the then very active research in social history. Studies of the cultural history of food were rare. When, in the early 1990s, I asked Natalie Zemon Davis, then Director of the Davis Center for Historical Research at Princeton where I held a visiting appointment, if she knew of any academic historians working in this area, she replied that the only name that came to mind was Barbara Wheaton, author of *Savoring the Past: The French Kitchen and Table from 1300–1789* (1983), and herself an independent scholar.[9]

Outside the universities, I found friends among the loosely knit circles of intellectuals interested in food history that began forming in the 1980s. Some seized on the new technology of word processing to publish newsletters.[10] Others found intellectual companionship in groups of culinary historians.[11] For publication, the chief outlet was the small journal *Petits Propos Culinaires* founded in 1979 by a retired British diplomat, Alan Davidson, to which the more scholarly cookbook writers such as Elizabeth David and Richard Olney contributed.[12] When Alan Davidson with French historian Theodore Zeldin founded the Oxford Symposium on Food and Cookery in the early 1980s, it drew food historians from around the world. In the United States, the International Association of Culinary Professionals welcomed food historians in those years.

Yet among these interlinked groups of intellectuals, the homegrown theory of culinary change reigned supreme. Food evolved from the bounty of the land (or *terroir*) developing from simple peasant cuisines to high cuisines refined in the courts and city restaurants. In its place of origin, the cuisine was at its finest; the further from that place, the more compromised and abased it became. Thus in spite of massive migration from Italy in the late nineteenth and early twentieth centuries, historians of Italian cuisine did not even mention how it evolved in places such as the United States and Argentina. Similarly, the authors of the flood of cookbooks that appeared in the 1970s instructing

THE FOODWAYS OF HAWAI'I

Americans how to prepare Italian, Chinese, Mexican, Indian, Thai, Vietnamese and Japanese food described the cuisines as those of a territory, ignoring people who had migrated beyond that territory. The "authenticity" of "ethnic" restaurants, which proliferated after immigration to the United States eased with the passing of the Hart-Cellar Immigration and Nationality Act of 1965 was judged by how closely they reproduced what Americans understood from cookbooks to be the cuisine of the homeland. When it began publication in 1994, Saveur took as its slogan "Savor a World of Authentic Cuisine."

The United States, with its "melting pot" of dishes from different cultures, scored poorly among those who subscribed to the homegrown model. At one conference after another, anxious panelists discussed "Is there such a thing as American cuisine?," a question further confounded by the conflation of cuisine and high cuisine. If foodies doubted that you could talk about the cuisine of the United States, they were convinced that the Local Food of Hawaii was so debased as to be unworthy of study, inauthentic and thus déclassé. During my first visit to the Oxford Symposium on Food and Cookery, a fellow symposiast commiserated. "Poor you, interested in food and having to live in Hawaii: no peasant cuisine, no authentic food, just international hotel food." By that time, I was beginning to doubt the homegrown theory so I retorted that in few places in the world was the construction of a cuisine, surely of interest to historians of food, so open to study.

By now, my confusion about what my students were eating had crystallized into a precise question about how Local Food was created from three major diasporic cuisines.[13] I did not call them naturalized at the time, but I like the name, which echoes the other meanings of a migrant who has attained citizenship and a plant that has become established. I drafted a manuscript using two recent well-researched books as inspiration. *Pickles and Pretzels,* historically informed essays about Pennsylvania's foods, had been published in 1980 by Virginia Bartlett, the wife of a former colleague in the History Department at Carnegie-Mellon University.[14] *On Persephone's Isle*, a culinary history of Sicily in light of its conquests and politics by Mary Taylor Simeti, had appeared in 1986.[15]

My manuscript, after an introductory overview of Hawaii's culinary history, stressing the coherence of culinary philosophy, methods of cooking, ingredients, and dishes of each diaspora, consisted of essays that began with one or another of the puzzling ingredients, dishes, meals, farming, markets, and food stores in Hawaii as a prologue to a historical explanation.

Part One, Local Food, dealt with how Local Food—like pidgin—was a way to bridge cultural differences. It was necessarily public food because it was in public, not in the home, that the different cultural groups in the Islands met. The plate lunch was the signature meal, rice, SPAM, and seaweed (*limu*) common ingredients, *saimin* (noodle soup), *manapua* (steamed pork bun), *musubi* (nori-wrapped rice), crackers, and raw fish (*poke*) popular snacks; and *crack seed* (Chinese dried, salted "plums"); *mochi* (sweet rice "cakes"); and *malasadas* and *andagi* (donuts) beloved nibbles. Ingredients such as rice, fish, and seaweed that appealed to many different ethnic groups were central to Local Food. Home economists from the mainland had laid the groundwork for Local Food by training a generation of cooks in shared techniques.[16]

Part Two, Ethnic Food, turned to the cuisines of the last group of settlers to arrive in the Islands, largely, but not entirely, Asians who came to work on the plantations.[17] I based my essays on the festivals such as Chinese Ching Ming, Japanese New Year, and Okinawan village celebrations and on retail outlets such as Portuguese bakeries and Filipino vegetable markets where I had caught glimpses of these cuisines on my jaunts around town and my collection of spiral-bound cookbooks. I ended with the way Anglo canned goods had penetrated the plantation diet and Chinatown.

Part Three, Kamaaina Food, dealt with the cuisine of "kamaainas" (literally children of the land) the white or haole inhabitants of the Islands who had been there since the nineteenth century. It depended largely on library research since I had almost no contact with this rather enclosed community. Essays explored why Hawaii has so many botanic gardens and such a large cattle ranch, how missionary wives fed their families, the surprising lack of fruits, the sugar and pineapple industries, the gracious poi supper of the kamaaina elite, and the conflicting visions of contemporary tourists seeking paradise and Locals struggling to make ends meet in remote Islands that offered little employment.

Part Four, Hawaiian Food, described the first settlers' struggle with a dearth of indigenous edible plants, particularly carbohydrates, the introduced plants taro, coconut, arrowroot, candlenuts, the use of fish and seaweeds, and the life-sustaining miracle of fresh water in the middle of an ocean of salt water. I concluded with a paean to the courage of the waves of migrants who had turned a food desert into a culinary paradise. My initial befuddlement had changed to affection and to admiration for what the successive settlers of Hawaii had achieved.

Surely, I thought, the visitors relaxing on Waikiki beach would find the real Hawaii more interesting than the tourist fable, the food in the offices, on the street, and in the mom and pop stores tastier than the watery mai tais and chicken long rice of tourist luaus. In 1994 I sent query letters to New York editors, regional American food being very much in vogue in the 1990s. A couple asked for the proposal, only to reject it because it did not update the how-to-do-a-luau cookbooks of the 1960s.

It was time to pluck up my courage and see what people in Hawaii thought. Until then, I had not dared divulge to colleagues and students that I, an outsider, a mainland haole, had the temerity to write about their cuisines, nor did I anticipate that my wide-eyed newcomer's perspective would add anything to what Locals already knew. Diffidently I showed the manuscript to Charlene (Charlie) Sato, local Japanese and Associate Professor in Second Language Studies where she specialized in pidgin, and to Wanda Adams, local Portuguese and food editor at the *Honolulu Advertiser*.[18] I asked Doreen Fernandez, drama critic, leading chronicler of Filipino food, and friend of Alan Davidson, to read the Filipino chapter on one of her regular visits to UH from the Philippines.[19] All the readers said "go ahead," and Wanda even said "You've written my book."

The University of Hawaii Press editors, Iris Wiley, Patricia Crosby, and Bill Hamilton, had long wanted a book on Hawaii's culinary history. They sent the manuscript on to the Editorial Board. Its members, all professors at the university, thought that a book on Hawaii's Local Food by a mainland haole would set a political hornet's nest buzzing. They forwarded it to the distinguished marine botanist, Isabella Abbott, then at the University of Hawaii, emeritus professor at Stanford, Hawaiian-Chinese, and the first woman of Hawaiian ancestry to receive a PhD in science, an unassailable authority. She approved.[20]

I titled the book *The Food of Paradise* as an ironic commentary on the contrast between the tourist hype about tropical bounty and the effort that had gone into creating the Island's cuisines, so costly in terms of transport, labor, and processing. The subtitle carried none of the political or intellectual baggage that it now would because the food heritage industry was then barely underway. Some reviewers suggested I should have called it simply *Local Food*. I added sidebars with illustrative life stories, recipes that I labored to construct from the sketchy instructions in local cookbooks, and photographs, some that I had taken, some from the Hawaii State Archives, but all in black and white to get away from the paradise myth.

Both the University of Hawaii Press and I were intensely relieved that *The Food of Paradise* did not provoke the feared political uproar. On the contrary, Island reviewers expressed appreciation that one outsider had not condescended but had taken their food seriously. Several declared it the "definitive" study of Island culinary history. On the mainland, reviewers for the *LA Times* and *Gourmet*, for example, thought it might "light up some possible futures of American food more penetratingly than a dozen style-chasers' panels."[21] It was awarded the Julia Child/Jane Grigson Prize for research of the International Association of Culinary Professionals.

Hawaii as a Model for Global Culinary Change

Far from being marginal and debased, I had decided that Hawaii's cuisines offered the key to a new way of writing global food history. For the next couple of decades, as I struggled to pull such a history together, Food Studies inched into respectability and then hurtled into trendiness. Steven Kaplan, expert on bread in French history, launched the journal *Food and Foodways* in 1985. The first meeting of the Association for the Study of Food and Society was held in 1987 and its now flourishing journal, *Food, Culture and Society*, began publication in 1996 as *The Journal of Food and Society*. Departments were founded at Boston University and New York University and smaller programs sprang up in many universities. Heartening as it was to see interest in food as a subject of study, much of the research focused on the United States, and took as its problems the creation of identity and the reformation of the food system, neither of them directly useful for my project.

THE FOODWAYS OF HAWAI'I

On the other hand, I had been given a flying start in world history during my time in Hawaii. In most years, leaders in the field spent a semester at the University of Hawaii. All were interested in long-distance contacts, encounters, or exchanges. William McNeill, who had pioneered contemporary world history with *A World History* (1967) showed in *Plagues and Peoples* (1976) and *The Pursuit of Power* (1982) the power of following infectious disease or firearms across national boundaries in illuminating world history.[22] Alfred Crosby in *The Columbian Exchange* (1972) had famously traced the ecological consequences of exchanges between formerly isolated populations.[23] Philip Curtin, famous for the first quantitative study of *The Atlantic Slave Trade* (1969), had argued for a non-European-centric analysis in *Cross-Cultural Trade in World History*, asserting that "external stimulation ... has been the most important single source of change and development in art, science, and technology." Continuing, he said, "cross-cultural trade and communication pose special problems. People with a different way of life are strangers by definition; their ways seem unpredictable, and the unpredictable is probably dangerous as well."[24]

When I asked William McNeill whether he thought food might provide as much insight into world history as plagues or firearms, he was encouraging. Listening to Alfred Crosby made me think that a natural next step from his work was to explore in more detail what was involved in "exchange." Conversations with Philip Curtin allowed me to draw on his vast experience to put the cross-cultural problems of Hawaii in the context of other parts of the world. My colleague Jerry Bentley's questions about how religions gained converts in *Old World Encounters: Cross-Cultural Traditions and Exchanges in Pre-Modern Times* were directly relevant to how new cuisines gain purchase. As Jerry founded the *Journal of World History* and co-wrote a major world history text, *Traditions and Encounters*, I was lucky enough to discuss how to go about writing a world history when we had a working lunch every couple of months at what he called "a very haolified Japanese restaurant."[25]

My first question in writing a world history of food was: what was food history about? What had been transferred to Hawaii was not the individual plants and animals of the Columbian Exchange. They were not the commodities of the increasingly popular commodity histories. They were entire systems including beliefs about appropriate eating, meal patterns, techniques for preparing ingredients and dishes, plants and animals, and the ways of farming them. What should such a system be called? One possibility is "foodways," a term anthropologists and folklorists use to describe the culture, history, and economy of regional foods, or, as defined in the masthead of the journal *Food and Foodways*, "the history and culture of human nourishment." I found the term too folkloric, not suggestive enough of system (though perfectly acceptable for the miscellaneous foodways of a region as in "Texas foodways") and too suggestive of the homegrown model.

I opted for cuisine. This choice deserves a whole essay, but in brief my position is the following. Although when equated with high cuisine the term reeks of elitism, its original sense of "style of cooking" reflects my opinion that processing and cooking techniques are central to food systems. Already in common use in cookbook titles, "cuisine" had been adopted both by anthropologists such as Peter Farb and George Armelagos and by thoughtful food writers such as Elizabeth Rozin.[26] I differed from them in including ideas and beliefs (culinary philosophy) since in my opinion culinary philosophy, not agricultural resources, is the glue that holds a cuisine together. Each culinary philosophy specified relations between cuisine and the divine or the moral, the social world, and the environment, including human bodies. All elements of the cuisine came together in an archetypal meal, not necessarily eaten every day, but like Thanksgiving dinner exemplifying the values and resources of the society.

The second question had to do with culinary diffusion. In Hawaii, whole groups moved taking their cuisine with them. It seemed clear that this was not always the case. Quite small numbers of culinary agents—missionaries, military, and merchants in particular—could transfer a cuisine from one region to another provided certain conditions were met. Those conditions were usually political. Cuisines perceived as successful were more likely to be accepted than those that were not. Success was indicated by the power of the state (or region) that had developed or adopted the cuisine. Since empires were the most powerful states through most of history, they served as centers of culinary dissemination, with lesser empires and states emulating their cuisines. In any state prior to the last hundred years or so, the ruling class enjoyed a high cuisine, rich in meat, sweets, and sauces that distinguished them from their subjects, who consumed a humble cuisine largely composed of a carbohydrate staple.

Using the concept of cuisine and believing empires to have been the most important centers of culinary diffusion, I distinguished three major overlapping periods in *Cuisine and Empire*: sacrificial cuisines; theocratic cuisines; and modern cuisine. Sacrificial cuisines appeared in different places around the world as humans mastered the processing and cooking of the major carbohydrates staples, roots and grains. Their culinary philosophies had three planks. Relations with the gods were defined by the sacrificial bargain: the chief, king or priests offered food in sacrifice to the gods hoping to ensure in return food from plentiful harvests, fertile women, and success in war. Social relations were hierarchical, with different cuisines for each step in the hierarchy from the gods through humans to the lowliest creatures. The cuisines of humans were divided into high cuisines rich in meat or fish, fats, and sweets for the ruling class and humble cuisines based on staple carbohydrates for everyone else. Environmental relations were expressed in correspondences between compass directions, seasons, ages, and the heating and cooling effects of food on the body (the culinary cosmos and the humoral theory). Early sacrificial cuisines were to be found in chiefdoms. Their archetypal meal was the feast on the remains of the sacrifice, a meal that linked, gods, rulers and the people.

Grains, hard, dry, and relatively lightweight, permitted the transport and storage of sufficient food to provision the armies and courts so that over the centuries in areas of grain cuisines cities, states and empires were created.

The Roman and Chinese empires based on wheat and barley came to dominate Eurasia.

Theocratic cuisines followed from alliances between empires and the new universal religions (sometimes called religions of salvation) that began being created shortly before the birth of Christ. The practice of sacrificing to and feeding the gods declined, replaced with a set of rules governing fast and feast days, permitted foodstuffs, and preferred ways of processing. Sacrificial feasts disappeared, replaced by court banquets for the civil powers and ascetic collations for the religious elites. The new theocratic cuisines were disseminated across wide swathes of the earth's surface. Between 200 BC and AD 800 Buddhist cuisine swept across the eastern half of Asia and the related Hindu cuisine across much of South and Southeast Asia. Between AD 700 and AD 1800 Islamic cuisine expanded across the western half. In the fifteenth and sixteenth century Catholic cuisine, formed centuries earlier with the expansion of the Iberian empires, enlarged its territory dramatically to the Americas and the borders of Asia and Africa.

Then in the mid-seventeenth century modern cuisines began taking shape as states began to abandon enforcing the rules of universal religions, to replace the culinary cosmos and the humoral theory with scientific nutritional theory, and to experiment with republican and socialist alternatives to imperial or monarchical hierarchies. Monarchies did not disappear, but the archetypal court banquet was joined by fine restaurant dining, which anyone wealthy enough could enjoy. Republics, such as the seventeenth-century Dutch republic and the early American republic, favored a family meal during which children imbibed both physical nourishment and the intellectual elements of citizenship. By the late nineteenth century, middling cuisines, like high cuisines in their abundant meat, sauces, and sweets, unlike them in being available to all citizens, began appearing in the richer countries of the world, reflecting the shift in status of ordinary people from subjects to citizens. *Cuisine and Empire: Cooking in World History* appeared in 2013.

Rethinking Hawaii's Culinary History in Light of Cuisine and Empire

How does Hawaii's culinary history stand in light of *Cuisine and Empire*? I would divide it into four periods: the sacrificial cuisine of the Hawaiian Chiefdoms; the aristocratic cuisine of the Hawaiian monarchy; the republican cuisine of the plantation oligarchy; and modern cuisine, Local Food, of an American state.

The sacrificial cuisine of the Hawaiian chiefdoms, practiced from several centuries AD to the beginning of the nineteenth century, was in most respects typical of sacrificial cuisines elsewhere in the world. Chiefs and priests offered their most valued foods—pork, coconuts, bananas, and fine fish—to the gods in sacrifice hoping to assure victory in battle and fertile lands and fertile women, and feasted on the leftovers.[27]

Hawaiian cuisine, like other sacrificial cuisines, was sharply hierarchical. High cuisines for the gods, chiefs and priests were distinct from the humble cuisines of the much larger numbers of commoners and outcasts. Chiefs and priests enjoyed mullet and other delicate pond fish. The everyday meals of both men and women were poi (pounded taro) and fish, with condiments of salt and seaweed. Gender divisions were just as marked. Women, forbidden to eat pork, coconut, bananas and certain fish, faced death if they dined with men. Of the culinary cosmos and the humoral theory there is little sign, perhaps because it disappeared after contact, perhaps because this is not a universal feature of sacrificial cuisines.

Most striking is just how far Hawaiian sacrificial cuisine had travelled and how ingeniously it was naturalized, supplementing the limited resources of Hawaii. The ancestral cuisine had been shaped in Southeast Asia, whence it had been carried out across the Pacific Islands, as far as Easter Island in the west, Hawaii in the north and last of all New Zealand in the south.[28] After a heroic journey, probably from the Marquesas, the Hawaiians unloaded a small portmanteau of plants and animals from their outriggers, most importantly taro as their main source of carbohydrate, but also bananas, breadfruit, coconut and other species, as well as pigs, dogs, and chicken, to create an agriculturally, but not biologically, local cuisine.

While waiting for their plants and animals to multiply sufficiently to provide a source of food, the Hawaiians survived on fish and flightless birds, most of which quickly became extinct.[29] Lacking both clay and metal, they cooked in earth ovens, or with potboilers in calabashes. Drying, salting, grilling, and pounding were other important techniques. Elaborate irrigation systems watered the taro patches and fresh or brackish water fish were farmed in ponds. A sophisticated system of land utilization allowed access to different ecological zones and a division of power within the political system. Given that the staple taro, like other roots, corms and tubers, was too wet and heavy to transport and store for urban provisions, cities never developed, nor did states let alone empires.[30]

Aristocratic Hawaiian cuisine was created during the nineteenth century, reaching its zenith with King David Kalakaua's coronation banquet on 12 February 1883. It proceeded from mulligatawny, turtle, Windsor, and à la Reine soups, through fish, and meats such as wild duck, pheasant, fillet of veal, turkey with truffle sauce, beef à la mode, ham, roast goose, and curry followed, served with potatoes, peas, tomatoes, corn, asparagus, spinach and taro. For dessert, guests were offered wine jelly, sponge cake, and strawberries and cream. Sherry hock, claret, champagne, port, liqueurs, tea and coffee were served.[31] Except for the taro and the local fish, this was a typical Anglo-French modern monarchical banquet.

FOOD, CULTURE & SOCIETY

Hawaii had been re-connected to the global culinary world when Captain Cook landed in the Islands in 1778, quickly followed by other westerners, most importantly Congregational missionaries from New England. The Kamehamehas quickly united the Islands under a single rule. The Hawaiians, having been isolated from the theocratic cuisines that had ruled for centuries in most grain-based states, were suddenly confronted with modern cuisine, based in scientific nutritional theory, employing ovens and metal pots, and using wheat, cattle, and grape vines.[32] The missionaries challenged the religious system underlying the sacrifice. The sacrificial feast disappeared within decades, and the rules separating the cuisines of men and women, nobility and commoner were jettisoned in 1819.

The Kamehamehas opted to make the Islands a kingdom on the English model introduced by Captain Cook, not a republic of the kind the New England missionaries came from. This enabled them to assert their place in the modern world while retaining hierarchy, albeit not as fierce a hierarchy as earlier.[33] Adaptations of Anglo-French cuisine demonstrated to dignitaries and foreign governments that theirs was a cosmopolitan kingdom that played on the world stage, an aspect of what is now called "soft power." They established fine restaurant dining, imported ice, as Hiʻilei Hobart shows in this issue, to show their modernity, and restricted ice and alcohol to the ruling class. Hence the apparent paradox of the Hawaiian ruling class naturalizing a cuisine from the other side of the world can be resolved by recognizing that Anglo-French high cuisine had been naturalized as culturally local, at least for ceremonial occasions, by states from Chile to Japan, from Thailand to the Ottoman Empire as a sign that they were modern.

Hawaii's cuisines ceased to be agriculturally local. Taro was joined and then surpassed by wheat and rice as staples of the diet. By the 1850s, wheat was being grown on Maui and milled in Honolulu. By the late 1860s, wheat was being imported from California. Western implements and ingredients entered the cuisine of ordinary Hawaiians. They found metal pots handier than underground ovens for cooking taro for poi. Hard tack was good for a quick snack, and when condensed milk became available toward the end of the century, it could be added to make a dessert. Beef, often as curry or stew, made a tasty meal. Salt salmon became a favorite.

At the end of the nineteenth century, King David Kalakaua continued earlier Hawaiian monarchs' practice of establishing credentials by adopting western diplomatic protocol, including the use of Anglo-French high cuisine for formal dining. He hired architects and builders to construct a palace in his capital Honolulu, which, now provisioned by grains, reached a population of 23,000 by 1890 and almost 40,000 a decade later.[34] He ordered oak Gothic Revival furniture from the Davenport Company in Boston, and sent to Paris for blue-bordered porcelain with the Hawaiian coat-of-arms. On a world tour in 1881, Kalakaua visited, among others, the Emperor of Japan, the Queen of England, President Chester Arthur of the United States, and the King of Siam, who had very successfully adopted western goods, including diplomatic dinners, to put his monarchy on an equal footing with western powers and ward off colonization.[35] Together Kalakaua's palace, dining paraphernalia, and a coronation in 1883 cost over $360,000 when total annual exports from the Island were valued at about $5 million.

The plantation owners and factors, the dominant faction among the resident foreigners, preferred middle-class thrift to princely magnificence, the meals of

THE FOODWAYS OF HAWAI'I

prosperous merchants to the banquets of kings, plain New England cooking to high cuisine.[36] Their everyday meals featured chowder, salmon ring prepared with canned salmon, spaghetti with meat sauce, curried dishes, devil's food cake, and brownies, taro as a substitute for potatoes, green mango sauce for applesauce, and taro leaves for spinach. In their view, a republic was a better model for a modern state than a monarchy. In 1893, a year after Kalakaua's coronation, a group of Hawaii-born men of European ancestry overthrew the monarchy and established an independent republic, which, in turn, was annexed to the United States in 1898. Although it would be disingenuous to suggest that a coronation dinner alone led to the downfall of the Hawaiian monarchy, it did throw into high relief political differences between haoles and the Hawaiian royalty.

Kamaaina Cuisine, with the gracious poi supper as its signature meal, was the cuisine of the political elite during the sixty years from 1898 to 1957 when Hawaii was a Territory of the United States. On special occasions, the elite abandoned their plain New England dining and gathered for a festive poi supper. Dressed in tuxedos and holokus (long dresses with trains), they sat around a table covered with ti leaves, strewn with flowers, and set with crystal for wine, polished coconut bowls for poi, and fingerbowls. To the dishes of laulau, kalua pig, chicken luau, and mullet baked in ti leaves that they delicately ate with their fingers, they added relishes of inamona (toasted ground nuts), red salt, green onions, and seaweed.[37] Ample but not extravagant, formal but distinct from Anglo-French manners, the meal expressed their complex loyalties.

From the republican New England tradition came the rejection of monarchical grandeur and the term "supper" not "dinner." From a still-to-be researched international plantation tradition came the formal dress, the crystal wine glasses, and a liking for curried dishes acquired as owners and managers went back and forth from Lousiana to Fiji, Mauritius to Indonesia, and to the Caribbean. From the Hawaiian tradition came the poi, the lomi lomi salmon, the relishes, and the use of fingers. The poi supper clearly proclaimed that although the Hawaiian monarchy had been overthrown, the Island's leaders identified as much with Hawaii as with the United States.

During the period of kamaaina cuisine, two other kinds of cuisine appeared in the Islands. One cuisine was "luau" cuisine, an exotic but unthreatening cuisine created for wealthy mainland vacationers who arrived on Matson steamers to stay in the Royal Hawaiian Hotel on Waikiki Beach.[38] Supposedly Hawaiian, in fact the cuisine was patched together from different elements in just the same way that provincial French cuisine was being put together to suit the tastes of the wealthy motorist. In Hawaii, hoteliers served readily acceptable kalua pork with long rice (Chinese rice noodles) and lomi lomi salmon, reducing the less popular poi to a small side offering. Similarly, in France, restaurateurs added more meat to regional dishes, replaced lard with butter, and eliminated strong flavorings such as garlic. In Hawaii, waitresses were expected to wear invented "traditional" dress such as sarongs as they offered food and exotic cocktails in coconut bowls to provide an "authentic" exotic experience.

THE FOODWAYS OF HAWAI'I

In France, waitresses were expected to don regional dress as they handed out regional pottery in dining rooms furnished with regional furniture, both pottery and furniture turned out in newly founded factories established for the purpose. In both cases, the aim was to present the tourists with an appealing meal that could be presented as homegrown.

The other new kind of cuisine was "ethnic" cuisine. As new diseases reduced the native population to around 60,000, the workers who came from many parts of the world to labor on the sugar and pineapple plantations brought their cuisines with them. Belatedly, variants of two theocratic cuisines were naturalized in the Islands: the largely Buddhist humble cuisine brought by the Asians; and the humble Catholic cuisine brought by the Filipinos, Portuguese, and Puerto Ricans. To process their food, the immigrants set up rice mills, sake factories, noodle shops, and bakeries. They bought their groceries from plantation stores carrying American processed goods or from the farmers, importers, peddlers, merchants, food processors and shopkeepers of their own ethnic group. Briefly these ethnic cuisines were agriculturally local as immigrants planted their staple, rice, in abandoned taro paddies, grew vegetables, and caught fish inside the reef. By the end of the century, though, rice was shipped in from Japan, Texas, Louisiana, and California.[39]

Although the different ethnic groups became aware of one another's cuisines when they shared lunch pails, the cuisines remained distinct. In the plantation camps, the housing was ethnically separated, deliberately maintaining rather than breaking down ethnic identity.[40] Indeed different ethnic groups can live in proximity for decades or centuries, coming to share certain foodstuffs and culinary practices over time without creating a new fusion cuisine. India, for example, had many longstanding ethnically or religiously distinct cuisines prior to, and continuing long after, it became a nation. When in 1947 the University of Hawaii home economist Katherine Bazore described the culinary scene in *Hawaiian and Pacific Foods*, she treated Hawaiian, Samoan, Chinese, Japanese, Korean, Portuguese, Filipino, and Haole quite separately.[41]

Local Food, the food of a modern American state, was created when political conditions changed to make it desirable to have a statewide cuisine. This occurred following 1959, when Hawaii was granted Statehood and the kamaaina Republicans were voted out, and in short order the plantation workers voted Democrat as a bloc.

The change in Island politics from an oligarchy to a democracy, from a colony to a state posed three challenges to the Asian-dominated Democrats. They had to unify different "ethnic" groups, which, except for a couple of generations in Hawaii, had nothing in common (and often longstanding differences in their regions of origin). They had to find a democratic alternative to earlier hierarchical cuisines, a way of asserting island identity that while not native Hawaiian did not exclude Native Hawaiians. They had to create a state identity different from the distant and somewhat threatening mainland.

Local Food, invented quickly by patching together elements of three layers of naturalized cuisines, the ethnic, the kamaaina, and the Hawaiian, neatly helped achieve all these goals. In terming the patchwork cuisine Local, the people of Hawaii were inverting the word's negative meaning as a name for the brown-skinned people of Hawaii, whether Hawaiian or Asian. Before World War II, although some island residents as well as mainland sociologists thought the mixed population to be a model for the future, powerful groups in the Islands disagreed.[42] In 1931 and 1932 in the widely publicized Massie trials, a white naval officer's wife claimed she had been raped by young men, one of whom was later severely beaten and another murdered when her family took the law into their own hands. "Local" was the word the press used to refer to the presumed perpetrators of the rape.[43] Kamaaina cuisine faded away as had Hawaiian monarchical cuisine earlier, luau cuisine was produced for thousands as airlines brought in tourists in ever-larger numbers, and ethnic cuisines continued to flourish in homes and in the festivals of different cultural groups.

The public cuisine of the state, though, was now Local Food. The plate lunch, the beach picnic, the garage party and the open-to-all buffets politicians offered at the start of the legislative session displaced the gracious poi supper as the archetypal meals. Politicians, such as Governor Waihee who referred to himself as "a Spam-and-rice kind of guy," took good care to identify with Local Food.[44]

Inexpensive and available to all from lunch wagons, Local Food became a secret code, something Locals knew about and mainlanders did not. It was the springboard for comedians' jokes, lovingly described in cartoon cookbooks that contrasted it to tasteless mainland food, while "it musubi your birthday" cards also played on the Local identity invisible to mainlanders.[45] And Local Food enabled locals to set to one side mainland stereotypes: a haven for military rest and recreation; home of canned pineapple; a tropical paradise enjoyed by Elvis Presley in *Blue Hawaii* in 1961, and in *Paradise Hawaiian Style* in 1966; a place where square-jawed Americans were supported by those of indeterminate other races in the popular television series *Hawaii 5-0* that ran from 1968 to 1979; inspiration for the exotic food in Trader Vics restaurants; and beaches where girls in sarongs and coconut shell bras danced while diners drank blue cocktails decorated with little paper umbrellas as they attended "authentic" Hawaiian luaus. Historians and sociologists use the term "banal" or "everyday" nationalism to describe the ordinary things, such as flags, anthems, and cuisine, that make people feel part of a nation.[46] Local Food was a triumphant expression of everyday Statehood.

Epilogue: Hawaii's Culinary Future

What does the future hold for the cuisines of Hawaii? As Local Food reached its peak popularity in the 1980s and 1990s, the economics, politics, and demography of the Islands shifted. The plantations, the Islands' economic base for a century, had begun closing in the 1970s and vanished by 2000, unable to compete against cheaper land and labor in other parts of the world. Young Locals whether part-Hawaiian, kamaaina, or Asian found it near impossible to get professional jobs. By 2000, a third of those born in the Islands were leaving for

THE FOODWAYS OF HAWAI'I

the mainland.[47] They were replaced as new, often wealthy settlers arrived from the mainland, Japan, and China. In addition, tourism continued to increase to seven million visitors a year. It is indicative of these changes that Linda Lingle, the governor elected in 2002, was neither a member of the old Republican oligarchy nor a Local, but a migrant from California.

New alliances were struck, new economic strategies tried, and history rethought. Hawaii felt the effects of a global indigenous rights movement.[48] For native Hawaiians, 1978 had been a crystallizing moment. Following a vigorous renaissance of Hawaiian culture, including the foundation of the Polynesian Voyaging Society soon to recreate the original Pacific migration, the Office of Hawaiian Affairs was created by the Hawaii State Constitutional Convention. In 1993, Bill Clinton apologized for annexation. Many Hawaiian and academic activists rejected the story of an upwardly mobile racially mixed society, symbolized by Local Food, in favor of one of oppressive Asian settler colonialism.[49]

Unaware of these local conflicts, many new residents who had come in search of a tropical paradise, as well as some longer-established ones, wanted a sustainable agriculture that made the Islands more self-sufficient in food. Hawaiian activists, as detailed elsewhere in this issue, claimed land to grow taro and other traditional crops. Both groups clashed with corporations that wanted to take advantage of a climate which allowed three crops a year to establish plant-breeding (including GMO) programs and with Locals growing GMO papaya for export to the mainland.

In response to these political changes, Hawaii's cuisines began shifting once again. The tastes of Locals, new residents, and tourists were no longer satisfied solely with the egalitarian, but rough and ready, plate lunches or with commercial luaus at which a thousand people were served. Already in 1992, a group of chefs had formed to promote a new high cuisine, Hawaii Regional Cuisine. Some, such as Alan Wong, Roy Yamaguchi, and Sam Choy, were Local. Others were mainlanders working in the hotels and restaurants of the hospitality industry. What Hawaii Regional Cuisine meant was fluid. Alan Wong and Roy Yamaguchi took the Local tradition of combining foods of different ethnic groups upmarket. Others turned to local ingredients in the sense of ingredients brought to the Islands by the first settlers. "Canoe foods" were introduced to restaurants. "Pa'i'ai [fresh, hand-pounded poi] has been taken to a new level by frying in butter to attain a crispy caramelization. Ulu (breadfruit) is now mainstream when in season," explained Lori Wong on the culinary staff of Windward Community College.[50] Yet others used local fruits and vegetables grown in the Islands, local cuisine in the mainland sense of local. New farmers' markets, ones that sold tomatoes and lettuce, ran in parallel with the rotating farmers' markets that supplied "ethnic" ingredients. While the menus of, say, Alan Wong, Sam Choy and Roy Yamaguchi reflect island history as well as newly locally grown foods, other chefs offer a cuisine attuned to mainland tastes with Hawaiian, Asian and tropical touches. As the population becomes more typical of the mainland United States, it seems likely that a mainland-oriented cuisine will overtake and displace Local Food.

Meanwhile, Local Food has migrated to the mainland and beyond as Locals have left the Islands. Roy Yamaguchi opened a score of restaurants across the mainland. L & L Hawaiian Barbecue, a small plate-lunch place on Liliha Avenue when I was in the Islands, now has dozens of franchises from California to New York. Mainlanders, who understandably have no idea of the complex culinary politics of Hawaii, call this Local Food "Hawaiian Cuisine." Although the distinctions between homegrown, naturalized, and invented cuisines, and the tripartite meanings of local may be a little over-schematic, they do make clear why, from the Local point of view, this is as way off mark as calling the barbeque, chili, and chicken fried steak of Texas "Comanche Cuisine."[51]

Acknowledgements

I would like to thank Hi'ilei Hobart for inviting me to reflect on how I came to write *The Food of Paradise*, for her patience as I struggled to reconstruct the state of food studies in the 1980s, and for her careful editing.

Disclosure statement

No potential conflict of interest was reported by the author.

Notes

1. Rachel Laudan, *The Food of Paradise: Exploring Hawaii's Culinary Heritage* (Honolulu: University of Hawaii Press, 1996). Neither in my book nor in this article have I chosen to insert diacriticals on Hawaiian words. My reason is that I want to make the text as easy as possible for readers to understand. Few readers of either have any knowledge of the Hawaiian language and adding diacriticals makes words already familiar in English seem strange and distant. So for these readers I use Hawaii, not Hawai'i, just as I would use Mexico, not México. If I were writing for native speakers or those learning the language, then I would consider the use of diacriticals essential.
2. Rachel Laudan, *Cuisine and Empire: Cooking in World History* (Berkeley, CA: University of California Press, 2013).
3. Francine du Plessix Gray, *Hawaii: The Sugar-Coated Fortress*, 1st ed. (New York:

THE FOODWAYS OF HAWAI'I

Random House, 1972); Richard L. Rapson, *Fairly Lucky You Live Hawaii!: Cultural Pluralism in the Fiftieth State* (Lanham, MD: University Press of America, 1980); Randall W. Roth, James Mak, and Jack P. Suyderhoud, eds., *The Price of Paradise: Lucky We Live Hawaii* (Honolulu: Ku Pa'a Pub, 1992).

4. Chinese migrants from Guangdong had introduced rice, may have run the first sugar mills, and practiced as bakers using skills they had learned in the Treaty Ports. Susan Kim, ed., *We Go Eat a Mixed Plate from Hawaii's Food Culture* (Honolulu, Hawaii: Hawaii Council for the Humanities, 2008).
5. Edward D. Beechert, *Working in Hawaii: A Labor History* (Honolulu: University of Hawaii Press, 1985); Ronald T. Takaki, *Pau Hana: Plantation Life and Labor in Hawaii, 1835–1920* (Honolulu: University of Hawaii Press, 1983).
6. Rachel Laudan, ed., *The Nature of Technological Knowledge: Are Models of Scientific Change Relevant?* (Dordrecht, Holland: Reidel, 1984); Thomas Parke Hughes, *Networks of Power: Electrification in Western Society, 1880–1930* (Baltimore, MD: Johns Hopkins University Press, 1988); David F. Noble, *Forces of Production: A Social History of Industrial Automation* (New York: Oxford University Press, 1986).
7. Eleanor C. Nordyke, *The Peopling of Hawaii* (Honolulu: University of Hawaii Press, 1977); John F. MacDermott, Thomas W. Maretzki, and Wen-Shing Tseng, eds., *People and Cultures of Hawaii: A Psychocultural Profile* (Honolulu: University of Hawaii Press, 1980); Lawrence H. Fuchs, *Hawaii Pono: A Social History* (San Diego: Harcourt Brace Jovanovich, 1984).
8. The state of anthropology and history of food at the time is usefully summarized in Jack Goody, *Cooking, Cuisine, and Class: A Study in Comparative Sociology* (Cambridge: Cambridge University Press, 1982), chap. 2; K. C. Chang, ed., *Food in Chinese Culture: Anthropological and Historical Perspectives* (New Haven: Yale University Press, 1977); E. N. Anderson, *The Food of China* (New Haven: Yale University Press, 1988).
9. Barbara Ketcham Wheaton, *Savoring the Past: The French Kitchen and Table from 1300 to 1789* (Philadelphia: University of Pennsylvania Press, 1983).
10. Jackie Newman's *Flavor and Fortune* (1994 on) was a wealth of information about Chinese traditions little known in the United States. I was delighted to be able to contribute a short piece on crack seed, a Hawaiian dried, salted fruit snack of Chinese origin. R. W. (Bob) Lucky's *Asian Foodbookery* (1996 on), with its historical extracts and personal observations, made it quite clear that distinct, unchanging national cuisines were no more than a myth. Other important newsletters were Ed Behr's *Art of Eating* (1986–), which concentrated on fine dining and Sandy Oliver's *Food History News* (1989 on), which concentrated on the mainland United States.
11. The Boston Culinary Historians was founded in 1980 in Boston by Barbara Wheaton and Joyce Toomre, who was to publish *Classic Russian Cooking: Elena Molokhovets' A Gift to Young Housewives* (Bloomington, Indiana: Indiana University Press) in 1992. It was followed in 1983 by the Ann Arbor group, at the instigation of the antiquarian cookbook dealer and historian of American community cookbooks, Jan Longone, and the New York Culinary Historians in 1985. A talk to the latter group gave me a chance to try out my ideas about three diasporas and fusion foods, as well as treating them to Spam musubi and other Local delicacies. There I met a kindred spirit in Cara de Silva, then pioneering writing on immigrant foods of New York in *New York*

Newsday. When I was at the Shelby Cullom Davis Center for Historical Studies at the University of Princeton and the Princeton Institute for Advanced Studies in 1994–5, I noticed that Betty Fussell's recently published book *The Story of Corn* (New York: Knopf, 1993), mentioned that she done her PhD at the university. With this tenuous connection, I ventured to write to her to ask if anyone else in the New York area was working on food history. A week later I was sitting in her book-lined apartment in Greenwich Village. She introduced me to Elizabeth Andoh, *An American Taste of Japan* (New York: William Morrow, 1985) and Raymond Sokolov.

12. Tom Jaine, "Obituary: Alan Davidson," *Guardian*, accessed June 29, 2015, http://www.theguardian.com/news/2003/dec/04/guardianobituaries.food. When I plucked up my courage to send him a letter asking if he would be interested in a piece on Hawaii's food for *PPC*, I received an enthusiastic midnight call.
13. *Wall Street Journal* Leisure editor, cookbook author, and food historian Ray Sokolov had already been thinking along similar lines. He put me to the test by taking me to a then still-exotic-on-the-mainland Korean restaurant but after nearly a decade in Hawaii it was a breeze. Raymond A. Sokolov, *Why We Eat What We Eat: How the Encounter between the New World and the Old Changed the Way Everyone on the Planet Eats* (New York: Summit Books, 1991).
14. Virginia K. Bartlett, *Pickles and Pretzels: Pennsylvania's World of Food* (Pittsburgh: University of Pittsburgh Press, 1980).
15. Mary Taylor Simeti, *On Persephone's Island: A Sicilian Journal* (New York: Knopf, 1986).
16. Judith Midgley Kirkendall, "Hawaiian Ethnogastronomy: The Development of a Pidgin-Creole Cuisine," PhD dissertation, University of Hawaii, 1985.
17. I am aware of the problems of the term "ethnic." However, this was common usage at the time. Besides, a satisfactory alternative to the storefront restaurants and small shops of recent immigrants has yet to be found.
18. Accessed June 15 2016. http://www.hawaii.edu/satocenter/pace/pace_news/7-charlene.htm. Wanda A. Adams, *The Island Plate: 150 Years of Recipes and Food Lore from the Honolulu Advertiser* (Island Heritage Publishing, 2006).
19. Doreen Fernandez, *Sarap: Essays on Philippine Food* (Aduana, Intramuros, Manila: Mr. & Ms. Pub. Co, 1988).
20. "Isabella Abbott," Accessed June 15, 2016. http://news.stanford.edu/news/2010/december/izzie-abbott-obit-120710.html.
21. Joan Clark, *Honolulu Advertiser*, December 25, 1996; D10,9; Anne Mendelson, "Aloha, food fusion," *Los Angles Times*, June 18, 1997.
22. William McNeill, *A World History* (New York: Oxford University Press, 1967); McNeill, *Plagues and Peoples* (Garden City, NY: Anchor Press, 1976); McNeill, *The Pursuit of Power: Technology, Armed Force, and Society since A.D. 1000* (Chicago: University of Chicago Press, 1982).
23. Alfred W. Crosby, *The Columbian Exchange: Biological and Cultural Consequences of 1492* (Westport, CT: Greenwood Press, 1972).
24. Philip D. Curtin, *The Atlantic Slave Trade: A Census* (Madison: University of Wisconsin Press, 1969); *Cross-Cultural Trade in World History* (Cambridge: Cambridge University Press, 1984), 1.
25. "Jerry H. Bentley (1949–2012)," *American Historical Association*, accessed August

2, 2015, http://blog.historians.org/2012/07/jerry-h-bentley-19492012/; Jerry H. Bentley, *Old World Encounters: Cross-Cultural Contacts and Exchanges in Pre-Modern Times* (New York: Oxford University Press, 1993); Jerry H. Bentley and Herbert F. Ziegler, *Traditions and Encounters: A Global Perspective on the Past* (Boston: McGraw Hill, 2000).

26. Peter Farb and George J Armelagos, *Consuming Passions: The Anthropology of Eating* (Boston: Houghton Mifflin, 1980); Elisabeth Rozin, *Ethnic Cuisine: The Flavor-Principle Cook-Book* (Lexington, MA: S. Greene Press, 1983).

27. Kaori O'Connor, "The Hawaiian Luau: Food As Tradition, Transgression, Transformation and Travel," *Food, Culture and Society: An International Journal of Multidisciplinary Research* 11, no. 2 (June 1, 2008), 4–7; Laudan, *Cuisine and Empire*, 43–7, for the philosophy and practice of culinary feasts.

28. For the foods of other parts of this diaspora, see Nancy J. Pollock, *These Roots Remain: Food Habits in Islands of the Central and Eastern Pacific Since Western Contact* (Laie, Hawaii; Honolulu, Hawaii: Institute for Polynesian Studies, 1992); Helen Leach, *From Kai to Kiwi Kitchen: New Zealand's Culinary Traditions and Cookbooks* (Dunedin, New Zealand: Otago University Press, 2010), chap. 1; Patrick Vinton Kirch and Jean-Louis Rallu, *The Growth and Collapse of Pacific Island Societies Archaeological and Demographic Perspectives* (Honolulu: University of Hawai'i Press, 2007). Gwen Skinner, *The Cuisine of the South Pacific* (Auckland: HarperCollins, 1985); Jennifer Brennan, *Tradewinds and Coconuts: A Reminiscence and Recipes from the Pacific Islands* (Boston: Periplus) 2000.

29. Storrs L. Olson and Helen F. James, "Fossil Birds from the Hawaiian Islands: Evidence for Wholesale Extinction by Man Before Western Contact," *Science* 217, no. 4560 (August 13, 1982): 633–35.

30. 40. Laudan, *Cuisine and Empire*, 35–6.

31. The menu comes from a printed version that I purchased at Iolani Palace during my time in Hawaii. For other Kalakaua menus, see Rachel Laudan, "Two Reasons Why I Am Interested in What King Kalakaua of Hawaii Ate," *Rachel Laudan*, accessed June 7, 2015, http://www.rachellaudan.com/2014/01/two-reasons-why-i-am-interested-in-what-king-kalakaua-of-hawaii-ate.html.

32. Others came too, such as Mexicans from California, then still part of Mexico; imported plants such as mangoes and avocadoes increased the range of fruits and vegetables.

33. Gavan Daws, *Shoal of Time: A History of the Hawaiian Islands* (New York: Macmillan, 1968), 55–60.

34. "2010 Census—Honolulu CCD Population," United States Census Bureau, Population Division, April 1, 2010.

35. See Maurizio Peleggi, *Lords of Things: The Fashioning of the Siamese Monarchy's Modern Image* (Honolulu: University of Hawaii Press, 2002) for consumption, and David Thompson, *Thai Food* (Berkeley, CA: Ten Speed Press, 2002), for their clever use of French cuisine.

36. Laudan, *Cuisine and Empire*, 2013, 289–90.

37. Maili Yardley, *Hawaii Cooks* (Rutland, VT: Tuttle Publishing, 1970), 18.

38. For the complex history of the luau, see O'Connor, "The Hawaiian Luau," op. cit., 149–72.

39. David Livingston Crawford, *Hawaii's Crop Parade: A Review of Useful Products De-

rived from the Soil in the Hawaiian Islands, Past and Present* (Honolulu, Hawaii: Advertiser Pub. Co., 1937), 287; 217–18.

40. Arnold Hiura, Rao Huo, and Dawn Sakamoto Paiva, *From Kau Kau to Cuisine: An Island Cookbook, Then and Now* (Honolulu: Watermark Pub., 2013).
41. Katherine Bazore, *Hawaiian and Pacific Foods; a Cook Book of Culinary Customs and Recipes Adapted for the American Hostess* (New York: M. Barrows, 1947).
42. Shelley Sang-Hee Lee and Rick Baldoz, "'A Fascinating Interracial Experiment Station': Remapping the Orient–Occident Divide in Hawai'i," *American Studies* 49, no. 3 (2008): 87–109; Lawrence H. Fuchs, *Hawaii Pono: A Social History* (New York: Harcourt, 1961).
43. John P. Rosa, "Local Story: The Massie Case Narrative and the Cultural Production of Local Identity in Hawai'i," *Amerasia Journal* 26, no. 2 (January 1, 2000): 93–115.
44. http://ethics.hawaii.gov/wp-content/uploads/2014/06/LegislativeAllowanceFunds.pdf, p. 15, retrieved 20 April 2015. *Food of Paradise*, 69.
45. Pat Sasaki, Douglas Simonson, and Ken Sakata, *Pupus to Da Max* (Honolulu, Hawaii: Bess Press, 1986).
46. Michael Billig, *Banal Nationalism* (London; Thousand Oaks, CA: Sage, 1995).
47. http://www.nytimes.com/interactive/2014/08/13/upshot/where-people-in-each-state-were-born.html?smid=tw-share&_r=0&abt=0002&abg=0#Hawaii, accessed August 20, 2014.
48. For a review of these developments, Paul Lyons, "'They Will Eat Us Up': Remembering Hawai'i," *American Literary History* 16, no. 3 (2004): 543–57.
49. Candace Fujikane and Jonathan Y. Okamura, *Asian Settler Colonialism: From Local Governance to the Habits of Everyday Life in Hawai'i* (Honolulu: University of Hawai'i Press, 2008).
50. Personal communication, Lori Wong, Food Business Feasibility Planner, Windward Community College, November 11, 2014.
51. http://ny.eater.com/2015/4/24/8490575/hawaiian-food-nyc-where-to-eat, accessed April 24, 2014.

FOOD, CULTURE & SOCIETY

Snowy Mountaineers and Soda Waters: Honolulu and Its Age of Ice Importation

Hi'ilei Julia Hobart

Abstract

In 1850, Honolulu received its first shipment of cold, clear ice for public sale. Used to chill cocktails and other refreshments, comestible coldness underwent a process of intense meaning-making that reflected the discourses concerning race and civility that played out across Hawai'i's growing urban environment. This article analyzes the political and social dimensions of ice's introduction to Honolulu in order to show how taste, and particularly the taste for coldness, emerged from, responded to, and pushed back against a burgeoning American settler colonial project. It shows that before coldness became so unremarkably common in Hawai'i, a place where water freezes only atop its three tallest mountain peaks during the coldest months of the year, the early introduction of ice cut across the deeply moralized and highly politicized foodscape of mid-nineteenth century Hawai'i.

"It is evident," opined an 1871 editorial in the *Hawaiian Gazette*, "that to have ice, purchasable as a regular and cheap commodity, we must rely upon its being manufactured here; and as such manufacture has been demonstrated in other places to be possible at a commercial profit, we see no reason why it should continue to be a luxury here, or at times not obtainable at any price however large."[1] A full two decades after comestible ice had been introduced to Hawai'i, the city of Honolulu still had not secured a reliable source for frozen water. Many of its residents, including the royalty and business class, had developed a taste for it in their drinks and so resigned themselves to impatiently waiting for the promise of still-nascent freezing technology to be fulfilled. The alternative had already proved unsuccessful: shipping in great blocks of frozen glacier and lake water from Alaska and the American Northeast. The effort could not be sustained, largely because ice shipments were remarkably unprofitable and lengthy; indeed, before construction of the Panama Canal a trip from Boston, Massachusetts, always included a harrowing pass around Cape Horn, and usually a stop in San Francisco before crossing the blue expanse of the Pacific Ocean to the Hawaiian archipelago. Yet for a time ice came, much to the delight of the city's elite, who found its refreshing qualities to be most agreeable when used for chilling cocktails, wines, and (for the temperate) soda waters. Before it came into popular use as a food preservative, the social practice of refreshing oneself with chilled drinks drove the demand for ice in warm, remote Hawai'i, encouraging an infrastructure of coldness that, by the turn of the century, permeated its foodscape.

Recalling the early history of ice in Hawai'i is central to understanding its modern food system. Hawai'i not only depends on, but *thrives* on coldness. Hawai'i's people take for granted the ice that has come to be expected in their grocery stores, their kitchens, or after a Sunday at the beach. Economists and activists alike recognize the precariousness with which residents depend on the shipment of refrigerated or frozen fruits and vegetables from overseas markets to feed its dense population; only about ten percent of food is produced locally.[2] However, little consideration has been given to the *symbolic* importance of coldness in Hawai'i's food system. A taste for coldness, developed globally in the nineteenth century as a practice of refreshment, also silently structures life in the Islands today. Ice is a vital element of the tourism industry, where it is a popular practice for visitors to cool themselves with maitais and Blue Hawai'is served in coconuts and tiki glasses on the artificial expanse of Waikiki beach.[3] It is celebrated as part of local cuisine in the form of shave ice (a product that cannot help but declare its affinity to Hawai'i's complicated history with sugar). This article argues that before coldness became so *unremarkably* common in Hawai'i, a place where water freezes only atop its three tallest mountain peaks during the coldest months of the year, the early introduction of ice cut across the deeply moralized and highly politicized foodscape of mid-nineteenth-century Hawai'i.

Although ultimately unprofitable and summarily abandoned, the ice trade's relationship with the alcohol market created a small but fertile battleground within a much larger war over political power—including commodity regulation, native rule, and a vigorous temperance movement. Questions over *who* would consume ice, *how*, and for *what reasons* spoke eloquently to the developing colonial landscape in Hawai'i; American interests vied for a favored trade relationship over Great Britain and France, foreign businessmen whispered their dissent from the monarchy, and laws prohibiting the native population from consuming alcohol created discriminatory consumption patterns. The very properties of ice in Hawai'i—its ephemerality, coldness, and newness—and its cultural associations—with whiteness, alcohol, and leisure—greatly shaped its complicated reception in the Islands. Ali'i (royalty) and the business class ordered iced cocktails at Honolulu hotels and saloons at the same time that temperance advocates sang "cold water hymns" in protest at immoral consumption; the Hawaiian government enforced laws prohibiting the sale of alcohol to "natives" while simultaneously collecting tax revenues from imported liquor (and the ice used to chill it); and questions that connected sovereignty with the taste for coldness, however far-fetched, reverberated long after this moment in Hawai'i's history. Through an analysis of the social, material, and legal contexts of ice's introduction to Honolulu society, I show how Western ideas about race, civility, and temperature became central to the development of taste in Hawai'i.

An account of Hawai'i's "first" ice shipment, which appeared in the American journal *The Californian* in 1881, provides a cogent example of how frozen water existed at the very intersection of these national and international concerns.[4] The article, entitled "Schemes to Annex the Sandwich Islands," makes one most curious assertion: that a single shipment of ice drove King Kamehameha III (Kauikeaouli) to his death and inadvertently preserved the Hawaiian Islands' sovereignty during a time of precarious political change. In fact, if one reads contemporary accounts that circulated through the popular press at the time of the mō'ī's (monarch's) death—around mid-December 1854—it is difficult to ascertain exactly *what* happened.[5] Newspaper articles generally focus on reactions: the grief of his nation, funeral details, and the business of appointing his successor, but actually say very little about the King's extended illness or his swift decline.[6] Perhaps it is this very lack of information that made it possible for this particular article to take considerable liberties with its telling of how ice meddled with international politics. Its narrative, though generously fictionalized, is tellingly animated by food: ice, butter, and alcohol.

The author, a teetotaler named James O'Meara, claimed witness to the events that he believed frustrated American desires for colonization. His story can be summarized as follows: on October 2, 1854, the Honolulu-bound steamer *Sea Bird* departed San Francisco carrying O'Meara, three unnamed US representatives tasked with negotiating a treaty of annexation, and a treacherously short-changed fuel store. The mission seemed doomed from the start when the ship ran out of coal two hundred miles from its destination, leaving the vessel bobbing helplessly in the middle of the Pacific Ocean. However, and as luck would have it, one day later a passing whaling ship offered a quantity of blubber scraps that powered the men past Maui Island and into the Moloka'i (Ka'iwi) Channel. With O'ahu nearly in sight and the blubber spent, the men hoisted sail and began breaking up any spare wood. Desks, trim, and chairs went into the furnace. As they approached land with the *Sea Bird* stripped to her bones, the food stores offered a last resort. At approximately 6:30 p.m. in the dusk of October 14, 1854, she limped into Honolulu harbor burning a final, lone keg of butter.[7]

FOOD, CULTURE & SOCIETY

In what O'Meara called "the warm days of November," about a month following the *Sea Bird*'s appearance, a cargo of natural ice arrived to be sold exclusively by local drinking establishment the Merchants' Exchange. So thrilling a novelty, O'Meara claimed, incited what can only be described as a royal bender:

> [The ice] was a luxury of untold gratification to the American and European residents; a marvel of uncommon curiosity and interest to the natives, from the King to the lowest.... Peck Cutrell was shrewd enough to discover and utilize this novelty. He made a large punch-bowl full of champagne cocktail, iced and decocted to appetizing completeness, and sent it to the Palace for the King's own delectation.[8]

The King, enchanted by the chilled alcohol, immediately put in a standing order for iced punch to be delivered regularly to the palace. After a number of days enjoying the cocktail in private, he honored Cutrell's saloon with a personal visit. O'Meara claimed that the punch provoked such a severe drinking binge that it eventually caused the monarch's death a few weeks later on December 15, 1854. He reports that:

> On Saturday the King complained of indisposition.... Sunday he was recuperating. Monday he was able to sit up. Tuesday morning his faithful personal attendant was giving him a hand-bath of brandy ... at half-past 11 o'clock the signal announced from the Palace that the King was dead.[9]

Kamehameha III allegedly sent his servant out during a brandy bath designed to revive him and, unsupervised, consumed the bathwater that sealed his fate. According to O'Meara, the King was scheduled to sign a treaty of annexation to the United States the day before his death on Monday, December 14.

It is worth mentioning at this point that no other public accounts of Kamehameha III's death mention iced cocktails or the almost-signing of an annexation treaty. On the contrary, Hawai'i historian Ralph Kuykendall shows that debates over American treaties had resulted in general *opposition* to an agreement, illustrated most obviously by Kamehameha III's proclamation published on December 8 of that year in *The Polynesian*, which affirmed his commitment to the Kingdom's sovereignty.[10] O'Meara's narrative is therefore unreliable at best, not least because it was published in 1881 several decades after the alleged events, but also because of the strong Protestant views evidenced in his other publications, which include passionate temperance tracts. Regardless, ice functions in this story as a potent symbol of western power: coldness is presumed to be the quality that pushes the monarch's immoral liquor consumption to a deadly conclusion. Kamehameha III's fondness for alcohol—or so the story leads us to believe—provided a convenient and fatal example of indigenous shortcomings in the face of colonial pressure. Even taken as a piece of fiction, this story offers a potent vantage point into understanding how ice, a relatively minor trade commodity in Hawai'i, intersected with the very real and complex ideologies of race and 'civility' that affected its metropolitan center in the mid-nineteenth century.[11]

THE FOODWAYS OF HAWAI'I

In its 1931 issue, *Thrum's Hawaiian Annual*, the long-running almanac of Hawai'i's business, commerce, and people, summarized the Honolulu ice trade in three short paragraphs. The article, entitled "Honolulu Yesterdays," states that "Honolulu's introduction to the use and comfort of ice" could be located to three specific moments. First, a few tons, which arrived on consignment from San Francisco in June 1852. Second, less than two years later a full cargo of ice shipped from Sitka at the consignment of the local ship chandlery Swan and Clifford, resulting in "an unfortunate loss of several thousand dollars." And finally, the small ice business established after a time by C.H. Lewers, who provided semi-regular shipments from Boston between October 1858 and July 1859, and from which he failed to turn a profit.[12] In this same spirit, nearly all documentation connected to Hawai'i's age of ice importation is notably sparse and somewhat perfunctory. Newspaper research indicates that although *Thrum's* neglected to capture a full portrait of the ice trade in its short recollections, it would have been equally challenged to fill in the gaps. Without anticipated—let alone regular—shipments, Honoluluans did not spent much ink or concern on ice during the long months when its saloons and hotels returned to tepid imbibery. But when ice *did* come to town, remarks about its luxury reflect an enthusiasm for coldness that grew among the moneyed classes.

Contrary to *Thrum's* assertion that the first ice arrived in Honolulu in 1852, sources indicate that city residents had their earliest tastes of coldness in 1850. In fact, the first flurries of ice in Hawai'i must have seemed to Honolulu residents to be happening all at once, even if it would continue on at a glacial place for the next eight years. On August 24, 1850, Henry Macfarlane published an advertisement for an ice-making machine alongside an announcement for the grand re-opening of his Commercial Hotel.[13] While the functionality of his machine is questionable, considering that the earliest experiments with freezing technology operated only as prototypes in 1850, it nevertheless exists as the first *promise* of its kind.[14] For his clientele, which consisted largely of local and foreign elites, he boasted "a patent ice machine having been purposely imported at a great expense, in order to afford this luxury to the frequenters of this establishment."[15] As the advertisement ran throughout the remainder of the year, and the editorials remained silent on whether the alcohol was, indeed, "placed on the table in a state of delicious coolness" at the Commercial, the *Polynesian* announced that ice from Boston had also arrived by way of San Francisco aboard the American brig *Fortunio* on September 14, less than a month after the ice machine appeared.[16] The quantity may have been small, since the papers note no tonnage—just that the ship proceeded on to Sydney a few months later, presumably after unloading and re-stocking its cargo.

Such brevity about what should have been, at the very least, a remarkable event is not very surprising in the context of the global ice market. These early shipments to Hawai'i came at the peak of the American ice trade, which did brisk business out of Massachusetts and Maine throughout the nineteenth century.[17] The most prominent figure of this industry was Frederic Tudor, a determined man of fluctuating finances, who developed methods for shipping

FOOD,
CULTURE
SOCIETY

frozen lake water across long distances and eventually succeeded in making a small fortune from lakeside real estate (purchased for ice harvesting), though he struggled to profit directly from exports in the international market.[18] Reflective of other global sites, most of Hawai'i's imported ice accordingly arrived as an afterthought, packed into ships bound for Honolulu with extra space in their holds. As one resident recollected in 1903:

> Ice was a cargo, taken only when it was cheap in Boston and when the ships could get no other cargo for the Pacific.... The ships bringing ice, from Boston that is, would take home whale bone and oil, and usually made a good thing of it. But they did not come often. Not more than once a year, as I remember.[19]

While it is possible, then, to imagine that the earliest auction of ice blocks must have been a curious and exciting event for the city of Honolulu, any documentation of the event is simply concerned with the perfunctory business of its arrival and quick sale.[20]

For example, the *Polynesian* noted a cargo of ice in its Saturday issue on June 26, 1852, writing that "this is the first importation of its kind, in any quantity, to this market, and but the beginning, it is to be hoped, of a regular supply of this luxury to the inhabitants of this city."[21] The quantity amounted to only a few tons packed aboard the *Harriet T. Bartlett*, a bark described in 1847 as a "trim, staunch little ship" measuring about 190 tons that arrived on June 18 after a 13-day crossing from San Francisco.[22] The ice soon went to auction at the room of prominent auctioneer Fred W. Thompson at a minimum bid of 25 cents per pound. While Honolulu papers do not discuss any additional details of the ice's provenance, who purchased the ice, or how long it lasted, a contextual approach provides some likely scenarios. It is almost certain that it originated from a Russian settlement in Sitka, Alaska (from February 1852 to 1859 the Russian American Commercial Ice Company shipped an estimated 50,000 tons of natural ice to California, and particularly to the trade hub of San Francisco).[23] The ship's captain, Edward Heeren, would have most likely taken the small quantity of ice on speculation upon discovering he needed ballast for a small cargo and hoping for a quick sale. At the time, Honolulu would not have had an icehouse prepared for its storage, and perhaps for this reason little time was wasted upon its arrival and it was probably scooped up by the few bidders who could afford to spend their money on quick-melting luxury items.

No other announcements of ice appear until October of 1854, when Honolulu ship chandlers Swan & Clifford busily prepared to offer the city an ice supply with some greater regularity. A few days before the arrival of their first cargo of 500 tons, they still rushed to complete their ambitious ice house, a building designed to hold up to 1,000 tons that sat near the "Lime Kiln" at the base of Maunakea Street on land leased from the Hawaiian Kingdom.[24] On October 17, and again on November 4, 1854, Swan & Clifford advertised in the *Polynesian* they possessed ice "in quantities to suit," arrived from Prince Frederick's Sound.[25]

All of this investment of time and infrastructure intimated that the operation would be long-lasting, but four months later on March 26, 1855, Swan & Clifford closed shop and quietly left behind $40,000 of forged bills of exchange and $80,000 of "other liabilities" for a total of $100,000 in fraudulent business.[26] In this manner, ice fades in and out of the business news of Honolulu, providing little information on the practices of consumption.

To understand what the reception of ice might have actually been like in 1850s Honolulu requires, again, a contextual approach to the commercial and social environments into which it arrived: a booming port city that had recently become caught up in the throes of early capitalism. Identified by many scholars as the "critical" era of its modern development, mid-nineteenth-century Hawai'i encountered an explosive exchange with the western world of goods, people, and ideas.[27] Rudimentary wooden structures cobbled together with lumber imported from the Pacific Northwest edged in on the thatched grass hale (houses) that lined Honolulu's narrow, unpaved thoroughfares. A Court House, Market House, and the McKee & Anthon Building, which would all last into the mid-twentieth century, had been recently completed to accommodate a commercial boom brought by the whaling ships crowding Honolulu's harbor.[28] It was the most populous settlement of the Kingdom, with approximately 10,000 of O'ahu's 73,000 or so residents packing in among foreign settlers, of which there were 1,180 (about half being American).[29] This number would increase significantly throughout the decade as several important events of the time amplified Hawai'i's position within the global economy, making it an attractive outpost for westerners hoping to capitalize on Pacific trade.

Between 1845 and 1855, the land division known as the Māhele made possible fee-simple ownership of land by both foreigners and Kanaka Maoli through the dismantling of the traditional Hawaiian land tenure system.[30] In the middle of this process, Honolulu became the Kingdom's capital and soon development of its harbor began by widening and deepening in order to accommodate larger and more numerous ships.[31] These transitions reflected not only an overall orientation toward international business and trade through proximity to its generously sized harbor, but also an early racialization of the political and economic center of the Kingdom. Gavan Daws, in his study of nineteenth-century Honolulu development asserts that, "the raw data [of the Māhele] shows that in the down-town area foreigners were awarded about 50 percent of lots, and that the percentage of awards to foreigners decreased steadily as distance from the harbor increased."[32] By the end of the Māhele, the city's population had correspondingly redistributed along blurry, but discernibly racial lines, particularly where the shipping industry had made land desirable for foreigners looking for business opportunities.[33] For many, Honolulu began to increasingly resemble what some described as a western, "semi-European" town.[34]

A lively downtown area catered to revelers both high- and lowbrow: those seeking relief from the boredom of seafaring attended back alley grog shops selling cheap bootlegs, and those conducting business sipped champagne and brandy at respectable hotels. Between 1825 and 1869, over thirty hospitality

FOOD,
CULTURE&
SOCIETY

establishments in Honolulu opened their doors to accommodate visitors.[35] A lithograph created in 1854 by Swiss artist Paul Emmert provides a useful guide to the growing city and how ice might have transited across it (Figure 1).[36] Its view of the city center is given from the harbor, framed by details of notable buildings that include the new constructions mentioned above. The waterfront buildings shown *in situ* at the center of the illustration housed nearly the entire ice business and everyone in it. Starting from the left of the image: the Honolulu Iron Works, where Hawai'i's first ice machine would have been manufactured in the 1870s, and in front of which its first ice house was built before the year's end; then, to the left, the Customs House, where bills of lading and taxes for ice imports were assessed and applied; the wide building just right of center belonged to the firm Swan & Clifford who imported ice from Alaska in 1854; the ground floor of the "Waikiki side" of the Swan & Clifford building contained the office of liquor dealer Cyrus W. Jones, who applied for an ice importation license in 1856; the Merchant's Exchange from which Cutrell advertised iced champagne in 1856 would have been located in the cluster of buildings set back from the harbor just slightly to the left of Swan & Clifford.[37] Finally, just beyond the right edge of the frame sat Kamehameha III's palace, Hale Ali'i. In 1854, then, a quantity of ice could go from ship to table in a space of no more than about five city blocks.

Advertisements by confectioners, restaurants, and saloons provide additional information about who might have been consuming ice as it circulated the urban space. As a relatively rare and costly accompaniment, ice performed a legitimizing function for the beverages that it cooled. For liquor drinkers, it elevated transgressors to cosmopolitans. For soda-water tipplers, it transformed conservatism to indulgence. Enjoyed by each of these opposing groups, the newness of ice in Hawai'i meant that its social meaning had not yet been fully codified, and so groups divided on the question of alcohol's morality each embraced the appeal and novelty of coldness. To borrow the concept of anthropologist Sidney Mintz, it is possible to trace, in the wake of ice's introduction to Hawai'i, how Honolulu consumers negotiated the extensification and intensification of ice and its developing meaning.[38] By taking Euro-American uses of ice and then translating those uses into a local context, points of access within the city existed along both racial and class lines.

Upon arrival, ice appeared immediately and most notably as a coolant for alcohol in elite drinking establishments or for sale at luxury auction prices. In addition to cash-and-carry markets, it also soon found its way to consumers in decidedly more chaste forms. For example, in 1854 Hoffman's drug store advertised, "Ice! Ice! Ice!" for their "very delicious" iced sodas. Newspapers show that a confectioner boasting a supply of ice-cream opened up on Maunakea Street near the recently built ice house.[39] These two primary outlets—alcohol and ice-cream—reflected a polarity that responded not only to the powerful missionary presence that for many decades past had influenced Honolulu society, but also to contemporary American attitudes in general about the pleasures and dangers of consuming coldness. Anxieties about maintaining gender

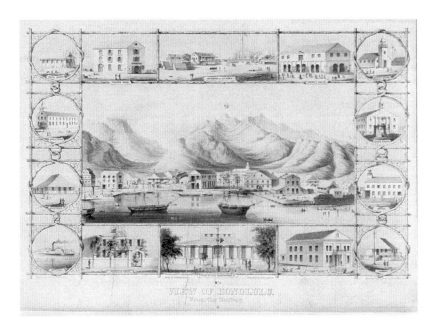

Fig 1: "View of Honolulu from the Harbor, No. 1." Paul Emmert, Lithograph, 1854. Courtesy of the Hawai'i State Archives.

and racial boundaries in both Honolulu and the United States rose to the surface when ice transited between temperate and transgressive spaces.

The ever-popularizing consumption of ice caused considerable debate within the United States, particularly in regards to appropriate female consumption, and these attitudes were quickly conveyed within Honolulu society. Attention to the effects of cold refreshments had increased as the ice industry gained momentum; it reached even higher velocity once frozen concoctions became widely available to the American middle class. According to popular belief, heat (the affective threat to morality) preyed most hazardously upon the many young women engaging in public culture. An 1858 article in the popular American magazine *Godey's Lady's Book* cautioned female readers against indulging in the iced or "very cold" beverages that had been become popular at social events. "In the present mode of living, all who indulge in iced beverages are in great danger…[of] *incurable disease* or *sudden death*," (emphasis original) wrote Dr. Jonathan Stainback Wilson in a regular column entitled the "Health Department."[40] Even as nineteenth-century cookbooks buzzed with recipes for ice-creams and ices, many authors felt compelled to add words of warning to their readers. Isabella Mary Beeton, in her ubiquitous domestic treatise *Beeton's Book of Household Management* (1861), notes that the consumption of ice must be altogether avoided for "the aged, the delicate, and children," but concedes that "the strong and healthy" can have iced drinks in moderation—though only well after dining, any kind of exercise, or warming of the body.[41] In both overt and subtle ways, gendered ideologies inflected the social rules of cold consumption, and carried over into the colonial context in contradictory, gendered, and racialized ways.

By 1858, the *Pacific Commercial Advertiser* had also begun to educate its readership on responsible ice consumption. A shipment of ice had arrived that day and would be available for sale the next, and so with an article entitled "A Few Words About Ice," the editors set about describing the benefits and dangers that Honoluluans would soon encounter:

> It would be idle to say a word in recommendation of it; it speaks for itself as eminently adapted to gratify the senses, invigorate the system, and lessen the effects of a prolonged or excessive heat, be the same produced by a tropical sun or by an internal fever. But a word of caution against its *abuse* may not be out of place, *particularly for those born on these islands*, who never or seldom have had an opportunity to indulge in iced drinks.[42]

Abuse of ice, according to the paper, included drinking iced beverages immediately after physical or mental exertion, or eating ice-cream after a full meal when one's body temperature would be warmer than usual.[43] While these ideas about diet and temperature reflected common precepts of the day, the racial divisions that inflected the *Advertiser*'s interpretation committed a subtle indictment of kanaka consumers: safely navigating ice consumption required a modicum of self-control that island natives were often thought to lack.[44]

Tracing the social meaning of ice in Honolulu during this time therefore proves slipperier than tracking shipments and tonnage, not least because of how race and cosmopolitanism in Hawai'i formed in contradictory ways during the midcentury. Legal restrictions regarding the consumption of alcohol are one salient example of how sociality—particularly forms linked to foreignness—could not be separated from the politics of control and safety. Most notably, Kanaka Maoli certainly patronized Honolulu's elite saloons and back-alley grog shops alike, even though laws made illegal the sale of alcohol to any native person. The 1850 *Penal Code of the Hawaiian Islands* established under Kamehameha III stated that, "Whoever shall sell, give, purchase, or procure for, and on behalf of any native of this kingdom, for his use, any spirituous liquor, or other intoxicating drink or substance, shall be punished by a fine not exceeding two hundred dollars."[45] Such prohibitions, however, existed in spite of a drinking culture within the capital city that proved not to be as cut and dry. Indeed, by 1854, the Hawai'i Supreme Court's *Annual Report of the Chief Justice* relayed that the past year had seen an increase of "natives fined for drunkenness in Honolulu" from 113 to 686; the earliest extant menus from 'Iolani Palace list wines and liquors as part of regular fare by the 1860s; and there had been no apparent concern for repercussion when (and if) Cutrell sent over the ill-fated champagne punch to the King in 1854.[46] But even if alcohol could be had by most men regardless of legal restriction, ice only appeared in elite, legal spaces. As an accompaniment, it legitimized an otherwise illicit practice.

To complicate the pretense of legal restrictions even further, the alcohol trade created a system of native criminalization at the same time that the Hawaiian government profited from its importation. Treaty agreements negotiated with England and France throughout the 1840s and 1850s permitted the controversial importation of alcohol under a graduated tariff scale. Even though such agreements had initially been resisted by the Hawaiian government, which at one time had sought the prohibition of liquor and spirits altogether, opposition relented once profits were realized. Because of its association with the liquor industry, ice soon became imbricated in these agreements—in 1855 the "Act to Provide Revenue from Imports, and to Change and Modify Existing Laws Imposing Duties on Imports," includes for the first time ice in a schedule listing "goods, wares, and merchandise" related to alcohol.[47] Gavan Daws estimates, in fact, that during the mid-century, "liquor duties and liquor licenses between them were in many years the biggest direct money earners for government." The monetary benefits were, however, often neutralized by the criminalization of Native Hawaiian drinkers, who soon filled the jails. Daws notes that, "those revenues were often matched dollar for dollar by the costs of running Honolulu's courts and prisons, whose business came in fair measure from crimes associated with liquor."[48] Alcohol was therefore not only seen as a simultaneous boon and scourge, but also as the lynchpin that held together Hawai'i's tenuous relations with powerful global empires.

During the midcentury, temperance advocates—some descended from Calvinist missionaries, some part of the ali'i nui (high-ranking royalty), others simply religious residents[49]—furthermore viewed the presence of liquor in Hawai'i as a political weakness, and one that endangered both the health of the Hawaiian people and the Kingdom's sovereignty.[50] To that effect, prominent politician and annexationist Lorrin Thurston explained in his 1909 review of Hawaiian liquor laws that:

> Foreign powers alone forced her [Hawai'i] to permit the liquor traffic which was destroying her people. So far as she could do so, she prevented her people from using liquor, but with a market open to all the world, and liquor available at all principal points, the prohibition to the natives was only partially effectual.[51]

FOOD,
CULTURE
SOCIETY

Opinion was polarized on whether such restrictions would have a positive effect on Hawai'i's declining indigenous population. Furthermore, many felt painfully aware of the exceptional rights afforded to the rich and the foreign, despite established racial divisions.[52] A large grey area furthermore existed for the Hawaiian elite, whose taste for chilled wines and spirits was cultivated within the courts, thereby stratifying alcohol consumption by class as much as race and allowing some Kanaka Maoli to transcend legal restrictions ostensibly enacted to "protect" native commoners from vice.[53] Sociologist Marilyn Brown argues that such laws created "a striking example of a unitary system of legal governance that produced a parallel legal code, one for Whites whose drinking could be regulated through licensing and permits and another for native subjects of the Kingdom whose drinking was criminalized."[54] The Māhele furthermore placed increased emphasis on the exchange of currency for consumer items and, as a result, monetary systems excluded the makaʻāinana even as cash exchange became the commercial standard in Hawaiʻi.[55] In addition to being illegal, cocktails would have simply been unaffordable for many, though certainly not all, indigenous residents.

In response to the social ills of the liquor industry, and likely boosted by concerns about ice's association with it, quantities of frozen water also found conservative audiences. Ice featured prominently at Honolulu Temperance League charity events, such as the one attended by Sybil Augusta Judd, daughter of the noted missionary Gerrit P. Judd. In 1855 she chose to sell iced soda water at a fundraising event for the construction of the Honolulu Sailor's Home Society, which offered alcohol-free housing to seamen on leave.[56] After answering a call placed in the newspaper by the organization's Trustees for donations of "any curiosities which they may possess," Sybil and her sister Laura settled on selling home goods and iced refreshments for the public fair.[57] The iced soda water, she remarked, brought in an especially tidy sum:

> The fair has come off, Laura made a pillow and I hemmed six towels and made some fancy lamplighters. Aunt Hattie made a smoking cap and a housewife. Laura and Hattie made some cake which was very nice. Laura sold iced soda water down stairs and father Akay and Ahea sold up stairs.... The soda water brought 1 hundred [sic] and two dollars.[58]

Refreshments served at the Sailor's Home fundraiser sent a message of moral purity to attendees by utilizing the product for charitable means and creating an anti-liquor association to counter the ice consumption patterns developing elsewhere in the city.

In contrast to the temperance fundraisers of 1855, the Honolulu saloon Merchant's Exchange featured ice prominently in sensational advertisements printed in October of 1856, in which proprietor Peck Cutrell announced his acquisition of "a quantity of that greatest of luxuries in a tropical climate—*ice*." (emphasis original).[59] The frozen cargo meant cocktails: "Mint Julips [sic], Mountaineers, Cobblers, Smashes, Punches, Stone Fences, Queen Charlottes, and numerous others."[60] The drinks conjured up a cool fantasy that promised to transport their thirsty patrons:

> Straightaway we are in Dreamland, and visions of "mint juleps," "iced punches," and other delicious compounds float before our enchanted visitor. When we awake, we find Randall Smith, the incomparable Randall, proffering to our eager grasp a snowy "mountaineer!"[61]

THE FOODWAYS OF HAWAI'I

At least three shipments of ice arrived that winter for exclusive use at his tavern, for which he had "spared neither pains nor expence [sic] to render the most popular place of resort in Honolulu."[62] As one of the few establishments in the city to hold a license for the selling of alcohol—which came at no small cost—the Merchant's Exchange retained a degree of social respectability.[63] There, patrons of the upper classes could legally consume alcohol, though options for cheap brandies abounded, dispensed liberally by back-alley grog shops to those with less capital.[64] These contrasting consumption patterns between temperance and alcohol made subtle but recognizable statements about how access to ice reflected, at times, class divisions as much as it did the legal racial divisions that presided over the city.

The contingent social categories that shaped alcohol consumption and, by extension, ice consumption in Honolulu meant that those who had the most ready access to iced drinks were relatively limited in numbers by either legal or economic means. In order for ice to become a regular fixture in Hawai'i's foodscape, its consumer base had to grow in order to overcome the challenges of transport and sale. With enthusiasm for ice increasing and the global market peaking, Hawai'i became an interesting new market for those seeking a permanent place in the ice trade business. Several potential importers submitted applications to the Hawaiian government in hopes to secure exclusive agreements that would prevent competition, inspire sufficient confidence to build storage and distribution infrastructure, and stabilize prices at an affordable level. Many applicants therefore took pains to argue that comestible ice would not only positively contribute to Hawai'i's economy, but that it could (and should) be readily available to all of the Kingdom's subjects regardless of race or cost. To bid for an agreement in 1858 for exclusive permission to import ice-making machines, for example, ship captain John Paty sent a letter to Prince Lota Kapuāiwa, who was at that time the Minister of the Interior, explaining that:

> ... [because] they have become acquainted with a method of fabricating ice by artificial means, at any and every degree of atmospheric temperature in the warmest climates of your Kingdom [that] ... the inhabitants thereof can be supplied with abundance of that healthful and refreshing article, at a rate of cost so cheap as to authorize its general consumption.[65]

FOOD, CULTURE & SOCIETY

Jones and Davis, American businessmen who applied for an exclusive trade license in 1856, likewise promised that their ice would be kept affordable enough "to furnish to all those willing to buy, the aforesaid article of importation at the most reasonable rate" (or, as they reiterate in the accompanying letter, that ice "may come within the reach of persons of limited income").[66] These letters, while cautious enough to not promise a specific sale price, acknowledged how important a broad consumer base would be to a sustainable ice business, particularly because of the product's perishable nature. Depictions of early ice shipments to Hawai'i thereby narrated responses to the shifting markets and manners of urban Honolulu. Advertisements that played up luxury, either on their own or in combination with ideas of health, purity, or comfort, at once spoke to a particular kind of consumer (white, moneyed, and cosmopolitan) and remained open to new markets (non-white and temperate). Racial divisions among ice consumers, or potential consumers, much like the distribution of residents in downtown Honolulu, proved to be drawn but not firm.

The first government support for a Honolulu ice business came in 1858. A young Irishman named Christopher Hamilton Lewers had arrived in the Islands about eight years prior as a building contractor and applied to the Privy Council for an exclusive license that many had been previously denied. Why he was successful in receiving the Kingdom's approval for his ice business in 1858 can only be speculated, though his reputation as a longtime Honolulu businessman *without* prior ties to the liquor business may have helped. Indeed, he had no vested interest in a racially segregated ice market. Records show that Lewers owned a lumber business, knew Council members rather intimately through his various construction contracts, and had the resources to handily erect his own ice storage facility.[67] Lewers' first shipment of commodity ice arrived with much fanfare that October after he received a government land lease, which allowed him to build an icehouse at the foot of Nuʻuanu Avenue near the boat docks (the icehouse constructed by Swan & Clifford had been located two blocks north).[68] Both white and non-white residents offered votes of confidence in Lewers' capability to offer a steady supply. One editorial stated that, "Mr. Lewers deserves credit for his venture, and we are sanguine enough to believe that he will be sustained in it."[69] Liquor retailers had already begun taking measurements for the construction of permanent iceboxes in their various establishments; newspapers in both Hawaiian and English detailed delivery options to their readers; and *Ka Hae Hawaiʻi* admired the quantities that arrived with hopeful skepticism, noting that "some ice has been obtained here before, but not as much as this—a little, and soon gone."[70]

Such announcements signaled the beginning of ice's popular use beyond the domain of public life and into the private sphere. The *Polynesian*, for example, anticipated an era of common household use, even for citizens of the most meager means:

> The great desideratum of civilized life in Honolulu is about to be supplied, and ice is shortly to become a "household word," expanding through every ramification of society down to the smallest "cobbler" and no longer stared at as a curiosity, or monopolized by the gentlemen at the bar.[71]

That discussions of the ice trade begin to surface in Hawaiian-language newspapers furthermore emphasizes how ice was not just associated with alcohol or piety (which ostensibly excluded Kanaka Maoli) but with general household use. To evidence, *Ka Hae Hawaiʻi* circulated one of Honolulu's first editorials that, along with announcing the arrival of 200 tons of ice to Lewers' shop, explained how to use ice for food preservation by describing how new ice storage units kept foods like meat, fish, milk, butter, and pie fresh. The editors notably made no references whatsoever to cocktails, saloons, or alcohol:

> No ka mea, i ke komo ana o ka hau iloko o ka waihona-hau, lilo koke ia i wahi anuanu loa a kupono no na mea a pau e pilau koke i ka wela—Ina e waiho ka io iloko o ka waihona-hau i ma la ekolu paha, aole pilau iki, no ka anuanu.
>
> (By placing the ice in the ice-box, it soon becomes a very cold place and preserves all of the things that spoil in heat. If meat is left in the ice-box for even three days, it does not spoil at all because of the cold.[72])

Ice had, at last, begun its migration from racially segregated public spaces and into Hawai'i's homes.

The press expressed dismay, then, that in May 1860 Lewers handed out his last 'ice-flake' before permanently shuttering his ice business. Despite his best efforts, he could not make a profit in the frozen water trade.[73] Still locked into a land lease, he began searching for another firm interested in taking over the icehouse along with his existing business the following March. Between the cost of constructing his icehouse and dismal revenue, his debt had climbed to over $7,000. Writing to the Department of the Interior, he asked that he might be forgiven his unpaid rent on the land leased beneath the icehouse until new tenants could be found.[74] This final and public failure meant that, at last, an exclusive government contract landed in the hands of business partners Henry Hackfield and J. Charles Pfluger, who exchanged a ten-year trade license for Lewers' extrication.[75]

With infrastructure already in place, Hackfield and Pfluger needed only to find a more reliable supply. They confidently reported that ice from the Russian American colonies in Alaska could be had directly (presumably without a transfer in San Francisco). Hackfield, who had been running an agency for Russian business interests in Honolulu since the early 1850s, intended to export items like sugar, coffee, beef and salt in return.[76] In exchange for an exclusive agreement, a free lease, and additional frontage, they would, "import into the Kingdom not less than 300 tons of Ice annually, and the price thereof shall not exceed six cents per pound."[77] The Hawaiian Privy Council approved the proposal's terms in full on April 13, 1861, with the only caveat that the land be used only for ice storage and sale, and that "a constant supply … shall be kept on hand."[78] For reasons unknown, however, that exclusively imported ice never arrived and a once-coveted contract languished, unused, in the government record office. No evidence exists that suggest Hackfield and Pfluger ever resumed Lewers' ice business. The *Saturday Press* reported in 1882 that Lewers' loss was the final nail in the coffin of ice shipments, writing that the business proved "not of much profit and importing of ice was abandoned."[79]

FOOD,
CULTURE
SOCIETY

While the ice market temporarily but most certainly failed, the impact upon Hawai'i remained profound as ice machines began to fill in the gaps in the market that imported ice left in its wake. The business records and news editorials that sporadically chart this brief industry offer only glimpses at what must have been vibrant public and political dialogues about ice's introduction to the Hawaiian foodscape. To understand the impact of a minor commodity market, it is thus necessary to attend to silences as well as texts: the apparent resistance by the Privy Council, the lack of reporting in the generally prolific Hawaiian newspapers, and the dearth of personal accounts from hotels and saloons in Honolulu. While discourses about foreign ice and what it meant as a comestible during these early encounters occasionally appear in printed records, affective experiences of both Kanaka Maoli and haole with coldness in the mid-nineteenth century are nevertheless difficult to assess. Indeed, the practical advice for food refrigeration in *Ka Hae Hawai'i* does not preclude indigenous residents from taking pleasure in coldness, and the insistence on ice's necessity for white settlers to survive the heat might reveal more about colonial marketing strategies than it does about actual climatological discomfort. If anything, records point towards the racial and economic tensions that gripped the Hawaiian Kingdom throughout the nineteenth century.

During these years, ice appeared sporadically; no one importer produced more than a few shipments, which melted away almost as quickly as they arrived. It was only after ice-making machines began local production near the end of the nineteenth century that iced refreshments like ice creams and soda fountains become embedded within Hawaiian food culture. Before that, the ice business tried, and failed, to sustain itself through foreign importation for over a decade despite an enthusiastic reception by the wealthy of Honolulu. To that end, a few interlocking points within this shadowy history emerge. First, a previously overlooked and profoundly influential facet of Hawai'i's rich food history is brought into focus. Second, commodity ice is shown to cut across the politics of taste as Hawai'i's government negotiated its place on the world stage. Hawai'i's imported ice market offers insights into the complex process of meaning-making applied to new foods when they are introduced to communities in transition. Would-be traders and distributors sought ways to generate both consumer desire and government support for an ice business by experimenting with discourses of affordability and luxury. Consumers, in turn, developed their own associations with ice by responding to its use within a highly racialized alcohol industry as well as its occasional cooption by temperance advocates. Over time ice began to inhabit a more popular place within Honolulu culture even though the industry remained unprofitable. Although the language of ice as a "tropical necessity" did not disappear from public discourse (it would, in fact, remain central for many decades as ice machines began manufacturing the commodity locally), a new and more inclusive way of talking about ice emerged that began to naturalize its place within Hawai'i's homes and everyday foodscape.

Even as iced refreshments became more commonplace in Honolulu in the following decades, ice's cultural association with political and social power continued to resonate with the Hawaiian monarchy. At the time James O'Meara published his description of the death of Kamehameha III and the troubles it caused for an American annexation project in Hawai'i, David Kalākaua ruled the Hawaiian Kingdom. His reign became known for its strong revitalization of Hawaiian nationalism and cultural practice, as well as the monarch's embrace of cosmopolitanism and modern technology. One of the most spectacular displays of this legacy occurred on the evening of July 21, 1886 when a grand celebration was held to show off the newly installed electric lights at 'Iolani Palace. As Hawai'i society in their evening finery paraded around the Palace Square to the music of the Hawaiian Band, the King, on horseback, conducted a battalion drill in the Government Building's yard. There the volunteer companies broke rank, stacked their arms, and settled under canopy tents for a grand tea party that included tea, coffee, and, most decadently, ice-cream.[80] The display literally and metaphorically projected power from the seat of a government still sovereign, and the selection of refreshments featured ice in its most socially virtuous form. Ice-cream had become the delight of the temperate, the innocent, and the pure. If iced alcohol allegedly ended one king's life in 1854, then thirty years later ice-cream served to affirm political strength and virtue. The final lines of O'Meara's article aptly concede the point: "Now reigns Kalakaua. He declares he will never sell his kingdom. It remains to be seen what he will do with it."[81]

Acknowledgements

I thank New York University's Center for the Humanities for their support during the completion of this article, as well as Lisa Gitelman, Krishnendu Ray, Dean Saranillio, David Chang, and the three anonymous reviewers for their indispensable feedback.

Disclosure statement

No potential conflict of interest was reported by the author.

FOOD, CULTURE & SOCIETY

Notes

1. "Ice," *Hawaiian Gazette*, October 11, 1871.
2. PingSung Leung and Matthew Loke, "Economic Impacts of Increasing Hawai'i's Food Self-Sufficiency," *Economic Issues* (December 2008): 2.
3. Tara L. Miller and Charles H. Fletcher, "Waikiki: Historical Analysis of an Engineered Shoreline," *Journal of Coastal Research*, vol. 19, no. 4 (2003): 1026–43.
4. In 1875, the commodity flow had been formalized with a Treaty of Reciprocity, and American businessmen confidently speculated over the eventual outcome of this intimate economic relationship. Merze Tate, *Hawai'i: Reciprocity or Annexation* (East

Lansing: Michigan State University, 1968) provides an overview of the ongoing debate of the second half of the nineteenth century.
5. See C. C. Bennett, "Death of King Kamehameha III," *Sketches of Hawaiian History and Honolulu Directory* (Honolulu: C.C. Bennett, 1871), 38, and *Polynesian*, December 30, 1854, 134.
6. Private correspondence from the time connects the King's death to alcoholism. For example, missionary John S. Emerson wrote in a letter to his son Samuel that, "The King Kamehameha III died a bout [sic] one month since, disease mania potu"—a nineteenth-century term to describe alcoholism. John S. Emerson to Samuel Emerson, letter, January 23, 1855. Bishop Museum Archives.
7. James O'Meara, "Schemes to Annex the Sandwich Islands," *Californian*, vol. 4 (1881): 257–8.
8. O'Meara, "Schemes to Annex the Sandwich Islands," 264.
9. Ibid.
10. Ralph S. Kuykendall, *The Hawaiian Kingdom*, vol. 1 (Honolulu: University of Hawai'i Press, 1938), 426. Kamehameha III's ultimate decision on whether to cease annexation negotiations before his death remains unclear. According to archival evidence referenced in Kuykendall, cabinet members were under the impression that all negotiations had been terminated. Meeting minutes, however, show that the discussion had simply been tabled for further consideration. Certainly, no prepared annexation document had been waiting for signature.
11. On nineteenth-century Hawaiian history, see Noenoe Silva, *Aloha Betrayed: Native Hawaiian Resistance to American Colonialism* (Durham, NC: Duke University Press, 2004) and Jonathan Kamakawiwoʻole Osorio, *Dismembering Lāhui: A History of the Hawaiian Nation to 1887* (Honolulu: University of Hawai'i Press, 2002).
12. Thomas G. Thrum, "Honolulu Yesterdays," *Hawaiian Annual for 1931* (Honolulu: Thos. G. Thrum, 1930), 33–4.
13. At this time, the term "hotel" referred to a place for socialization and entertainment more than sleeping accommodations. Laws put into effect in the years 1845–6 determined that places "for the ordinary entertainment of sailors" would be called inns or victualing houses, and that a hotel would be "a house of public entertainment for the higher classes of society." In 1856 "respectable" retailers, including Cutrell, Bartlett, and Macfarlane, complained that the inadequate enforcement of harsh liquor license laws bred illegal competition with "numerous illicit vendors diffused among all the classes of society." Richard A. Greer, "Grog Shops and Hotels: Bending the Elbow in Old Honolulu," *Hawaiian Journal of History*, vol. 28 (1994): 46–8.
14. Florida physician John Gorrie filed the earliest ice machine patents in the United States and England in 1851, but the machines did not go into production. George D. Howe, "The Father of Modern Refrigeration," *Publications of the Florida Historical Society*, vol. 1, no. 4 (1909): 19–23.
15. The notice is specifically directed toward "the gentlemen of Honolulu, Captains of vessels, and strangers visiting Oahu." "Notice," *Polynesian*, August 24, 1850, 59.
16. Ibid. and advertisement, *Polynesian*, November 16, 1850, 108. The cargo, perplexingly, does not appear in any other records in contemporary publications. This may be simply due to a lack of reporting, or perhaps the cargo did not last long enough

for it to make significant news. *Polynesian*, September 21, 1850, 74 and December 14, 1850, 123.

17. Jonathan Rees reports that Tudor's largest foreign market, India, peaked in 1856 with 146,000 tons shipped that year, though the ice trade continued to grow domestically in American markets until the end of the nineteenth century. *Refrigeration Nation: A History of Ice, Appliances, and Enterprise in America* (Baltimore: Johns Hopkins University Press, 2013), 23–4.
18. Gavin Weightman, *The Frozen Water Trade: A True Story* (New York: Hyperion, 2003), 173.
19. "How Ice Was Had Here in Old Pioneer Days," *Advertiser*, April 19, 1903.
20. Through searches in the archives of University of Hawai'i's Hamilton Library, the Hawai'i State Archives, and the Bishop Museum Library Archives, I have come to the conclusion that there are no known first-hand accounts that exist of this ice shipment.
21. "Ice," *Polynesian*, June 26, 1852. It seems, though, that the mail the *Harriet T. Bartlett* brought with it excited Honoluluans even more than the ice, which gets no mention in an announcement of the bark's arrival published in *Polynesian*, June 19, 1852.
22. *The Life and Adventures of a Free Lance* (Burlington, VT: Free Press Company, 1914), 64. The *Polynesian* notes that the bark was captained by "Edward Hereen" (spelled Heeren in *The Friend*'s "Marine Journal," July 2, 1852), which could have been a misprint.
23. "Seaborne Commerce of Pacific Coast of North America in Pioneer Days," *Monthly Review Mercantile Trust Company of California*, October 15, 1923, 218. The Russian American Commercial Ice Company reportedly sold the ice for $25–$35 per ton (a good deal cheaper than the $75 per ton that could be bought from Boston by way of Cape Horn), and sold to consumers for 5 cents per pound. Sven D. Haakanson and Amy F. Stefiian, *Giinaquq Like a Face: Suqpiaq Masks of the Kodiak Archipelago* (Fairbanks: University of Alaska Press, 2009), 45. One publication reports that San Francisco's first ice shipment arrived via the *Backus* on April 11, 1852 along with 800 pounds of halibut at the consignment of the newly formed Pacific Ice Company. Louis J. Rasmussen, *San Francisco Ship Passenger Lists: November 7, 1851–June 17, 1852* (Baltimore, MD: Genealogical Publishing, 2003), 244.
24. *Polynesian*, October 14, 1854, and Thomas G. Thrum, *Hawaiian Almanac and Annual for 1914* (Honolulu: Thos. G. Thrum, 1913), 52. Additional details of the ice house's structure cannot be found in the popular press, government documents, or city maps, though it continued to change hands for some time afterward and was eventually occupied as a shipwright's shop run by George Emmes. Thomas G. Thrum, *Hawaiian Almanac and Annual for 1882* (Honolulu: Thos. G. Thrum, 1882), 9.
25. One of their notices claimed that "the Agents will be prepared to furnish Ice at the Houses of all who may desire this indispensable luxury." Shipments advertised via the American brigs *Mallory* and *Noble*. *Polynesian*, October 28, 1854, November 4, 1854, and February 3, 1855. News of the icehouse built in anticipation of its arrival reached as far as California in "Further from the Sandwich Islands," *Sacramento Daily Union*, November 9, 1854, 3.
26. Circular, "Swan & Clifford…" [Honolulu 1855], Hawai'i State Archives. Also see

David W. Forbes, ed., *Hawaiian National Bibliography*, vol. 3 (Honolulu: University of Hawai'i Press, 2001), 156.

27. Kuykendall calls vol. 2 of his *Hawaiian Kingdom* trilogy "The Critical Years" (1953) and Sally Engle Merry also makes this reference in *Colonizing Hawai'i: The Cultural Power of Law* (Princeton: Princeton University Press, 2000), 4.
28. Baker reports that in the year 1853, 110 vessels entered the harbor and Honolulu's custom receipts numbered over $100,000, with total Kingdom revenue of $234,169. Ray Jerome Baker, *Honolulu in 1853* (Honolulu: Ray Jerome Baker, 1950), 5.
29. Ibid., 6.
30. The historical literature on the Māhele is extensive; here I use Stuart Banner, "Preparing to be Colonized: Land Tenure and Legal Strategy in Nineteenth-Century Hawai'i," *Law & Society Review*, vol. 39, no. 2 (2005): 281.
31. Kuykendall, vol. 2, 19–20.
32. Daws explains in footnote 11 that during the period of the Māhele, "the outlines of a town committed to western property practices became visible." Gavan Daws, "Honolulu in the 19th Century: Notes on the Emergence of Urban Society in Hawai'i," *Journal of Pacific History*, vol. 2 (1967): 80.
33. Banner, "Preparing to be Colonized," 284.
34. S. S. Hill, *Travels in the Sandwich and Society Islands* (London: Chapman & Hall, 1856), 96.
35. Don Hibbard, *Designing Paradise: The Allure of the Hawaiian Resort* (New York: Princeton Architectural Press, 2006), 8.
36. Accessed January 23, 2015, "View of Honolulu from the Harbor, No. 1," *Hawaiian Historical Society Historical Photograph Collection*, http://www.huapala.net/items/show/4711. Reprinted in Ray Jerome Baker's *Honolulu in 1853* (1950).
37. It is difficult to pinpoint the exact location of the Merchant's Exchange since coordinates do not appear in newspaper advertisements, and buildings of this time tended to change hands rather rapidly. In Richard Greer's detailed history of Cunha's Alley, located between Merchant and King Streets, he traces Cutrell's ownership of a building that is either the Merchant's Exchange or the Union Hotel (or both). Richard A. Greer, "Cunha's Alley: The Anatomy of a Landmark," *Hawaiian Journal of History*, vol. 2 (1968): 144.
38. Sidney Mintz, *Sweetness and Power: The Place of Sugar in Modern History* (New York: Penguin Books, 1985).
39. *Polynesian*, November 4, 1854. Horace Crabb advertised "Ice Cream!" to be served at 7:30 p.m. on the same date.
40. Jonathan Stainback Wilson, "Health Department," *Godey's Lady's Book*, vol. 57 (1858): 560.
41. Isabella Mary Beeton, ed., *The Book of Household Management* (London: S.O. Beeton, 1861), 761.
42. Emphasis added. "A Few Words About Ice," *Pacific Commercial Advertiser*, October 21, 1858.
43. This year also saw the opening of an ice cream parlor on the corner of Nu'uanu and Chaplain Streets by Mr. William Huddy, "where pleasant rooms and gentlemanly attendance greet the lady and gentleman visitors." *Pacific Commercial Advertiser*, November 11, 1858.

44. I must acknowledge here that although I interpret this passage to be in regards to Native Hawaiians, they are not named as such. Per my conversation with Historian David Change, it is possible that the passage could instead be referring to first- or second-generation haole. For a good analysis of the feminization, sexualization, and infantilization of Hawaiian bodies, see Sally Engle Merry, *Colonizing Hawai'i: The Cultural Power of Law* (Princeton, NJ: Princeton University Press, 2000). Prohibition of alcohol consumption for Kanaka Maoli began almost as soon as foreign rum arrived on the shores of Kailua, O'ahu in 1791. Kimo Alama Keaulana and Scott Whitney, "Ka wai kau mai o Maleka 'Water from America': The Intoxication of the Hawaiian People," *Contemporary Drug Problems* (1990): 168.
45. Marilyn Brown, "'Aina Under the Influence: The Criminalization of Alcohol in 19th-Century Hawai'i," *Theoretical Criminology*, vol. 7, no. 1 (2003): 89–110. Greer, "Grog Shops and Hotels," 46, and Hawaiian Government, *Penal Code of the Hawaiian Islands* (Honolulu: Government Press, 1850), 101.
46. Hawai'i Supreme Court, *Annual Report of the Chief Justice* (Honolulu: Hawai'i Administration of Justice), 3.
47. *Laws of His Majesty Kamehameha IV, King of the Hawaiian Islands, Passed by the Nobles and Representatives, at their Session* (Honolulu: Hawaiian Government, 1855), 15. A good analysis of what trade agreements did to the Hawaiian economy, and ultimately its political independence, can be found in Sumner J. LaCroix and Christopher Grandy, "The Political Instability of Reciprocal Trade and the Overthrow of the Hawaiian Kingdom," *Journal of Economic History*, vol. 57, no. 1 (March 1997): 161–89.
48. Gavan Daws, "Decline of Puritanism at Honolulu in the Nineteenth Century," *Hawaiian Journal of History*, vol. 1 (1967): 37.
49. The social landscape of temperance is more complex than I have space to represent here, but can be found illuminated by Jennifer Fish Kashay in, "'We will banish the polluted thing from our houses': Missionaries, Drinking, and Temperance in the Sandwich Islands," in *The Role of the American Board in the World: Bicentennial Reflections on the Organization's Missionary Work, 1810–2010*, eds. Clifford Putney and Paul T. Burlin (Eugene, OR: Wipf & Stock, 2012), 287–311.
50. Letter, [James J. Jarves] to Robert C. Wyllie, November. 25, 1849, F.O. & Ex., Hawai'i State Archives. These views undoubtedly stemmed from the negotiation of international treaties with England, France, and the United States that preoccupied kingdom politics for much of the 1840s, and did much to shape alcohol importation. Encouraged by temperance reformers in 1846, the Hawaiian Kingdom proposed amendments to treaty agreements made with France and England in 1839 and 1844, respectively, that included the prohibition of liquor importation. After a wholly unsatisfactory debate with representatives of the two powers, including complaints of favoritism, the Kingdom not only allowed alcohol importation, but eventually lowered the tariffs outlined in their first concession. Ralph S. Kuykendall, *The Hawaiian Kingdom, 1874–1893: The Kalākaua Dynaisty*, vol. 3 (Honolulu: University of Hawai'i Press, 1967), 372–3. Also see "The Struggle for Equitable Treaties," in Kuykendall, *Hawaiian Kingdom*, vol. 1, 368–82.
51. Thurston, *The Liquor Question in Hawai'i*, 8.
52. See Isabella Bird, *Six Months in Hawai'i* (New York: Routledge, 2013), 290.

53. Caroline Ralston argues that, "Progressively the interests of chiefs and people had diverged until, by the 1850s, it would appear to a modern-day western analyst that in many senses two classes with opposed interests had emerged." "Hawai'i 1778–1854: Some Aspects of Maka'ainana Response to Rapid Cultural Change," *Journal of Pacific History*, vol. 19, no. 1 (1984): 36. Daws, "Honolulu in the Nineteenth Century," 88.
54. Brown, "'Aina Under the Influence," 315.
55. Ralston, "Hawai'i 1778–1854," 22.
56. For more, see Gerrit P. Judd IV, *Dr. Judd: Hawai'i's Friend, A Biography of Gerrit Parmele Judd, 1803–1873* (Honolulu: University of Hawai'i Press, 1960).
57. *Polynesian*, September 15, 1855.
58. S. A. Judd to L. Fish [October 1855]. Bishop Museum Archives.
59. The cargo arrived on the American clipper *Yankee*, along with letters and dry goods. *Polynesian*, October 25, 1856, 98–9. Cutrell owned both a liquor retail business and a boarding house called the Union Hotel. The Merchant's Exchange appears to have operated as a tavern only; however, the Union Hotel and the Merchant's Exchange may have operated under the same roof. Greer, "Cunha's Alley," 144, 149–50.
60. The concoctions would have been familiar to many hollow-legged colonialists; contemporary reports from Australia list beverages of the same name. For example, a "stone fence" contained ginger beer and brandy, and a "smash" comprised ice, brandy, and water. "The Literature of the Bottle," *Titan* (January—June 1859): 506.
61. *Polynesian*, October 25, 1856, 98.
62. *Pacific Commercial Advertiser*, February 26, 1857, and *Pacific Commercial Advertiser*, October 30, 1856.
63. An 1856 petition signed by a dozen or so liquor license holders, including Cutrell, complained against the "numerous illicit vendors diffused among all the classes of society" that they believed were negatively affecting the profitability of their business. Greer, *Grog Shops and Hotels*, 47.
64. American sea captain E. E. Adams wrote in 1850 that, "Wherever I go [in Honolulu], I meet men lying on the floors, in the streets, in the forecastles, perfectly helpless and senseless; but brandy is so CHEAP." "Honolulu—Cheap versus Dear Spirits," quoted from the *Honolulu Friend* in *Bristol Temperance Herald* (January 1851): 91.
65. "A Few Words About Ice," *Advertiser*, October 21, 1858.
66. Cyrus W. Jones and Charles G. Davis, Draft Agreement, 1856, Hawai'i State Archives; C. W. Jones and C. G. Davis to The Privy Council of his Hawaiian Majesty, Privy Council Petitions, April 17, 1856, Hawai'i State Archives.
67. Charles E. Peterson, "Pioneer Architects and Builders of Honolulu," *Annual Report of the Hawaiian Historical Society*, vol. 72 (1964): 12, and "A Honolulu Hardware Store," *Hardware Dealer's Magazine*, vol. 40 (1913): 1237.
68. Per details indexed in Hawai'i State Archives card catalog under heading "Ice," with incomplete reference to article in *Honolulu Advertiser*, February 1931.
69. Ibid. and *Polynesian*, October 16, 1858.
70. My translation. "Hau! Hau!," *Ka Hae Hawai'i*, November 3, 1858, 122.
71. "Cool," *Polynesian*, March 20, 1858.
72. My translation. *Ka Hae Hawai'i*, November 3, 1858, 122.
73. "The Ice, and What Came of It," *Polynesian*, May 26, 1860.
74. C. H. Lewers to Hawaiian Minister of the Interior, March 18, 1861, Hawai'i State Archives.

75. H. Hackfeld and J. C. Pfluger to Hawaiian Minister of the Interior, March 25, 1861, Hawai'i State Archives. For more on Hackfeld's business in Hawai'i, see "History of the House of H. Hackfeld & Co.," *All About Hawai'i, Thrum's Hawaiian Almanac and Annual for 1900* (Honolulu: Thos. G. Thrum, 1902), 43.
76. H. Hackfeld and J. C. Pfluger to Hawaiian Minister of the Interior, March 25, 1861, Hawai'i State Archives.
77. In contrast, a note in *Paradise of the Pacific* regarding the death of Lewers' widow in Kansas City, MO mentions that Lewers recalled that his ice cost him ten cents per pound. "The First Ice Importer," *Paradise of the Pacific* (November 1909): 23.
78. Cabinet Council Records, vol. 5, 13 April 1861, 217. Hawai'i State Archives.
79. "Ice," *Saturday Press*, April 22, 1882.
80. "Electric Light," *Daily Bulletin*, July 22, 1886, 3.
81. The alternate spelling of Kalākaua here reflects the punctuation used in the quoted text. O'Meara, "Schemes," 265.

Dairy's Decline and the Politics of "Local" Milk in Hawai'i

Clare Gupta

Abstract

This paper uses the case of Hawai'i's dairy industry to examine the history of food production in Hawai'i, contemporary interest in re-localizing Hawai'i's food system, and the conflicting agrarian imaginaries that challenge this endeavor. The evolution of the dairy industry in Hawai'i illustrates how over the past several decades the US dairy industry has become consolidated in the name of economic efficiency, regardless of the potential environmental and human health impacts. As elsewhere in the United States, Hawai'i consumers are pushing back against this economic transformation, and advocating for greater protection of local dairy farms. Most local food advocates do not value local purely on a geographical basis, but for its potential to capture desirable attributes such as sustainably produced, supportive of local economies and/or freshness. This can make it difficult to establish a local food system when community members hold different visions, or agrarian imaginaries, for how best to produce local food, and for where or by whom it should be produced. I highlight the history and political economy of milk production in Hawai'i in order to demonstrate both the challenges and opportunities for reforming—and more specifically re-localizing—the dairy industry in Hawai'i, and in the United States more broadly.

Introduction

The politics of food looms large in the United States today, as a growing number of Americans are increasingly conscious of the ways in which food and agriculture affect human and environmental health. This awareness has spurred initiatives led by a diversity of actors, from the First Lady Michelle Obama to guerrilla gardeners, to use the food system as a tool to address and improve health inequities, hunger, environmental degradation, rural economic depression and a host of other socio-ecological ills. While many agree that the current industrial model of food production in the United States is unsustainable and broken (Shiva 2000; Pollan 2006; Carlisle 2015), there is no consensus as to what a "sustainable" food system might look like. However, there is a growing popular movement oriented towards the re-creation of regional or "local" food systems, captured by popular slogans such as 'buy local,' that associates localized systems of production and consumption with improved sustainability (Henderson 2000; Hinrichs 2003). Local food systems are touted as providing food that is good for people, the environment and the local economy. The growth of farmers' markets, Community-Supported Agriculture, and public procurement policies (Kneafsey 2010; Marsden 2010) all reflects the responses of producers to increased consumer awareness of and demand for locally grown food.

This paper uses the case of Hawai'i's dairy industry as a lens for examining the history of food production in Hawai'i, the contemporary interest in re-localizing Hawai'i's food system, as well as the conflicting visions for a local food system that challenge such an endeavor. Borrowing a term from Guthman's 2004 analysis of the organics industry, I show how individuals and groups within a community may hold competing "agrarian imaginaries" for how, where, by whom and at what scale food should be grown. These competing visions can create conflict amongst those otherwise collectively committed to the cause of "local food" and, in doing so, break apart any romantic notions of local food as an inherent social good, or a concept around which there is a cohesive singular movement. More specifically, I demonstrate how proponents of local food in Hawai'i disagree over production methods (e.g. organic versus conventional and scale of production), land-use planning (where it is appropriate to produce food) and even the definition of local (e.g. who or what counts as a "local" business). I argue that the case of dairy production in Hawai'i highlights that, in reality, most local food advocates do not value local purely on a geographical basis, but instead value locally grown food when it embodies other desirable attributes that they associate (or arguably conflate) with "local," such as organic or small-scale.

The trend towards local food is not without its critics. Empirical research on the environmental and economic impacts of local food has shown that a localized food system does not inherently provide such benefits (Purcell and Brown 2005; Edwards-Jones et al. 2008; Matthews et al. 2008; Weber and Matthews 2008). Local food's critics suggest the benefits of local food—lower carbon footprint or strengthened local economy in particular—are more a marketing claim than proven facts (Peterson 2013). Another strand of criticism, rooted in human geography scholarship, critiques the local food movement on the grounds that it tends to re-affirm racial and class-based inequities (Allen 2004; DuPuis and Goodman 2005; Allen 2008; Alkon and Agyeman 2011). The local food movement to date has reflected an affluent habitus of whiteness (Alkon and McCullen 2011; Guthman 2011) that in some cases precludes its ability to achieve equity and social-justice-oriented goals. The movement also has not (until recently) paid significant attention to issues of labor (i.e. farmworker, food service industry), which again has limited its ability to address a broad range of social concerns (Brown and Getz 2011). Lastly, there is little consensus on how to even define "local" food (Rushing and Goldblatt 2014), and critics have linked this ambiguity to the potential for corporate "local washing" that misleads consumers (Cleveland 2013; Gupta and Makov in review). This kind of portrayal of local food opens the door to examine the way in which efforts to develop a local food system can be complicated by differing definitions of and motivations for local food within a given community.

Despite the perils and pitfalls identified by critics of re-localization, in the state of Hawai'i the so-called "locavore" movement has gained particular traction. Hawai'i's acute geographic isolation and dependence on the globalized economy for its food supply, coupled with a longstanding indigenous sovereignty movement, have infused Hawai'i's local food movement[1] with a particular sense of urgency and political activism. Coalitions between indigenous Hawaiians and settlers around the issue of local food system development (Gupta 2015) complicate some of the common critiques of the local food movement as a place of white liberal dominance. For these reasons, Hawai'i is a particularly compelling place to study the politics of local food. Furthermore, the historical trajectory of Hawai'i's agricultural system, while unique in many ways, also serves as a magnified account of the global trend towards globalized food production and commodity export economies at the expense of regional self-sufficiency—which in turn has been the impetus for the overall resurgence of interest in re-localizing food systems.

Dairy in Hawai'i is a particularly interesting case to examine for several reasons. First, fluid milk is considered an essential component of the daily American diet, especially for children and the elderly (Lee 2007).[2] Access to safe, affordable milk is thus of widespread importance to the majority of consumers, including those in Hawai'i.[3] Second, milk supply chains for Hawai'i differ from those in the continental United States because of the extreme distances milk travels to reach Hawai'i, which is particularly notable given milk's perishability. On the continent, milk has historically been produced and consumed locally (DuPuis 2002). A host of federal and state regulations exist to establish geographically bounded "milksheds" that ensure a reliable supply of fluid milk (Sumner and Balagtas 2002; Cakir and Balagtas 2012). However, the trajectory of milk production in Hawai'i has precluded the survival of such regionalized milksheds, as it has become cheaper to import milk from the American continent than source it within the state. Quality is thus an issue in the debate over Hawai'i's current milk sourcing policies because imported milk travels great distances to reach the islands, with potentially serious implications for human health and nutrition.[4] Lastly, dairy production as a form of land-use has proved to be particularly contentious throughout the globe (Tilman et al. 2002; Eshel et al. 2014), and as the two cases elucidated below show, Hawai'i is no exception.

THE FOODWAYS OF HAWAI'I

This paper is laid out as follows: after tracing the historical decline of food self-sufficiency in Hawai'i and in the dairy industry in particular, I explain the underlying motivations and goals behind re-localization efforts in Hawai'i, in part drawing on data from 61 interviews I held with key players in Hawai'i's contemporary food system.[5] These motivations and goals, rooted in Hawai'i's unique history, geography and political economy, help shape the nature of agrarian imaginaries held by Hawai'i residents. I then use the case of the dairy industry to think through how differing agrarian imaginaries come to be expressed and how they have practical implications for local food movements on the ground. Specifically, I present two cases of local dairy production[6]—one on Hawai'i Island (hereinafter referred to as the Big Island to avoid confusion) and the other on Kaua'i—that have garnered particular attention and incited heated debate over local food production in Hawai'i. In the first case, protests over a local dairy growing genetically modified corn feed highlight a specific understanding of the value of "local" food predominant within the alternative agriculture community on the island. Within this agrarian imaginary, "local" is associated with, or arguably conflated with, non-industrial and/or organic-oriented practices. In the second case, resistance by Kaua'i rural residents to the placement of a dairy farm in close proximity to existing homes and hotels reveals that the historical and geographic context in which local food developments occur—especially a producer's relationship to the local community—matters hugely to any local food enterprise's fate. In the Kaua'i case, discord between the agrarian imaginaries of the dairy investors and certain segments of the local community reflect a deep-seated history of land struggles that significantly shapes contemporary land-use decision-making. These cases show that while there may be consensus amongst Hawai'i's residents regarding the need to increase their food production and self-sufficiency, there is great debate over how these goals should be achieved, especially amongst rural residents in the areas where local food production occurs. In this way, both cases serve as excellent illustrations of the competing values that can complicate any attempt to establish a local food system.

I argue that both cases reveal how local food movements can splinter when community members do not agree on the best practices for agricultural production, or when competing values and priorities within a community exist. Further, an analysis of these competing and sometimes conflicting visions for local food system development calls into question whether a "local food movement" as a cohesive social movement actually even exists, given the different priorities, interests and aims of the actors involved. Local food has become a much-lauded concept, but these cases show that localized food production is more easily realized in theory than in practice. This is not only because of the larger well-documented structural political economic and regulatory challenges that face nascent local food systems (Dupuis 2002; Dupuis and Goodman 2005; Freidberg 2009), but also because of the competing agrarian imaginaries within a community that can bog down the creation or development of food-producing enterprises. This can make it difficult to establish a local food system when community members hold different visions for how best to produce local food, and for where or by whom it should be produced.

While the presented cases serve as a cautionary tale against romanticism of the local food movement, they are not meant to dismiss the potential of local food systems entirely. Instead, the case of dairy re-localization in Hawai'i highlights the importance of understanding how and why rural residents value local food, and the potential trade-offs they associate with its production. Only through such geographically and historically specific understandings of rural priorities and politics can communities begin to develop viable strategies for the re-localization of their food systems.

Historical Shifts in Food Production in Hawai'i

The desire of Hawai'i's residents to become more self-sufficient and connected to "local" food stems directly from Hawai'i's history as a settler colony that became dependent on the outside western world for its survival, and that is now seeking greater independence and autonomy. This is not unlike large swaths of the Global South, where historically resources have flown from a "periphery" of poor and underdeveloped states to a "core" of wealthy states, enriching the latter at the expense of the former (Wallerstein 2000). As illuminated by Tongan scholar Epeli Hau'ofa (1994), there are growing efforts across the Pacific to resist the paradigm of an economic dependence of Oceania upon the rest of the world. Hau'ofa counters the dominant narrative that specialized production for the world market is necessary for the economic survival of islands in the Pacific. While he is referring primarily to small nation-states in the Pacific, his rejection of a global economic model in which small islands in the Pacific are perpetually trapped in dependency relations with the Global North resonates in Hawai'i as well.[7]

The following section traces the history of food production in Hawai'i—namely the decline in self-sufficiency—from the pre-colonial era (i.e. pre-contact with western explorers) through to the present day. Understanding the particular historical conditions associated with Hawai'i's loss of a local food economy helps to situate the unique expression of, and motivations for, the local food movement seen in Hawai'i today.

Since the late 1800s, Hawai'i has experienced a continued pattern of extraction of raw materials to meet the needs of the western world (i.e. provisions for whalers, then sugar) at the expense of local Hawaiians' ability to provision their own food (Kent 1993). As Hawaiian scholar-activist Noelani Goodyear-Ka'ōpua notes (2013), these structures of settler colonialism have inflicted a kind of violence on the relationship between Native Hawaiians (Kānaka Maoli) and their land, by eroding the ability of Kānaka Maoli to feed themselves from the land.

Thomas Kemper Hitch (1993) writes that when Captain James Cook arrived in the Hawaiian Islands in 1778, he encountered a people with "arguably the highest standard of living" and "the most varied cuisine" in Oceania. The most abundant food resource was, of course, marine life—reef and inshore fish, crustaceans, deep-sea fish and edible seaweed (Kamehameha Schools

Hawaiian Studies Institute 1982). Within ancient Hawaiian society, the basic land division was the *ahupua'a*,[8] a wedge-shaped unit of land following the natural boundaries of a watershed (i.e. mountains to ocean), which supported one or more extended family group(s), or *'ohana*. Each *ahupua'a* was:

> ... a complete estate, running from sea to the mountains, and hence providing a share of all the different products of soil and sea; fish from the seashore, taro, yams, sugarcane, breadfruit, and bananas in the fertile area of the lowlands; and further up in the forest belt, firewood, poles for houses, logs for canoes, bark for tapa cloth, *olana* and other plant fibers for cords and rope, and feathers. (Morgan 1948)

In this way, each *'ohana* was relatively self-sufficient within its wedge-shaped *ahupua'a*. In the pre-contact era, Native Hawaiians thrived on a nutritious diet, as evidenced by their stature and the rate of population increase (Hitch 1993).

In the years following Captain Cook's arrival, western influences and the teachings of Christian missionaries led the *ali'i*, or chiefs, to privatize and dismantle the *ahupua'a* (Akutagawa et al. 2012). Notably, in 1848, the Māhele was enacted, which established private ownership of land in Hawai'i (Kame'eleihiwa 1992) and provided the necessary preconditions to dispossess Native Hawaiians of much of their land. While the chiefs received their apportionment of lands, many commoners, out of ignorance, trust in their chiefs, or fear of reprisal, failed to register land claims to small *kuleana* parcels that would have allowed them to keep a comfortable piece of arable land to maintain their family (Akutagawa et al. 2012). Furthermore, these *kuleana* lands became isolated islands in the midst of large-scale ranching or commercial agriculture operations. Lacking access to previously cultivated areas, Native Hawaiian farmers were unable to earn subsistence living on their remaining small plots of land (MacKenzie 1991). At the same time, Hawai'i's entry into market relations with the outside world shifted the labor of Native Hawaiian commoners away from agriculture and towards deforestation of the upland forests to fulfill the kingdom's sandalwood trade with China. As Hawai'i was stripped of its sandalwood forests, the subsequent rise of the whaling industry further diverted labor from the production of food for local consumption to the production of items for sale to the ships (Hitch 1993). Like sandalwood, the whaling industry eventually went bust (by the 1870s), which gave way to the mass commercial production of sugarcane and then pineapple, two export crops that came to greatly shape Hawai'i's political economy and environmental landscape. Notably, as sugar planters diverted water from the lush windward valleys to the dry leeward plains for sugarcane and pineapple production, many Native Hawaiians were left without water to irrigate their taro fields, and were forced to abandon their land and move to the city (i.e. Honolulu) in search of work (Akutagawa et al. 2012).

By the late 1800s, the allocation of the majority of viable agricultural land to commercial agriculture had undermined the islanders' ability to be self-sufficient in food production. The economies of scale and capital investment necessary to further the commodity crop export economy precluded the cultivation of vegetables, fruits and grains, and the building of a local dairy (Kent 1993). As Kent (1993) writes, "in a group of islands containing thousands of acres of extremely fertile land ... eggs, cream and beans were imported from California." As he shows, the figures for Hawai'i's high degree of imports by the early 1900s reveal a society "unable to feed itself or even produce the basic capital goods necessary for its agro-industrial life." Hawai'i's dependent economy meant that it was vulnerable to economic fluctuations and developments (e.g. tariffs, trade agreements) from the mainland United States, a trend that continued for much of the remainder of the century and arguably continues today.

Towards the end of the twentieth century, monocrop plantation agriculture (e.g. sugar, pineapple) began to shut down in Hawai'i, as it lost its economic edge due to foreign competition. By the late 1990s, government economists, private businesses and farmers were advocating for the development of a new diversified agriculture industry (i.e. defined as any agricultural commodity besides sugar and pineapple) to take the place of the large corporate sugar and pineapple plantations. By 2000, only two sugar plantations and three pineapple companies were left, with about 35,000 acres in production (HDOA 2003). However, despite the vast amount of land that became available from the plantation closures, prime agricultural land in Hawai'i today remains relatively scarce. This is largely because of the strong oligarchic control of land (Suryanata 2002)—most of Hawai'i's agricultural land is owned by a handful of land trusts and large landowners, as well as managed or held by the State of Hawai'i—a legacy of the plantation economy days. As a result, small entrepreneurs who want to enter the diversified agriculture sector face a significant structural barrier.

Though the State committed to building diversified agriculture, this goal has been undermined by its policy of promoting massive resort development in rural areas, while keeping funding for agriculture low (Kent 1993). While the State Constitution of 1978 was supposed to protect good agricultural land and promote agricultural self-sufficiency, these aims have not been fully realized. This failure is in part due to the fact that landholders with designated agricultural land are rent seeking, and hold onto land for potential future development as opposed to using it as a working agricultural landscape (Suryanata 2002). Also, the dominant approach to developing Hawai'i's agricultural sector has focused on continuing the export-oriented strategy by diversifying into high-value nontraditional export crops, like tropical flowers, gourmet coffee, and tropical specialty fruits. While this approach seeks to capitalize upon niche markets for specialty products from Hawai'i, it does little to address Hawai'i's lack of food self-sufficiency. As Kent (1993) notes, the export of flowers and papayas, rather than the production of food crops, has been given priority. Furthermore, the state's water-use decisions, general land-use planning, and continued support of corporate agribusiness have undercut localized food production efforts. In this way, state-level decisions, along with the national US policies and dynamics of global capital that structure the current globalized food system, have made it particularly difficult for Hawai'i to achieve greater food self-sufficiency.

History of Dairy in Hawai'i

In a number of ways, the history of dairy in Hawai'i mirrors the path of food production in Hawai'i in general, though with some unique twists in its trajectory. Capt. George Vancouver first introduced cattle to Hawai'i in 1793 on his second trip to Hawai'i, as part of his voyage of discovery on behalf of Great Britain (Fischer 2007). On this trip and again in 1794, a total of eight female cows and four male cows from California were landed on the island of Hawai'i, though a few cattle died shortly after landing. The first landing was at the Kealakekua Bay, where a bull and a cow were turned loose to roam on the upland slopes of Hualālai. Once they started breeding rapidly, they were removed to the Waimea plains, and from there they gradually spread inland among the hills and valleys of Mauna Kea (Henke 1929). The goal of this "gift" to Native Hawaiians was to provide a return for the hospitality they had received as well as ensure the availability of beef for British sailors during future re-provisioning stops (Fischer 2007). After the initial importation, King Kamehameha I, at the request of Vancouver, placed a taboo on the slaughter of cattle in order to establish a reproducing population, so that by 1830 when it was removed, cattle were very numerous (Hugh et al. 1986). In 1869, the first commercial dairy was developed.[9]

Though the very first cattle introduced in Hawai'i were the longhorn Spanish type, the Holstein cattle (Figure 1) became the most numerous and popular among the dairy breeds in Hawai'i. According to a survey by Dr. Henke[10] (1929), published by the University of Hawai'i, no confirmed record has been found of the first Holstein imported to Hawai'i. The survey presents accounts of dairymen like Valdemar Knudsen (who in 1883 purchased two Holstein bulls for the herd at Kekaha, Kaua'i) and H. N. Greenwell (who in 1889 probably introduced the first Holstein to Kona). Along with Holstein, other breeds like Guernsey and Jersey cows were also used for dairy farming.

According to Henke's report (1929), there were 8,482 dairy cattle in Hawai'i by 1910, which increased to 12,244 by 1920 (Figure 2). In 1928, around 14,100,000 quarts of milk were being marketed at 10c per quart. Per-capita consumption of fresh milk in 1920 was estimated to be around 0.12 pint per person per day in the Territory, which increased to 0.23 pint per person per day by 1928. According to the First Progress Report of the Territorial Planning Board, Hawai'i (1939), an estimated 43.2 pounds of fresh milk was consumed per capita in 1919. In 1928, the per-capita consumption of fresh milk increased to 89.8 pounds, indicating that milk consumption in Hawai'i more than doubled over the span of a decade. In 1931, the per-capita consumption of fresh milk in Hawai'i was 102.0 pounds, which was considerably less than the per-capita consumption of fresh milk in the continental United States in the same year, recorded at 382.0 pounds (Territorial Planning Board, Hawai'i 1939).[11] This surge in milk consumption could be attributed to the growing awareness

Fig. 1: Joletta, one of the Holstein foundation cows at University of Hawai'i.
Source: Henke (1929).

regarding the value of milk spread by educational initiatives of public schools and nutrition workers, as well as due to improvements in the sanitary conditions for milk production. Moreover, as part of their welfare work, several plantations were known to have set up model dairies, supplying milk to their employees at lower costs.

A brief look at newspapers from the 1840s to early 1900s (before the Second World War) provides snapshots of the history of dairy in Hawai'i. These snapshots together create a larger mosaic that showcases the collective effort on the part of the government and dairy farms to promote consumption of "local" milk among the residents of Hawai'i. One of the earliest mentions of dairy products in Hawai'i's newspapers can be found in an advertisement for "Fresh Moloka'i Butter" imported from the Meyers' Dairy (*The Polynesian*, April 25, 1863). After introduction of the first commercial dairy in 1869, newspapers published articles, reports, letters and advertisements on various "local" dairy-related themes. While an article commended the operation of the Pond dairy farm (Figure 3) in Diamond Head near Honolulu (*Sunday Advertiser*, June 4, 1905), another criticized the Star dairy in Honolulu for selling adulterated "bad" milk (*The Pacific Commercial Advertiser*, April 28, 1900; February 7, 1901). Others included reports such as the Food Commissioner's inspection of the quality of milk (*The Pacific Commercial Advertiser*, July 11, 1901), ordinances regulating dairies and milk depots (*The Hawaiian Star*, July 26, 1909), recommendations for dairy testing (*The Sunday Advertiser*, October 31, 1909) and notices addressing an anthrax scare in dairy farms (*Honolulu Star Bulletin*, May 26, 1917).

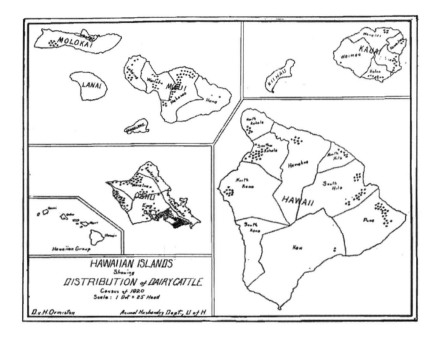

Island	Number of cows milked
Oʻahu	2,726
Hawaiʻi	628
Maui	263
Kauaʻi	319
Molokaʻi	68
Total	4,004

Fig. 2: Map showing distribution of dairy cattle in Hawaiian Islands, census 1920.

Source: From data furnished by M. B. Bairos, Food Commissioner of Hawaiʻi, 1928 (Henke 1929)

Advertisements ranged from announcement of the Honolulu Dairymen's Association proclaiming the supply of 'pure' and fresh milk (*The Hawaiian Star*, October 16, 1900) to an educational incentive of Kamehameha schools for teaching trade in dairy (*The Maui News*, August 23, 1918). Despite the

THE FOODWAYS OF HAWAI'I

Fig. 3: Cows going for milking at the Pond Dairy.
Source: *Sunday Advertiser,* June 4, 1905.

concerns voiced by news reports, bloated advertisements showcasing milk and milk products like butter, cheese and ice cream signify efforts of the then government and producers to assure Hawai'i's residents that consuming 'local' milk was healthy and safe. On July 10, 1885, *The Daily Bulletin*, Honolulu depicted a full page advertisement for 'Elite Ice Cream Parlors' (Figure 4). The naming and presentation of the advertisement in the paper implied that dairy products like ice cream made from milk were considered emblematic of a civilized way of life. While some of the contents hint at the presence of a "colonial gaze," these advertisements reached not just Native Hawaiians, but all the residents of Hawai'i in general. The discourse presented here is not separate from that promulgated on the continental U.S., but consistent with the American ideals of purity and civility, represented by the name 'Elite' ice cream parlors. The name is symbolic of the quality or value attributed to both the object (ice cream) as well as its consumers.

What emerges from the newspapers is that regardless of the difficulties involving producing milk locally in Hawai'i, inhabitants were highly encouraged to consume milk. Popular imaginaries in the newspapers highlighting the benefits of milk consumption along with warnings about "dirty" or "impure"' milk were not only oriented towards improving the dietary health of the population, but also aimed at promoting a modern and "civilized" lifestyle for the residents of Hawai'i.

During the Second World War, dairy farms played an important role in the health programs designed for the military based in Hawai'i, when milk was

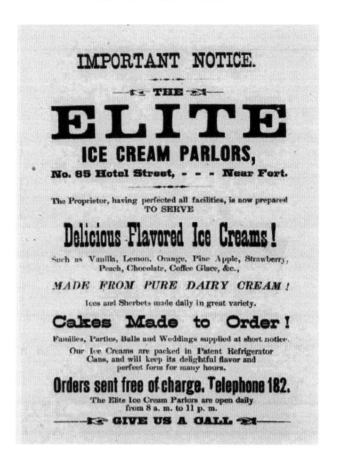

Fig. 4: *The Daily Bulletin,* July 10, 1885.

given freely to injured military personnel. These dairies remained and expanded after the war: by 1955 there were 86 dairies recorded and by 1965 cow populations peaked with 15,100 head. The rapid growth of dairy operations coupled with a limited number of processors led to discriminate purchasing practices and prices caused turmoil within the industry. Dairy producer protests at the state capital led to legislation that created the Hawaiian Milk Act, which was intended to ensure order in the marketplace (similar to federal milk marketing orders throughout the rest of the country, but which did not apply to Hawai'i). Like national dairy policies, the Milk Act was aimed at ensuring sufficient supply of fluid milk by ensuring a reasonable return to investment. This legislative support was justified according to the logic that fluid milk must be given special consideration as an essential component of the nutrition in the average American diet (Lee 2007).

The Milk Act, still in existence today, established quotas, which represent the fluid milk demand within a milkshed and set the base for milk production within a farm. Despite the price support of the quota system, by 1974 dairy operations in Hawai'i began to decrease. Hawai'i remained self-sufficient in milk production until 1982, when the milk supply was tainted with heptachlor, a pesticide chemical found in the pineapple-based roughage given to dairy cows. During the period of time in which Hawai'i-produced milk was recalled, consumers shifted to powder milk and reconstituted fluid milk, imported from the mainland. This event opened the gateway for processors to import milk from the mainland on a regular basis even after the heptachlor scare was over. Starting in 1984, when Safeway first imported processed milk into the marketplace, processors began to look outside of Hawai'i for its milk sources. While local processors initially remained loyal to local milk, they would import milk as "filler" during the summer months when local production was depressed. Then, when bulk shipment became possible in the mid-1990s, their purchasing practices shifted dramatically to cheaper imported milk sources (Lee 2007).

In the past several decades since the heptachlor incident, environmental issues, land-use policy (and subsequent limitations in land access), feed costs, transportation, milk prices to farmers, and an aging ownership in the industry, along with changing dynamics of the marketplace (e.g. national intensification and consolidation of the dairy industry), have led to the decline of Hawai'i's dairy industry. One particular point of contention for dairy producers in Hawai'i is the milk pricing system. Because no law compels a local processor to use locally produced milk, the remaining local dairies in Hawai'i (of which there are two—Big Island Dairy and Cloverleaf Dairy) are vulnerable to the whims of market forces and processor decision-making. While the processors' approach makes sense from a purely economic perspective, it introduces trade-offs in terms of milk's quality and consistency of supply available to Hawai'i consumers. For advocates of local food, whether motivated by economic, cultural, political, health or security-related reasons, the dairy industry is thus an obvious arena in which to focus re-localization efforts.

Explaining Preferences for Local Food in Hawai'i

Today, there is increasing concern amongst Hawai'i's residents over the state's ability to feed itself. While by 1937 self-reliance in food had already declined drastically—only 37.1% of Hawai'i's food supply was sourced locally compared with 100% in the pre-contact era—this percentage has continued to decline to the present day. As estimated in 2010, Hawai'i produces only 11.6% of its own food and is thus dependent upon imports for almost 90% of its food (Loke and Leung 2013). At any given time, Hawai'i, which is almost 2,500 miles from the mainland United States, has only a seven-day food supply (USDA 2011). This dependence, coupled with Hawai'i's geographic isolation, makes it particularly vulnerable to disruptions to food supply lines. Concern over this vulnerability, especially in the context of fear of increasing numbers of climate change-induced storms, has resulted in the higher prioritization of food

FOOD,
CULTURE
SOCIETY

self-sufficiency amongst island residents (Suryanata 2002; Costa and Besio 2011). Increasingly, consumers in Hawai'i are exhibiting preferences for locally produced food. For example, in a recent study on food preferences of Honolulu residents, 81% of respondents stated that they believed too little food was grown locally (OmniTrak Group Inc. 2011). As the demand for locally grown produce increases, the number of farmers' markets and community-supported agriculture (CSA) ventures emerging across the state has also risen (Loke and Leung 2013). The Hawai'i Department of Agriculture also has developed two statewide branding programs (*Island Fresh* and *Buy Local, It Matters*) that encourage shoppers to buy local. This trend towards local purchasing is bolstered by more recent state-level documents such as the Hawai'i State Plan, the New Day Plan, Hawai'i Green Growth Initiative, and Hawai'i Comprehensive Economic Development Strategy (CEDS), which all support, at least on paper, strengthening Hawai'i's local food system in order to promote food self-sufficiency.[12] From chefs to environmentalists to social justice activists, local Hawai'i-grown food has become a platform that civil society on the islands is using to advocate for improved economic, environmental and human health in the state (North Kohala Community Resource Center 2009, The Kohala Center 2010).

Primary data from 61 interviews by the author with key actors involved in efforts to re-localize the food system in Hawai'i re-affirm a local agrarian imaginary in which the globalized food system poses a threat to island sustainability, and a localized food economy is envisioned as critical to the islands' well-being and survival. When asked why local food is important, the most commonly cited reason amongst interviewees was food security (25.2% of responses), followed by reasons relating to support for the local (Hawaiian) economy (16.8% of responses).[13] (Table 1). Many of these respondents emphasized that because Hawai'i is a geographically isolated island chain, the islands should produce more food as a way to reduce vulnerability (i.e. dependence on mainland imports) and increase food security. For example, one interviewee explained that:

> [Agriculture] is the industry that should be supported and not just by lip service ... because if these people are not going to produce the food, where are you going to get the food? We buy it from somewhere else. But what if the barge is not coming in here? That is the reason why there is this push of, "We have to feed ourselves, because if the barge is not coming in, we've got only three weeks, or at most a month, of food that we have." If we're going to have a tsunami, and we got isolated here, because we are in the middle of nowhere, we don't have a source of food. We don't have a source of food.

Those that cited support for the local economy expressed that locally grown food is important because it keeps money in the state, creates jobs, and gives Hawai'i residents greater control over their economy. As one interviewee explained, a local food system is important because, "it keeps the money here,

THE FOODWAYS OF HAWAI'I

Table 1. Frequencies and percentages of responses to the interview question, "Why do you think developing a local food system in Hawai'i is important?"

Motivation for Local Food	Frequency	Percent
Economic		
$ stays in state	8	9%
Jobs	2	2%
Control instead of vulnerable to plantation economy	1	1%
Save money by growing own taro	1	1%
Support our farmers	1	1%
Support local economy	7	8%
Sub-total	**20**	**22%**
Quality		
Better taste	3	3%
Freshness	9	10%
Superior product	2	2%
Sub-total	**14**	**15%**
Health benefits		
Healthy, balanced nutritional plate	3	3%
Seasonal food has better nutrition	1	1%
Sub-total	**4**	**4%**
Community well-being		
Community cohesion	5	5%
Community resilience	3	3%
Community development	1	1%
Maintain rural character	2	2%
Relationships	1	1%
Responsibility to preserve cultural heritage	2	2%
Hawaiian empowerment	1	1%
Sub-total	**15**	**16%**
Environmental		
Less extractive	3	3%
Sub-total	**3**	**3%**
Food Security		
Food security	2	2%
Security, less vulnerability	23	25%
Self-sustaining	5	5%
Sub-total	**30**	**32%**
Accountability		
Transparency/Credibility	5	5%
Trust	2	2%
Sub-total	**7**	**8%**
Total	**93**	**100%**

Table 2. Frequencies and percentages of responses to the interview question, "What are your goals related to the development of a local food system in Hawai'i?"

Goals for Local Food	Frequency	Percent
Farmer livelihoods		
Getting youth interested in agriculture	1	3%
Increasing # of farmers	1	3%
Lease land to get people farming	2	6%
Maintain legacy of ranch	1	3%
Making agriculture productive viable career	1	3%
Helping with small farm sustainability	2	6%
Sub-total	**8**	**25%**
Import substitution/self-provisioning		
Creating agriculture-based value chain	1	3%
Import substitution	5	16%
Recovering from plantations/self-provisioning	1	3%
Self-provisioning	1	3%
People growing more of own food	6	19%
Reduce imported food to state	1	3%
Larger percent of food grown locally	6	19%
Sub-total	**21**	**66%**
Economic development		
Stimulate economy	1	3%
Save papaya industry	1	3%
Keep Hawaii products competitive	1	3%
Sub-total	**3**	**9%**
Total	**32**	**100%**

pure and simple. It keeps the money right here and if the money's here, the economy's good."

In regards to specific goals related to the development of a local food system, almost half of responses (42%) fell into the broad category of import substitution/self-provisioning (Table 2). This finding dovetails with the above finding that the most commonly cited reason for local food's importance related to food security. As succinctly put by one interviewee, "basically the goal for any farmer within the state of Hawai'i is to produce enough of any given crop to stop imports from the mainland."

However, interviews also reveal that local food advocates are divided in terms of the agricultural production methods they espouse and employ. On the one hand, some interviewees believe that the goal of food security warrants the use of all available technologies, including the use of genetically modified organisms, to allow Hawai'i-based farmers to compete with mainland imports. Others, however, believe that local food should be produced using "sustainable" farming practices, which interviewees described as organic, diversified (versus monocropping) and inclusive of native crops (e.g. taro, breafruit), which they tended to contrast with conventional farming in the continental United States. For example, one interviewee on the Big Island explained that:

> For me and us and all my work, we're not just about local. We're about local, sustainable; sustainably grown meaning without chemicals. So I think that that is a huge issue.

In contrast, another interviewee who had worked for many years for an agricultural biotechnology company in Hawai'i voiced a very different sentiment. He strongly supported agriculture as an economic activity in Hawai'i, but did not equate local with agro-ecological farming methods. He emphasized instead that:

> Today in America the use of pesticides is safer and more careful than it's ever, ever been in the history of man, so how do I feel about it? I know them. I use them. I welcome them and they're an integral part of American agriculture across the board.

These results reveal both the particularity of the local food movement in Hawai'i as well as its commonalities with the broader continental US trend towards re-localization. Like on the continent, local food advocates associate locally grown food with support for the local economy and in particular for farmer livelihoods. Many also equate locally grown food with food that uses farming methods that are more "sustainable" and ecologically friendly than those employed in industrial agriculture. However, beyond these commonly documented nationwide motivations for supporting local food, Hawaiian residents are also particularly compelled to re-localize their food system out of unique concerns over their dependence on imported goods that must travel long distances and which make them vulnerable to disruptions in food supply chains. This vulnerability is accentuated by Hawai'i's geographic isolation as well as its historic legacy of devoting its agricultural lands towards export commodity crops and, more recently, towards tourism.[14]

Along with what is colloquially referred to as the "if the barge doesn't come" mentality, Hawai'i's political sovereignty movements also influence the desire for self-sufficiency and resource independence. These movements date back to Hawai'i's overthrow by sugar barons in 1893 and its annexation to the United States in 1898. They focus on self-determination and self-governance for Hawai'i as an independent nation and/or for people of Hawaiian descent (Daws 1968). The politics of re-localization are therefore very much intertwined with long-standing questions relating to Hawai'i's sovereignty and political power (see Gupta 2015 for a detailed analysis of this intersection). As

Goodyear-Ka'ōpua has written (2009), "our [Native Hawaiian] traditions cannot be divorced from a renewal of our collective capacity to feed and sustain ourselves from our āina [land].... Sustainably providing food and water from our own lands is fundamental to the long-term survival and independence of Kānaka Maoli." Interviews with Native Hawaiians involved in re-localizing Hawai'i's food system re-affirmed this point; they articulated as this interviewee did that:

> We want to keep open space and keep the island sustainable by feeding ourselves. Recently we have gotten the word "sustainable" but that's just how we live—our parents taught us to live off the land.

Native Hawaiians and settlers[15] have thus found themselves aligned in their efforts to renew, or "re-localize," food production in Hawai'i, despite their different historical subjectivities and varied contemporary motivations for such action. However, as elucidated below, this alignment does not guarantee that proponents of re-localization share the same agrarian imaginary as to how or where local food production in Hawai'i should occur.

The Value of Local Milk

Reflective of the broader local food movement in Hawai'i, the struggling dairy industry is working to capitalize on increased consumer interest in purchasing local products. For example, in a recent study of consumer food preferences on O'ahu, consumers stated that if they understood all the characteristics of local milk—freshness, level of pasteurization—they would be willing to pay up to $1.25 more per each quart of local milk (OmniTrak Group Inc. 2011). Already there are some branding programs that identify local milk and receive a premium at the retail level, because of consumer willingness-to-pay. For example, the Mountain Apple brand, sold at a regional chain grocery store, has had great success in marketing local products, and local milk sales at its stores in particular continue to increase. The growing sales of the Mountain Apple brand, coupled with the introduction of Whole Food's branding of local milk, attest to consumer preference to buy local when available. At the same time, the two remaining local dairies face significant hurdles in maintaining their businesses as feed costs continue to rise, making it increasingly difficult to compete with mainland milk imports. Their ability to remain viable rests on their ability to gain a premium for their milk from consumers who believe that purchasing and consuming local milk provides benefits such as support for the local agricultural economy, freshness and greater nutritional value.

However, while consumers in Hawai'i appear to value local milk in theory, in practice conflict over local dairy practices reveals that residents do not support local milk production unequivocally. Instead, as the two cases below illustrate, the value consumers associate with local milk is constructed in relation to the ability of local dairies to live up to a whole suite of expectations and priorities, which are not necessarily contingent upon (local) geography.

This highlights an important point—that few individuals value "local for local's sake," and that, instead, embedded in most people's understandings of local food are assumptions about the qualities believed to be inherent in local food—i.e. fresh, supportive of the local economy, or sustainably produced. When local food production does not meet these expectations, fissures in the social construction of local food as a panacea to the globalized industrial food system are made visible.

Seeds of discontent: dairy protests on the Big Island

Illustrative of this tension within the local food paradigm, a dairy farm on the Big Island called Big Island Dairy, a subsidiary of Idaho-based Whitesides Dairy, came under fire in 2011 when nearby residents discovered that the farm was growing genetically modified (GM) corn to feed to its dairy cows. Activists concerned about both the environmental impact and indirect health effects on milk consumers of cows fed GM corn held a protest and staged a concert to voice their opposition to the dairy farmer's practices. As farmer and anti-GMO activist Eden Pearl explained to the press, "Around the world, people are documenting genetic crime scenes, and we've got one here in Ookala. Big Island Dairy is growing GMO corn here … and it has to stop right away." As another local organic farmer explained, "We can't be self-reliant if corporations like Monsanto pollute the resources." For Big Island residents like Pearl—especially organic-oriented farmers—a local food system is not sustainable if it is dependent upon corporate-owned GM seeds.

In response, the dairy farmer and his supporters countered that by growing their own feed and avoiding the high cost of importing feed they were creating a viable model for localized milk production on the Big Island. This factor—the cost of inputs, notably feed—has to date strained Hawai'i's dairy and livestock industries. Indeed, the State Department of Agriculture Chairman Russell Kokobun was quoted as stating that:

> One of the real issues for them, and for any protein producer, actually, or livestock producers, is the cost of feed…. It's the high cost of feed that is amongst the major causes of livestock producers giving up. So the idea of being able to produce our livestock feed is one of the keys to insuring that our livestock industry will be able to continue here. (Burnett 2012)

In this way, the protests against the dairy were constructed by those in favor of GM technology as "anti-farmer"—a portrayal that the protesters, many of whom are farmers themselves working to re-build local food production on the island, found particularly galling. These recent events illustrate the contrasting agrarian imaginaries held by rural community members on the Big Island, particularly in regards to the role of GM technology in "sustainable" farming.

Indeed, the debate over GMO technology is particularly divisive amongst producers and consumers alike. This is the case across various parts of the globe, and particularly true in Hawai'i, where many biotechnology firms conduct their seed testing (see Gupta 2015). On the Big Island in particular, there is an especially vocal and active group of organic farmers who oppose the use of GM crops. For these farmers, GMOs pose a threat to the viability of alternative agricultural systems that produce "clean," safe food. They decry the use of GMOs in favor of organic practices and are suspicious of technological "quick-fixes" that do not address the deeper systemic problems that accompany monocropping and other industrial-oriented conventional forms of agriculture. As one interviewee articulated:

> Because not everything that's local is sustainable.... It might have economical benefits, but it might not have ecological benefits ... there's been five generations of farming with pesticides here, you know? It's been a very coming down from the university, just like any other big Ag state, where all the research and all the science comes down and now you have the Monsantos and all that, with their special seeds and all that. So they give all this stuff, pesticides, and modified seeds to all the big farmers. And they've been using them. And they're believers. It increases their yield. And, sure a virus might come in and wipe out an entire crop one year, but they just chop it all down and start over. They don't really think like, "Oh, there's a flaw." They're not just switching over to organics. They're not—they're holding firm with the way it's always been done.[16]

Yet at the same time there is a base of farmers—several of whom are some of the larger producers of locally consumed fruits and vegetables on the island—who believe that food self-sufficiency on the Big Island is a pipe dream without the utilization of genetically modified organisms as tools for combating agricultural challenges such as new plant pathogens and adequate feed supply for livestock. For example, one local government official in the Hawai'i Department of Agriculture rhetorically questioned:

> How much production is there [in Hawai'i] if you're going to [try to] be self-reliant? With organic, everybody's going to starve.... How much production do you actually get from organic farming?

These two camps of farmers are united in their desire to strengthen their island's ability to feed itself, yet vehemently divided on how to achieve this goal. The recent debate over the local dairy's agricultural practices is just one such conflict that highlights the difficulty of building a local food system, given that communities—whether in Hawai'i or elsewhere—rarely hold uniform views.

"Local but not in my backyard": dairy politics on the Garden Isle
Controversy over a proposed dairy on the island of Kaua'i also illustrates the challenges to re-localizing milk production in Hawai'i. In December of 2013, Ulupono Initiative, a Hawai'i-focused impact investing firm backed by

eBay founder Pierre Omidyar, announced plans to invest US$17.5 million in the creation of Hawai'i Dairy Farms (HDF) on Kaua'i. Their mission, rooted in a belief that Hawai'i's milk should come from Hawai'i, is to provide "fresh nutritious milk that's affordable for local families—produced in Hawai'i for Hawai'i" (http://www.hawaiidairyfarms.com). They aim to "transform the dairy system in the state" (Datta quoted in Tanaka 2013) by doubling the local milk supply through a New Zealand-based pastoral model of what they are describing as sustainable production. Rather than feed its cows imported grain, the proposed dairy plans to feed its cows grass, which will reduce reliance on imported inputs. Like Big Island Dairy, by substituting imported grain for local inputs, it intends to be able to make its production of milk cost effective and thus competitive with imported mainland milk. However it differs from the Big Island dairy in that cows will be fed locally grown (non-genetically modified) grass, as opposed to locally grown genetically modified corn.

Yet nearby residents have found other reasons to contest the proposed dairy farm. Ulupono plans to develop HDF in Maha'ulepu, an area of historical and environmental significance to Hawaiians that has been the focus of community struggles to stave off commercial development for decades. Local residents and other environmentalists say that the dairy will generate more than three million pounds of manure each month, which could cause runoff problems and noxious odors for neighbors and nearby hotels (Daysog 2014). A member of the Kaua'i chapter of the Surfrider Foundation was quoted in the local newspaper as saying that "We think it's inappropriate to have an industrial-sized dairy in that particular place. For us, it's a public health problem. That much manure with that many diseases, viruses and bacteria…" (Daysog 2014). The owner of the nearby Grand Hyatt Kaua'i Resort and Spa has filed a lawsuit against Hawai'i Dairy Farms, claiming its business will be adversely affected by the wastewater treatment unit, the dairy farm and its effluent ponds (Shimogawa 2014). Residents worry also about the proximity of the dairy and its waste to the ocean.

FOOD,
CULTURE
SOCIETY

The Big Island Dairy Farm has defended its enterprise, arguing that the proposed dairy represents the best practices for sustainable dairy farming. It issued a statement explaining that "we've heard [the community's] concerns and we're planning a dairy that goes beyond compliance to ensure the operation is environmentally protective [and] adaptable to operating conditions" and that it is working with regulators "to ensure we are meeting and exceeding all requirements under federal and state law" (http://www.hawaiidairyfarms.com/news_posts/hawaii-dairy-farms-plans-for-phased-approach). Its response to concerns about the dairy has focused on the project's pastoral-based model, in which manure produced by the grazing cows will be left in the pasture as fertilizer (while manure produced by cows being milked will go into an effluent pond and eventually be put back into pasture). As Datta of Ulupono Initiative explained, in this pastoral system, "cow manure from dairies and ranches is broken down by biological organisms and turns into nutrients that feed the grass and create rich organic soil" (Shimogawa 2014). They also point to the fact that the dairy has implemented a number of protective measures such as large setback areas and containment berms to prevent runoff. A spokeswoman from the Ulupono Initiative stated that HDF would be "much better for the environment, much better for the cows and more financially sustainable" (Daysog 2014).

Ulupono has criticized Kawailoa Development (the owner of the Hyatt) for its "malicious attack on local food by commercial resort interests." In response, they plan to "fight this insidious attack on local food on behalf of all of Hawai'i agriculture, because we care about the future of farming and we also care about the right for families on all of our islands to have fresh local milk" (http://www.hawaiidairyfarms.com/news_posts/an-update-from-the-farm). The dairy has received the support of the island's mayor Bernard Carvalho Jr. and Hawai'i's Farm Bureau. Carvalho opposes the hotel's lawsuit and has emphasized the importance of supporting the goal of statewide food self-sufficiency. Jerry Ornellas, vice-president of the Kaua'i Farm Bureau, stated that he supports the dairy farm "because at some point we're going to have to get serious about producing our food locally," and added that "this is a classic case of shifting the burden, not in my backyard. Let's put it in some other neighborhood" (Daysog 2014).

This last remark highlights the tension between local food in theory and local food in practice. While the concept of local food has gained support amongst Hawaiian consumers as a social, economic and environmental good, the realities associated with certain production models of local food—shifting land-use and associated (potential) environmental effects—are not always equally embraced. On the one hand, Ulupono has framed the reaction to Big Island Dairy Farm as a threat not only to the local dairy industry, but also to agricultural operations in Hawai'i more broadly. Datta was quoted as saying that:

> Ulupono Initiative believes the implication of the lawsuit from Kawailoa Development will impact all animal agriculture within the state… Nearly all of the locally owned and operated, family-run animal operations that have fed the people of Hawai'i for generations are considered animal feeding operations and could be put out of business. Further, the misguided legal concept that the owners of reclassified agricultural land can sue to have their agricultural neighbors declared a nuisance would impact every single farmer in the state, large or small, and is a direct assault on the rights of farmers under the laws of the State of Hawai'i.

From this perspective, tourism and other vested interests (i.e. those with real-estate values contingent on a certain kind of non-agricultural landscape) are juxtaposed against agricultural interests and the statewide imperative to become more food self-sufficient. The criticism of those who oppose the dairy then becomes about pointing out the self-interest and naiveté of those who envision the benefits of local food production as consumers, without imagining the activities associated with certain kinds of food production taking place near their backyard. In other words, they want food production to be close, but not too close.

On the other hand, many of the community members who oppose HDF are actively involved in food systems re-localization efforts in other realms and take issue with this characterization. Their primary points of contention are not about animal agriculture in and of itself, but stem from concerns over the influence of what are perceived to be large outside investors (i.e. Ulupono Initiative, funded by the Omidyar family) in determining the future of the island and what does or does not develop. They have taken issue with a perceived lack of transparency on the part of HDF, the intensity of production and in particular the proposed grazing density. Furthermore, they question whether Kaua'i should be producing milk for the entire state (or whether production should be localized at the island level instead), particularly in an area—Maha'ulepu—that has been the focus of long-standing preservation efforts by local community members. They see this "right to farm" argument, articulated in the quote above, as a continuation of discursive efforts by historically powerful large agricultural interests (namely plantation sugar) to minimize any form of regulation.

In this way, while residents of Hawai'i have shown renewed interest in locally grown food, there are individual, community or business-related concerns related to the expansion of agricultural industries that may trump this preference. The backlash to HDF reveals that islanders are not willing to support the cause of local agriculture in any form—they are discerning about the models of development and potential environmental costs that may accompany certain types of production. The case of HDF has opened up tricky conversations about what type of local food system the community can collectively embrace, and where/in whom it wants to invest its resources. Indeed, while Hawai'i Dairy Farm considers itself to be a "local" enterprise (Ulupono Initiative is based in Honolulu), many community members on Kaua'i consider it to comprise "outside" investment capitalists. As islanders weigh trade-offs—the value of locally produced milk against the threat (real or perceived) of environmental or even aesthetic degradation by an outside entity—the challenges to re-creating a self-sustaining agricultural-based economy in contemporary Hawai'i come into focus. More broadly, the Kaua'i dairy case highlights the difficulties in creating local food systems, which require stakeholders to come together to decide how food should be grown. In practice, community conflicts, rife with political contention, can preclude the development of robust local or regional food systems, despite the best intentions and aspirations of community members.

Discussion

Food activists and practitioners increasingly tout local food systems rooted in community values and relationships as a social good—yet as the case of the dairy industry in Hawai'i shows, in practice they can become mired in debates over how and where this food should be grown. In this way, local food as a concept is fraught with tension. Conflicting agrarian imaginaries can create divisions amongst farmers, as in the Big Island example, as well as between agricultural investors and rural residents, as in the Kaua'i case. These imaginaries are conceived of differently by different groups for economic, social, and cultural reasons and are tempered by wider historical, ecological, economic, and technological constraints. In the context of Hawai'i, they fit themselves to particular yet shifting discourses about public health, production, food safety, sovereignty, security, and cultural heritage. More specifically, on the Big Island, resistance to a local dairy's use of GM corn highlights the fact that the value local food advocates ascribe to locally produced food is about more than just food's geographic origins. Instead, local food is socially constructed as a vehicle for achieving a whole host of broader goals, many of which are intended to challenge the status quo industrial agricultural model. In turn, certain models of local food production are then perceived as harmful—and as something to resist—when they run counter to other anti-industrial agriculture movement concerns. And as the Kaua'i case shows, individuals may support the notion of local food as a vehicle for greater food self-sufficiency, but may resist certain models of local food production when it interferes with their priorities and values as rural residents living in a (relatively) pristine area, especially one of historical cultural importance.

While the rhetoric of local food is one that many people, both in Hawai'i and beyond, unite around, the political coalitions that actually come together around various issues and agendas related to food production suggest that there is no singular and monolithic local food movement. Notably, while some local food advocates are part of a social movement looking to transform the corporate industrial food system, others are more supportive of industrial-style agriculture (including the use of GMOs) and see local food production as beneficial for other reasons (e.g. food security, economic development). In other words, "local food" is a discourse that is frequently mobilized by different actors with different priorities and interests. This raises the question, which warrants further exploration, of whether the concept of a "local food movement" in fact works to obscure political controversies over resource use, power and historical legacies, and to what effect.

In conclusion, the complexity of social relations embodied in local food systems does not necessarily preclude the viability of a regional food system; however, awareness of divisions between and amongst local farmers, nearby rural residents and other food system stakeholders is essential to the development of realistic expectations and goals for such a system. The sustainable and steady production of local foods requires not only appropriate ecological conditions but also a certain social ecology. In the case of Hawai'i, this means recognizing the forms of land-use that compete with agriculture, especially high-end real estate, tourism and its vested interests. It requires that attention be paid to the context in which local agricultural enterprises are developed. More specifically, sensitivity to the extent to which such developments re-entrench versus challenge long-standing struggles over land and associated historical injustices is critical, given Hawai'i's history of land dispossession. It also means taking seriously the current debates over best practices for agriculture that have created divides both within Hawai'i's farming communities and between farmers and their rural neighbors. In particular, the use of genetically modified organisms in agriculture has become a lightning-rod issue in Hawai'i (see Gupta 2015). Without addressing and taking into account these entrenched points of discord, proponents of food re-localization—whether in Hawai'i's dairy industry or beyond— will face an uphill battle in realizing their agrarian vision.

Acknowledgements

I thank The Kohala Center for their support of my fieldwork as well as Alice Kelly, Mez Baker-Medard, Lindsey Dillon, Laura-Anne Minkoff-Zern and the two anonymous reviewers for their helpful comments on this paper. I would also like to thank Tanaya Dattagupta for her help with archival analysis.

Disclosure statement

No potential conflict of interest was reported by the author.

Funding

This work was funded by National Science Foundation [award number 1215762].

Notes

1. Though there is no consensus around the definition of "local," for the purposes of this article (and based on stakeholder interviews and document analysis) I define local as produced within the state of Hawai'i and do not assume local to inherently imply any other specific attributes (i.e. organic, small-farm produced) other than this geographic boundary.
2. However, there is some debate over milk as an "essential part of the American diet"—see DuPuis (2002) for an account of the social construction of milk as a major dietary practice in the United States.
3. Again, it is important to note that while today milk is consumed widely across the state of Hawai'i (though to varying degrees amongst Hawai'i's various ethnic populations), milk was not historically part of the Native Hawaiian diet and was only introduced by white settlers in the nineteenth century.
4. Milk quality can be measured in two broad categories: (a) bacteria-related issues and (b) nutrient changes in milk following handling. Bacteria-related issues result

in spoilage and potential illness. Handling, such as through the extended heating of milk, can denature proteins or amino acids and thus change the values of the nutrients in milk. The pasteurization process itself does alter some proteins and enzymes. Hawaiʻi milk is unique in that it is pasteurized *twice*—first before being shipped to Hawaiʻi and then second it is re-pasteurized prior to bottling for retail in Hawaiʻi. It is worth noting that California specifically prohibits the re-pasteurization of fluid milk for fluid purpose. Milk imported to Hawaiʻi has also been shown to exceed federal regulatory limits in bacterial counts five days prior to expiration. While the source or site of this contamination has not been determined, Lee (2007) notes that the duration of time the milk at retail in Hawaiʻi would have left a cow if this milk were imported might be quite lengthy. He estimates that the age of milk after it left a CA cow and at its expiration date is at minimum 24.7 days, and at maximum 30 days. While it is unlikely that any other state in the nation has 25–30-day-old milk sold to consumers unless ultrapasteurized, no law is actually broken with this duration because no states regulate shelf-life (Lee 2007).

5. These actors are from the islands of Hawaiʻi and Molokai and include farmers, restaurateurs, grocers, distributors, government officials involved in food and agriculture policy, researchers, non-profit practitioners advocating for local food and community leaders. They reflect the diversity of Hawaiʻi's ethnic fabric, as they include members of the Native Hawaiian, Asian immigrant and white settler communities. They also come from varying economic backgrounds, ranging from struggling farmers to tenured university professors. Interviewees were asked why "local food" is important and what goals they held vis-à-vis local food production. They were also asked the metrics they use to assess progress towards achieving these goals.

6. The analysis of these two cases is based on research conducted between 2012 and 2014 while based primarily on Hawaiʻi Island. Along with the semi-structured interviews mentioned above and document analysis (e.g. media reports, internal community organization documents), an integral component of my research involved participant observation, a key methodological tool for qualitative research that involves intense involvement with people in their cultural environment through both observation of and participation in daily activities over an extended period of time (Guest et al. 2013). Specifically, I worked closely with a local non-profit focused on food self-reliance in Hawaiʻi. As well as with interacting with my interlocutors on a regular basis, I attended numerous community food system events and sustainable agriculture workshops. The empirical data gathered through these processes—both formal interviewing and informal participant observation—informs the following narrative, which I present in some places through direct quotes and in other places through paraphrasing or synthesis.

7. His stance also reflects broader analytical efforts to denaturalize dominant discourses on "development" that serve as mechanisms of control over the "Third World" and instead to offer alternative visions for the post-development era (Escobar 1995).

8. While I am in solidarity with sovereignty advocates who choose not to italicize Hawaiian words (see Silva 2004 for the rationale behind this), I have chosen to italicize Hawaiian words based on the logic that italicization is conventionally used to indicate the use of a foreign language, which is relational to the author and the place one is writing about and from where (which in my case is the place of an English-speak-

ing author writing about Hawai'i from the continental United States).

9. There were, however, a number of unintended negative environmental consequences, including destruction of native grasses and crops such as taro by grazing cattle (Fischer 2007).

10. Prof. Louis A. Henke was a professor of Agriculture at the College and University of Hawai'i. He was also known for developing the most outstanding herd of dairy cows in Hawai'i. The herd held the first place for all Hawaiian produced A.R.O records (*The Garden Island*, May 3, 1921).

11. The figures were computed by the Territorial Planning Board, Hawai'i (1939), based on running averages for five-year periods. Sources for the data include Board of Health, US Census and US Department of Commerce reports.

12. For example, in his New Day Plan, Governor Neil Abercrombie has called for an "agricultural renaissance" in which Hawai'i grows more of its own food and becomes increasingly self-reliant (Abercrombie 2010). More recently, the Hawaiian Department of Business Economic Development and Tourism (DBEDT) and the Department of Agriculture put forth a food self-sufficiency strategy report in 2012 that aims to increase the amount of locally grown food consumed by Hawai'i residents. The report's strategies include strengthening agricultural infrastructure, increasing support for Farmers' Markets and further developing a "Grow Local/It Matters" campaign (DBEDT 2012).

13. As smaller considerations, 12.6% of responses stated that local food was important because it was good for community well-being, citing community resilience, the maintenance of rural character and inter-community relationships as key benefits of a local food system. Some 11.8% of responses cited quality as the reason for supporting local food production—either in regards to better taste, freshness and/or superior product. Respondents also mentioned accountability (5.9%), health benefits (3.4%) and reduced environmental impact (2.5%) as reasons for local food's importance.

14. The critiques of re-localization discussed above call into question the logic behind the beliefs and goals of local food proponents in Hawai'i (e.g. an economist might argue that the principle of competitive advantage is more important than overall self-sufficiency). This article does not purport to assess or pass judgment on the empirical validity of their claims, but instead takes their re-localization efforts at face value as a starting point to analyze what is a growing and noteworthy social movement capable of producing outcomes that merit increased scholarly attention.

15. While the term *haole* (meaning "white" or "foreigner") is used colloquially to describe non-Native Hawaiians, the term "settler" is used in academic literature to describe non-Native Hawaiians and will be subsequently used in this paper.

16. This sentiment—criticism of local farmers who farm conventionally with pesticides—was voiced numerous times in interviews. See Appendix A for further quotes in this vein.

References

Abercrombie, N. 2010. "A New Day in Hawaii: A Comprehensive Plan." Unpublished paper, Honolulu.

"*Advertisement*". 1885. *The Daily Bulletin*, July 10.

Agricultural Water use and Development Plan. 2003. "State of Hawai'i Department of Agriculture." Prepared by Water Resource Associates. Unpublished report.

Akutagawa, M., L. Han, E. Noordhoek, and H. Williams. 2012. "Agricultural Needs Assessment. Sustainable Moloka'i." Unpublished report.

Alkon, A., and J. Agyeman. 2011. *Cultivating Food Justice: Race, Class and Sustainability*. Cambridge, MA: Massachusetts Institute of Technology.

Alkon, A. H., and C. G. McCullen. 2011. "Whiteness and Farmers Markets: Performances, Perpetuations ... Contestations?" *Antipode* 43: 937–959. doi:10.1111/j.1467-8330.2010.00818.x.

Allen, P. 2004. *Together at the Table: Sustainability and Sustenance in the American Agrifood System*. University Park: Pennsylvania State University Press.

Allen, P. 2008. "Mining for Justice in the Food System: Perceptions, Practices and Possibilities." *Agriculture and Human Values* 25 (2): 157–161.

Brown, S., and C. Getz. 2011. "Farmworker Food Insecurity and the Production of Hunger In California." In *Cultivating Food Justice: Race, Class and Sustainability*, edited by A. Alkon and J. Agyeman. Cambridge, MA: Massachusetts Institute of Technology.

Burnett, J. 2012. "GMO Corn Grower Spurs Protest." *Hawai'i Tribune Herald*. Accessed January 15, 2015. http://hawaiitribune-herald.com/sections/news/local-news/gmo-corn-grower-spurs-protest.html.

Cakir, M., and J. V. Balagtas. 2012. "Estimating Market Power of U.S. Dairy Cooperatives in the Fluid Milk Market." *American Journal of Agricultural Economics* 94 (3): 647–658.

Carlisle, L. 2015. *Lentil Underground: Renegade Farmers and the Future of Food in America*. New York: Penguin.

Cleveland, D. 2013. *Balancing on a Planet: The Future of Food and Agriculture*. Berkeley: University of California Press.

Costa, L., and K. Besio. 2011. "Eating Hawai'i: Local foods and Place-making in Hawai'i Degional Cuisine." *Social and Cultural Geography* 12: 839–854.

Daws, G. 1968. *Shoal of Time: A History of the Hawaiian Islands*. Honolulu: University of Hawai'i Press.

Daysog, R. 2014. "Opposition mounting to Kaua'i Dairy." *Hawai'i News Now*. Accessed January 15, 2015. http://www.hawaiinewsnow.com/story/27611904/exclusive-opposition-mounting-to-kauai-dairy.

Desrochers, P., and H. Shimizu 2012. *The Locavore's Dilemma: In Praise of the 10,000 Mile Diet*. New York: PublicAffairs.

DuPuis, E. M. 2002. *Nature's Perfect Food: How Milk Became America's Drink*. New York: New York University Press.

DuPuis, E. M., and D. Goodman. 2005. "Should we go "Home" to Eat?: Toward a Reflexive Politics of Localism." *Journal of Rural Studies* 21 (3): 359–371.

Edwards-Jones, G., L. M. Canals, N. Hounsome, M. Truninger, G. Koerber, B. Hounsome, P. Cross, E. H. York, A. Hospido, and K. Plassmann. 2008. "Testing the assertion that 'local food is best': the challenges of an evidence-based approach." *Trends in Food Science & Technology* 19 (5): 265–274.

Escobar, A. 1995. *Encountering Development: The Making and Unmaking of the Third World*. Princeton: Princeton University Press.

Eshel, G., A. Shepon, T. Makov, and R. Milo. 2014. "Land, Irrigation Water, Greenhouse Gas, and Reactive Nitrogen Burdens of Meat, Eggs, and Dairy Production in the United States." *PNAS* 111 (33): 11996–12001.

Fischer, J. R. 2007. "Cattle in Hawai'i: Biological and Cultural Exchange." *Pacific Historical Review* 76 (3): 347–372.

Freidberg, S. 2009. *Fresh: A Perishable History*. Cambridge, MA: Belknap Press.

Goodman, D., and E. M. DuPuis. 2002. "Knowing Food and Growing Food: Beyond the Production-Consumption Debate in the Sociology of agriculture." *Sociologia Ruralis* 42: 5–22. doi:10.1111/1467-9523.00199.

Goodyear-Ka'ōpua, N. 2009. "Rebuilding the 'Auwai: Connecting ecology, economy and education in Hawaiian schools." *AlterNatives* 5: 46–77.

Goodyear-Ka'ōpua, N. 2013. *The Seeds We Planted: Portraits of a Native Hawaiian Charter School*. Minneapolis: University of Minnesota Press.

Guest, G., E. Namey, and M. Mitchell. 2013. *Collecting Qualitative Data: A Field Manual for Applied Research*. Thousand Oaks, CA: Sage Publications.

Gupta, C. 2015. "Return to Freedom: Anti-GMO Aloha Aina Activism on Molokai as an Expression of Place-based Food Sovereignty." *Globalizations* 12 (4): 529–544.

Gupta, C., and T. Makov (under revision). 2015. "How Global is My Local Milk?: Compatibility between Perceived Attributes and the Reality of Local Food." *Journal of Agriculture and Human Values*.

Guthman, J. 2004. *Agrarian Dreams: The Paradox of Organic Farming in California*. Berkeley: University of California Press.

Guthman, J. 2011. "'If They Only Knew': The Unbearable Whiteness of Alternative Food." In *Cultivating Food Justice: Race, Class and Sustainability*, edited by A. Alkon and J. Agyeman. Cambridge, MA: Massachusetts Institute of Technology.

http://www.hawaiidairyfarms.com. Accessed January 15, 2015.

http://www.hawaiidairyfarms.com/news_posts/hawaii-dairy-farms-plans-for-phased-approach. Accessed January 15, 2015.

http://www.hawaiidairyfarms.com/news_posts/an-update-from-the-farm. Accessed Jan, 15, 2015.

Hau'ofa, Epeli. 1994. "Our Sea of Islands." *The Contemporary Pacific* 6 (1): 147–161.

Hawaii Department of Agriculture (HDOA). 2003. *Agricultural Water Use and Development Plan*. Honolulu: Water Resource Associates.

Henderson, E. 2000. "Rebuilding Local Food Systems from the Grassroots up." In *Hungry for Profit*, edited by F. Magdoff, J. B. Foster and F. H. Buttel. New York: Monthly Review Press.

Henke, L. A. 1929. *A Survey of Livestock in Hawai'i* (Research Publication No. 5, August). Honolulu: University of Hawai'i.

Hinrichs, C. 2003. "The Practice and Politics of Food System Localization." *Journal of Rural Studies* 19 (1): 33–45.

Hitch, T. K. 1993. *Islands in Transition: The Past, Present and Future of Hawai'i's Economy*. Honolulu: University of Hawai'i Press.

Honolulu Star-Bulletin. (Honolulu, O'ahu, Hawaii), 3:30 Edition. 1917. "Anthrax Deaths Now Number 22," May 26, p. 1.

Hopper, K. C. 1921. "The Extension Leaders." *The Garden Island (Lihue, Kaua'i, H.T.) Hawai'i Edition*, May 3, p. 4.

Hugh, W. I., T. Tanaka, J. C. Nolan, Jr., and L. K. Fox 1986. *The Livestock Industry in Hawai'i*. HITAHR Information Text Series 025. Hawai'i: College of Tropical Agriculture and Human Resources, University of Hawai'i.

Kame'eleihiwa, L. 1992. *Native Land and Foreign Desires: Pehea Lā E Pono Ai?*. Honolulu: Bishop Museum Press.

Kamehameha Schools Hawaiian Studies Institute. 1982. *The Ahupua'a*, 20–26. Honolulu: Kamehameha Schools Press.

Kent, N. J. 1993. *Hawai'i Islands Under the Influence*. Honolulu: University of Hawai'i Press.

Kneafsey, M. 2010. "The Region in Food—Important or Irrelevant?" *Cambridge Journal of Regions, Economy and Society* 3: 177–190.

Lee, C. N. 2007. *Issues related to Hawai'i's Dairy Industry*. Manoa: Department of Human Nutrition, Food, and Animal Science, College of Tropical Agriculture and Human Resources, University of Hawai'i.

Loke, M., and P. Leung. 2013. "Competing Food Concepts—Implications for Hawai'i, USA." *Food and Energy Security* 2: 3, 1–11.

MacKenzie, M. K. 1991. *Native Hawaiian Rights Handbook*. Honolulu: University of Hawai'i Press.

Marsden, T. 2010. "Mobilizing the Regional Eco-Economy: Evolving Webs of Agri-food and Rural Development in the UK." *Cambridge Journal of Regions, Economy and Society* 3: 225–244.

Matthews, H. S., C. T. Hendrickson, and C. L. Weber. 2008. "The importance of carbon footprint estimation boundaries." *Environmental Science & Technology* 42 (16): 5839–5842.

Morgan, Thomas. 1948. *Hawai'i: A Century of Economic Change, 1778–1876*, 17. Cambridge, MA: Harvard University Press.

North Kohala Community Resource Center. 2009. North Kohala Food Forum Data Book and Proceedings. Unpublished report.

Office of Planning Department of Business Economic Development and Tourism, State of Hawaii (DBEDT). 2012. *Increased Food Security and Food Self-Sufficiency Strategy*. White Paper.

OmniTrak Group Inc. 2011. *Local Food Market Demand Study of O'ahu Shoppers: Executive Summary*. Honolulu: Ulupono Initiative.

Peterson, G. R. 2013. "Is eating locally a moral obligation?" *Journal of Agricultural and Environmental Ethics* 26: 421. doi:10.1007/s10806-012-9397-8.

Pollan, M. 2006. *Omnivore's Dilemma: A Natural History of Four Meals*. New York: Penguin.

Polynesian (Honolulu [O'ahu], Hawai'i). 1863. "Moloka'i Butter," April 25, p. 3.

Porter, B. E. 1909. "The Milk Supply for Honolulu," *Pacific Commercial Advertiser. (Honolulu, Hawaiian Islands), Sunday Advertiser*, October 31, p. 4.

Purcell, M., and J. C. Brown. 2005. "Against the local trap: scale and the study of environment and development." *Progress in Development Studies* 5 (4): 279–297.

Rushing, J., and M. Goldblatt. 2014. "Ripe for Grocers: The Local Food Movement." Accessed 22 September 2014. http://www.middle-east.atkearney.com/consumer-products-retail/ideas-insights/featured-article/-/asset_publisher/KQNW4F0xInID/content/ripe-for-grocers-the-local-food-movement/10192.

Shimogawa, D. 2014. "eBay Founder Omidyar's Hawai'i Dairy Farms scales back Kaua'i Plans," *Pacific Business News*, Accessed January 15, 2015. http://www.bizjournals.com/pacific/news/2014/07/25/ebay-founder-omidyars-hawaii-dairy-farms-scales.html?page=all.

Shiva, V. 2000. *Stolen Harvest: The Hijacking of the Global Food Supply*. Boston, MA: South End Press.

Silva, N. K. 2004. *Aloha Betrayed: Native Hawaiian Resistance to American Colonialism*. Durham, NC: Duke University Press.

Sumner, D. A., and J. V. Balagtas. 2002. "United States' Agricultural Systems: An Overview of U.S. Dairy Policy." In *Encyclopedia of Dairy Sciences*, edited by H. Roginski, J. Fuquay, and P. Fox. Oxford: Elsevier Science.

Suryanata, K. 2002. "Diversified Agriculture, Land Use, and Agrofood Networks in Hawai'i." *Economic Geography* 78: 8–10.

Tanaka, C. 2013. "Dairy Farm coming to Kaua'i," *Hawai'i News Now*, Accessed January 15, 2015. http://www.hawaiinewsnow.com/story/24117696/dairy-farm-coming-to-kauai.

Territorial Planning Board, Hawai'i 1939. *First Progress Report. A Historic Inventory of the Physical, Social and Economic, and Industrial Resources of the Territory of Hawai'i*. Honolulu: Territorial Planning Board.

Tilman, D., K. Cassman, P. Matson, R. Naylor, and S. Polasky. 2002. "Agricultural Sustainability aand Intensive Production Practices." *Nature* 418: 671–677.

The Hawaiian Star (Honolulu [O'ahu]). 1900. "The Honolulu Dairymen's Association, Ltd.," October 16, p. 6.

The Hawaiian Star (Honolulu [O'ahu]) Second Edition. 1909. "An Ordinance Regulating Dairies, Milk Depots and the Delivery of Milk," July 26, p. 3.

The Kohala Center 2010. *The County of Hawai'i Agriculture Development Plan*. Hawai'i: Research and Development Department County of Hawai'i.

The Maui News (Wailuku, Maui, H.I.). 1918. "Practical Education for Hawaiian Boys," August 23, p. 6.

The Pacific Commercial Advertiser (Honolulu, Hawaiian Islands). 1900. "He Sold Bad Milk," April 28, p. 2.

The Pacific Commercial Advertiser (Honolulu, Hawaiian Islands). 1901a. "The Star Dairy Manager Sold Adulterated Milk," February 7, p. 9.

The Pacific Commercial Advertiser (Honolulu, Hawaiian Islands). 1901b. "Milk Below Standard: Dr. Shorey Describes Methods of Dealers," July 11, p. 11.

The Pacific Commercial Advertiser (Honolulu, Hawaiian Islands), Sunday Advertiser. 1905. "Small Farming Near Diamond Head," June 4, p. 6.

United States Department of Agriculture (USDA). 2011. *Hawaii Fact Sheet*. USDA Farm Service Agency.

Wallerstein, I. 2000. *The Essential Wallerstein*. New York: New Press.

Weber, C. L., and H. S. Matthews. 2008. "Food-miles and the relative climate impacts of food choices in the United States." *Environmental Science & Technology* 42 (10): 3508–3513.

Appendix A. Interview quotes illustrating the agrarian imaginary of one segment of the local food movement in Hawai'i

Quote 1 (Beekeeper on the Big Island)
But I have to say that when I talk to people about farmers' markets, I say you know, don't be deceived. Like, you may assume that because a farmer is selling at a farmers' market that they're doing it organically and that's not true. Otherwise, you're buying this lettuce and it'll be filled with all kinds of toxins.... I only want to eat organic foods. I can't totally do that. But it's not locally available. And the choice is ... b etween buy local or get organic. So part of the thing you want to put under the farmers' market organization is the damage to the Earth and people that toxic stuff does and try to ... organize an organic farmers' market. Totally organic, based on that principle.

Quote 2 (Organic farmer on the Big Island)
You have a lot of people here with that third-world way of thinking. Chemicals are our savior.

Quote 3 (Professor of Soil Science, University of Hawai'i, Hilo)
A lot of the growers of things like sweet potatoes and ginger, they don't really care about the land.... Because they are just moving from one property to another. So they'll either plow up and down the hill or use nasty chemicals and ... they don't really care about chemical drift and things and you see the workers out in the field not using proper safety equipment.

Customary Access: Sustaining Local Control of Fishing and Food on Kaua'i's North Shore

Mehana Blaich Vaughan and Adam L. Ayers

Abstract

Where Hawai`i's land and sea once supported a population close to contemporary times, today 90 percent of food consumed in Hawai`i is imported and delivered on container ships. Once plentiful in the bays and coral reefs surrounding these islands, fish is now frequently shipped in and store bought. Yet, local families in parts of Hawai`i have maintained self-sufficiency in part of their food system through communal surround net fishing, employing ancestral knowledge, mobilizing community effort, and sharing catch from these collective harvests. This article examines the role of access in perpetuating surround net harvests and sharing through hō'ihi (respectful reciprocity); konohiki (inviting ability); and kuleana (rights based on responsibilities). It concludes by considering the implications of the findings for food systems and food security.

Introduction

> This place will feed you if you know how to take care of it. (Young Halele'a fisherman, 2012)

> The old man [name of *konohiki*] would sit up on the hill by the house and watch for the ball of *akule*. During the season, he'd just watch every day until the ball would come in, just this huge, huge massive ball of fish that would come and spawn in the bay. The [sugar plantation bell would] alarm and the entire town would run down to the beach. We had these big wooden

boats and we'd go out and he had 30-foot deep nets and you'd row and row and row. The guy out the back would be throwing out the net. Then the boats would circle the ball of fish and the whole ball would be circled and it wouldn't realize it yet. Then all of a sudden they'd realize it and hell would break loose. Fish just jumping everywhere into the boat, hitting you in the head. And everything's in there. Whatever was chasing the fish, the shark that was chasing the fish, turtles, everything in there—and so you have to [dive down to] try to get out the things like that. Then you'd bring the net closer and closer together, tighter and tighter. And so you dive down and sections of the net would come out and you'd have those hooked together with little bamboo chopsticks sort of. And you'd take out a section and get it tighter and tighter. By this time, the entire population of [the area] is on the beach. Everybody—man, woman, and child—everybody. And then the big bag net gets put in the water.... And you'd go dive down and sew that into one of those joints in the net. Then you'd pull the main net together until all the fish swam in this bag, as big as half this room. And then you'd bring the boats together, the nets together with the huge bag of fish and somebody would swim in the big rope and then they'd yell, "huki [pull]!"(Kilauea area community member)

Over three centuries of demographic, social and economic change, large catches from surround net fishing, locally referred to as *hukilau* (pulling together), have continued to provide an important source of sustenance that can be stored and shared throughout Halele'a, Kaua'i communities. Surround net fishing requires cooperation, social ties, cultural, and ecological knowledge sustained across generations. We examine how Halele'a families have continued this culturally important fishing practice into the present day, maintaining access to the benefits of near shore fisheries despite dramatic changes in property rights and governance. We explain changes in both land and coastal tenure systems under the Hawaiian kingdom, western contact, US annexation, and later statehood; then describe more recent changes in Halele'a. Using access analysis, we demonstrate how community members have perpetuated surround net harvests and sharing through *hō'ihi* (respectful reciprocity); *konohiki* (inviting ability); and *kuleana* (rights based upon responsibilities). We conclude by considering the implications of our findings for access and policy in near shore fisheries, and for food systems and food security in Hawai'i and beyond.

Food security is one of the most salient issues facing humans in the twenty-first century. Food security can be defined as "physical and economic access to food that meets people's dietary needs as well as their food preferences" (World Health Organization 2015). Food systems are a vital component of food security, encompassing the production, processing, distribution and consumption of food. Defined more broadly, food systems can include impacts on social welfare, the biophysical environment, and national security (Ericksen 2008). Globally, food systems are stressed by population growth, climate change, and economic uncertainty, placing the food security of billions of people at risk (Brown 2012; Godfray et al. 2010). Strategies are needed to enhance and support food systems at multiple scales (Born and Purcell 2006). Local-scale solutions are particularly important in Pacific islands, where locally sourced food is socially and culturally important and food systems are vulnerable to rising food costs, import prices, changes in land tenure, and increasing urbanization (McGregor et al. 2009). Indigenous groups such as Pacific Islanders are especially threatened by shocks or changes in food systems, in which are embedded indigenous culture, language, and ancestral knowledge (Kuhnlein, Erasmus, and Spigelski 2009). Hawai'i faces many of the threats to food systems described elsewhere in the Pacific. The archipelago's isolation and large population of Native Hawaiians make it an ideal place to examine indigenous knowledge, food systems, and food security. The closest landmass to Hawai`i, California, is 2,400 miles away and approximately 85–90 percent of food consumed in Hawai'i is imported (Leunga and Lokeb 2008), compared with a national average of 15 percent for the rest of the United States (Jerardo 2008), making the islands' food system vulnerable to both economic shocks and natural disasters. At any given time, Hawai`i food markets retain just a seven-day supply of food (USDA FSA 2014) for over 1.43 million residents (US Census Bureau 2015).

Coral reef fisheries provide a culturally significant source of protein and micronutrients across the Pacific and in Hawai`i, where they play a crucial role in food security (Bell et al. 2009). Seafood was a primary source of protein in pre-contact Hawai`i (Kittinger et al. 2011). Today, 90 percent of Hawai'i residents frequently consume fish, spending over twice the US national average annually to purchase fish (Geslani, Loke, Takenaka, and Leung 2012). Coral reef fish (caught near shore with nets, pole and line, or free-diving) continue to be a very important component of community food systems (Kittinger et al. 2015; Vaughan and Vitousek 2013). Further, recent studies suggest that 90 percent of Hawai`i coastal fisheries are subsistence-oriented, with most of the catch either consumed within fishers' households or shared, rather than sold commercially (McCoy 2015). However, overfishing has decreased the size and biomass of reef fish across the main Hawaiian islands (Friedlander, Brown, and Monaco 2007; Friedlander and DeMartini 2002), reducing the supply of locally sourced seafood. Reef fish, once found on over 60 percent of restaurant menus in Hawai`i, today are present on 5 percent or less (Friedlander, Shackeroff, and Kittinger 2013). Lack of enforcement and clearly defined harvesting rights have created de facto open access to most coral reef fisheries in Hawai`i (Finkbeiner et al. 2015). Studies show near 75 percent depletion of biomass in near shore coastal fisheries over the past decade (Friedlander et al. 2008; Maly and Maly 2003).

Before western contact, sophisticated tenure systems underpinned management of coral reef fisheries and food systems in Hawai`i. Harvest rights were well defined to enhance resource production and prevent resource exploitation (Beamer 2014). *Konohiki* (administrators of an *ahupua`a* land division appointed by the chief) made decisions to manage and distribute coastal resources at the local level and shared harvest rights with area residents (Higuchi 2008). Landmark historical events, including the introduction of western property rights, depopulation due to introduced disease, demographic change, and eventually annexation by the United States in 1900, eroded local-level coastal management.

Today, resources are managed by a centralized state resource management agency that is underfunded and understaffed (Jokiel et al. 2011). This agency implements uniform state-wide regulations, even though Hawai`i's coastal and marine areas exhibit tremendous diversity due to differences in geological age, rainfall, and wave exposure (ibid.). For example, state rules close harvest of single species at the same time across Hawai`i, though recent studies show different spawning times at different locations (Schemmel 2014). Ineffective state management affects fish assemblages and abundance (Friedlander and DeMartini 2002; Friedlander, Brown, and Monaco 2007), placing Hawai`i food systems at risk, and increasing user conflicts (Ayers and Kittinger 2014).

Access to fish, hunt, and gather local foods, key to food security in pre-contact Hawai`i, is becoming increasingly difficult. Development restricts entry to customary gathering areas despite Hawai`i Supreme Court rulings protecting Native Hawaiian gathering rights (Jarman and Verchick 2002). Control of fresh water critical to supporting health of near-shore fisheries through both ground and surface flows is also contested (Gopalakrishnan et al. 2005).

Despite management challenges, declining resource health, and access conflicts, some Hawai`i communities have maintained local control of a critical component of their food system, by retaining access to the benefits of coastal resources they have depended on for centuries. Narrow economic definitions of access focus on property rights to enter an area (Schlager and Ostrom 1992). Drawing on the field of political ecology, we present a broader definition of access as:

> ... the ability to benefit from things—including material objects, persons, institutions, and symbols. By focusing on ability, rather than rights as in property theory, this formulation brings attention to a wider range of social relationships that can constrain or enable people to benefit from resources without focusing on property relations alone. (Ribot and Peluso 2003, pp. 153–154)

One area where communities have maintained local access to seafood is the Halele`a *moku*[1] (district) on northwestern Kaua`i. Here, communities perpetuate a cultural fishing method, surround net fishing, often referred to as *hukilau*, as a key component of their food supply. Fishing families in Halele`a Kaua`i continue to employ ancestral knowledge, mobilize community effort, and share fish from these collective harvests. We apply the broader framework of access analysis to these surround net fisheries to understand how resources are being used and by whom, as well as why some receive benefits from resources and others do not (Ribot and Peluso 2003). Mechanisms of access include capital, markets, technology, identity, labor, social relations, knowledge, and authority (ibid.). Access analysis can be useful in small-scale fisheries, where studies of fishing effort, market rates, or formal fishing rights may not capture the dynamic flow of benefits (Seto et al. Forthcoming).

This study employs an embedded case study approach (Cox 2015) in which the main "case" aggregates data from several communities within the Haleleʻa *moku* on the north shore of Kauaʻi island gathered over the past ten years (2006–2016). The lead author grew up within the study area and worked with community members on place-based education and resource management efforts for ten years prior to beginning formal study of area fisheries (Vaughan 2014). This study employed a mixed method approach (Tashakkori and Teddlie 2003) combining interviews, focus groups, participant observation, oral histories of *kūpuna* (elders), observation of community meetings, beach surveys and catch logging by *lawaiʻa*, archival searches of Hawaiian-language newspapers, and analysis of legal and policy documents. Interviews, oral histories, and meeting minutes were transcribed and coded using HyperRESEARCH™ (ResearchWare Inc., Randolph, MA, USA) analytical software. Initial findings were critiqued by community members and then analyzed using Ribot and Peluso's (2003) mechanisms of access framework. How have local communities in Haleleʻa, Kauaʻi maintained access to near-shore fisheries and the key source of food they provide? Three themes emerge as key to perpetuation of surround net fishing and sharing: *hōʻihi* (respectful reciprocity); *konohiki* (inviting ability); and *kuleana* (rights based on responsibilities).

History of Near Shore Fisheries Governance

Land tenure in the Hawaiian Kingdom

In Hawaiian Kingdom times (1795–1893), a complex land tenure system supported food production for several hundred thousand Native Hawaiians, comparable to contemporary population levels on every Hawaiian island except Oʻahu (Dye 1994; Kirch and Rallu 2007; Stannard 1989). Islands in Hawaiʻi were divided into *moku* containing many *ahupuaʻa* (land sections). *Ahupuaʻa* were a "culturally appropriate, ecologically aligned, and place specific unit with access to diverse resources" (Gonschor and Beamer 2014, 71). This system of land division was devised by key *aliʻi* (chiefs) to enhance resource productivity following population increases across the archipelago (Beamer 2014). Annual tribute or taxes from each *ahupuaʻa* helped to sustain central government (Beamer 2014; Gonschor and Beamer 2014) and provided for a high level of resource productivity across Hawaiʻi (Kirch 1997, Vitousek et al. 2004). *Okana* (subdistricts within or apart from *mokus*) and *ahupuaʻa*, along with their subdivisions, such as *ili* (an *ahupuaʻa* subdivision consisting of individual farming parcels) established *palena* (boundaries or delineated place-based rights) to utilize natural resources (Gonschor and Beamer 2014). Trade between mountain and coastal areas within *ahupuaʻa* ensured food diversity as well as local-level self-sufficiency. Well-respected *konohiki* were selected to oversee and allocate key resources within an *ahupuaʻa* such as fisheries and water resources among *hoaʻāina* (*ahupuaʻa* residents) (Kirch 1990; McGregor 1996).

Near shore fisheries tenure in the Hawaiian Kingdom

Ahupua'a fisheries encompassed "certain areas of the sea, from the reefs and, where there happen to be no reefs, from the distance of one geographic mile seaward to the beach at low watermark…" (Kosaki 1954, 3). *Ahupua'a fisheries* were reserved for exclusive use of the hoa'āina and *konohiki* of that *ahupua'a* (ibid.). The earliest written kingdom laws continued to protect local-level rights to near-shore fisheries. The first constitution written by Kamehameha III in 1839 and the laws of 1842 officially recognized exclusive local-level rights to near-shore fisheries and ensured seafood access (Higuchi 2008; Jokiel et al. 2011). These laws conserved resources, while maintaining a defined social and religious system (Friedlander, Shackeroff, and Kittinger 2013). Most seafood harvested within the boundaries of an *ahupua'a* was reserved for *hoa'āina* and the *konohiki* residing within the *ahupua'a* boundaries (Higuchi 2008; Kosaki 1954). Certain fish species were *kapu* (restricted) and reserved for the *ali'i* (chief).

The *ali'i* appointed a *konohiki* and entrusted them with the right to make resource decisions. For their service to the *ali'i* and the *hoa'āina*, *konohiki* were entitled to one-third of the catch from the entire fishery, or the right to exclusively harvest one species of fish (Higuchi 2008). Upon consultation with *hoa'āina*, *konohiki* made decisions to open, close or place harvest restrictions on particular species (Akutagawa Forthcoming, Kosaki 1954). *Konohiki* could come from outside an *ahupua'a*, and their appointments were subject to changes in the larger political landscape. *Kilo* (master fishermen, fish spotters) from the area retained significant responsibility, serving as a counsel to the *konohiki*, leading communal fishing efforts, and ensuring equitable share of harvests (Jokiel et al. 2011; McGregor 2007). Some accounts reference shared management and decision-making across multiple *ahupua'a*, often at the *moku* level (Beamer 2014). For example, adjoining *ahupua'a* might alternate closures on a given species, allowing residents of both areas to continue harvesting in the *ahupua'a* where the species was open, while providing for replenishment of the other area.

Changes in land tenure: the Great Mahele

Three-quarters of a century after western contact, and one-quarter century after the arrival of the first missionaries in Hawai'i, King Kamehameha III co-created "The Great Mahele" with his advisors in 1848. The Mahele abolished the existing communal property system in favor of fee simple private land ownership, distributing land in Hawai'i to four groups: the *Mō'ī* (ruling King), the *ali'i* (chiefly class), *maka'āinana* (commoners), and foreigners living in Hawai'i. Although the Great Mahele may have paved the way for dispossession, foreign land ownership, and colonialism, King Kamehameha III and his advisors conceived of the division as a way to embed Native Hawaiian rights into the land within the changing property system (Perkins 2013). Shortly after the Great Mahele, agricultural plantations were established to cultivate large-scale crops such as sugarcane for export. Decimated by western-brought disease, the Native Hawaiian population was reduced to 82,000 by 1850, less than one-quarter of its pre-contact levels (Dye 1994). Thousands of foreign immigrants arrived between 1852 and 1924 to fill the plantation labor requirements. Many intermarried with Native Hawaiian families. Despite these demographic, social, and economic upheavals, *konohiki* continued to fulfill an important role in productive fishing areas by mobilizing labor—Native Hawaiians and immigrants alike—for communal harvests (Seto et al. Forthcoming).

Changes in near-shore fisheries tenure following US annexation

In 1893 the Hawaiian Kingdom was illegally overthrown by a small group of influential foreigners, including some American plantation owners, with military support from the US Government (Chock 1995). Following the illegal overthrow (Boyle 1994), a provisional government presided over Hawai`i from 1893 to 1900. In 1900, the Organic Act (1900) proclaimed Hawai`i a US territory and sought to open near-shore fisheries to public access by nullifying their associated "exclusive," or community-level rights (Kosaki 1954; Murakami and Tanaka 2015). However, a process for vesting private rights to near-shore fisheries allowed registration of *konohiki* fisheries within two years. Of nearly 400 "*konohiki* fisheries" across Hawai`i counted by the Territorial Government in 1900, just one-quarter (101) were officially registered by 35 owners (Higuchi 2008).[2]

The territorial government pursued systematic condemnation of these remaining registered *konohiki* fisheries through payment of "just compensation," "for the declared purpose of making all fisheries in the sea waters of the Territory free to the citizens of the United States" (Kosaki 1954, 5). One motivation was the perception that public access to fisheries was crucial to food security in Hawai'i, particularly in times of shortage such as the Depression or World War II. During that war, the commanding officer on the island of Kaua'i temporarily suspended *konohiki* fishing rights to give island residents more access to fresh fish (Kosaki 1954 citing *Honolulu Star Bulletin*, July 23, 1942). Though proponents of *konohiki* fishing rights argued that local-level management enhanced conservation of a declining inshore marine food supply, opponents countered that conservation was best achieved by uniform, large-scale government management (Kosaki 1954). There was also debate as to whether *konohiki* fishing rights were appurtenant rights, remaining attached to the lands of an *ahupua'a*, regardless of who owned them, or if they only applied to owners at the time fishing rights were vested with the Organic Act of 1900. These issues were legislated in a series of Hawai'i and US Supreme court cases in the first half of the twentieth century. Most involved not Hawaiian *konohiki* families, but American businessmen and missionary descendants who acquired *konohiki* fishing rights through purchase of adjoining *ahupua'a* lands. By 1953, the territorial government had condemned 37 *konohiki* fisheries on Maui and O'ahu (including multiple fisheries purchased to facilitate construction of Pearl Harbor) and the Attorney General had initiated condemnation of nine more on Maui and Kaua'i. Some of the last registered konohiki "*fisheries*" in all of Hawai'i exist in *ahupua`a* within our study site. *Konohiki* fishing rights remain an unresolved legal issue with aspects of these rights reaffirmed in Hawai'i's state constitution and other present-day laws (Murakami and Tanaka 2015).

Though Hawai'i kingdom, territorial, and state laws also state that *konohiki* share fishing rights with *hoa'āina* (ahupua'a residents) (Murakami and Tanaka 2015), the issue of *ho'aina* rights in *ahupua'a* fisheries remained largely unaddressed even as *konohiki* rights were slowly being eroded. Halele'a community members continued to respect *konohiki* families' rights to regulate harvest of particular species and exclusive near-shore fishing rights for *ahupua'a* residents well into the 1970s and later. Today, most *ahupua'a* near shore fisheries in Hawai'i are open to the public. Fishery regulations are largely uniform across the state despite variation in geology, habitat, fish-spawning seasons, and generations of place-specific knowledge. Most meetings and decisions regarding natural resources on the rural outer islands such as Kaua`i are made in the capital city of Honolulu, on O`ahu, by the Division of Aquatic Resources, which resides within the Department of Land and Natural Resources.

Study Site: Halele'a, Kaua'i

This study takes place in the *moku* of Halele'a, on Kaua'i's north shore (Figure 1), which comprises nine *ahupua'a* (Hā`ena, Wainiha, Lumahai, Waikoko, Waipā,

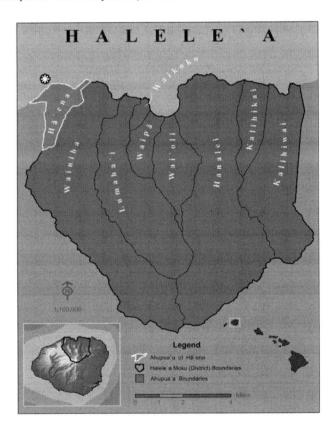

Fig. 1: Location of the Halele'a *moku* on the Island of Kaua'i, Hawai'i.
Source: H. Peter King

Waioli, Hanalei, Kahlihikai, and Kalihiwai). Kaua'i is geologically the oldest of the main Hawaiian Islands, and the coastal and marine areas along its north shore are unique. Two of the largest fringing reef systems in the main Hawaiian Islands are found within the Halele`a Moku: Hā`ena and Anini. Several large bays provide seasonal spawning areas and habitat for culturally and economically important schooling fish species targeted in surround net fishing, such as *Akule* (bigeye scad, *Sela crumenophthalmus*).

Description of surround net fishing in Halele'a: hukilau

There are many different types of net fishing in Hawai'i. Historically, most targeted specific fish species using nets of varying sizes woven from the fiber of endemic trees or shrubs such as *olonā* (Kahaulelio, Nogelmeier, and Kahaulelio 2005). *Hukilau* is a Hawaiian surround net fishing method that is labor-intensive, highly efficient, and yields large catches (Friedlander and Parrish 1997). The word *"hukilau"* comes from *huki*, to pull, and *lau*, leaves. The name refers to dried *ti* leaves (*Cordyline minalis*) tied to a long rope pulled across the surface of the ocean to herd schooling fish.[3] The shadows and movement of the leaves served to scare the fish into the shallows where a short length of hand-woven net could be used to surround and harvest part of the school (Kahaulelio, Nogelmeier, and Kahaulelio 2005). Over time, surround techniques, in which longer lengths of net were substituted for the rope and *ti* leaves, were also referred to as *"hukilau"* or simply "surrounds," with nylon then monofilament nets replacing those woven from fiber. Today, *lawai'a* in Halele'a continue this practice, using hundred-foot lengths of net to surround, herd, and harvest schools. They use small boats launched from shore to deploy nets, spotters on land to direct the boats, divers to disentangle rocks or untargeted marine species, and groups of people on the beach to help pull in the nets. It is important to distinguish between community-led surround net fishing and industrial commercial fishing techniques that indiscriminately capture entire schools of *akule* further offshore or when they arrive to spawn in Hawaiian bays. Some of these industrial fishing enterprises employ seine net fishing vessels and spotter planes, both launched from outside Halele'a. Their catch is sold in distant commercial markets rather than shared communally.

Economic and demographic change in the Halele'a Moku

Today, Kaua`i's rural north shore beaches within the *moku* of Halele`a are visited by upwards of 2000 tourists a day, mainly to swim and snorkel (Vaughan and Ardoin 2014). International recognition of the area's natural beauty has caused an influx of luxury coastal development. Increased demand for coastal property has forced many local families to move due to inability to pay taxes tied to rising property values (Andrade 2008). Many new homeowners from outside of Hawai'i have gated their properties or shut off informal easements to access public beaches, some of which were used to launch boats for surround net fishing. A large number of homes are vacant or primarily used as vacation rentals. For example, in one area community, Hā'ena, just half of 322 homes in 2010 were owner-occupied (US Census Bureau 2010). Likewise, over half of Hā`ena's population (431 residents) relocated to the area since 2002 (US Census Bureau 2010). These demographic and economic changes have caused local families to move away from their ancestral lands and fishing grounds, while simultaneously decreasing coastal access. Despite changes in land tenure and demographics, government efforts to terminate local-level *konohiki* management, and imposed centralization of state agency control, some features of local-level near-shore fisheries management are now being reinvigorated in parts of Halele'a. Though near-shore fisheries regulation is now centralized and overseen by the State of Hawai`i, *kilo* and *lawai`a* (fishermen and women) in many areas continue to employ ancestral knowledge and organize area families for surround net fishing.

Perpetuating social and cultural ties through surround net fishing

This article opens with one community member's account of how surround net fishing took place within one Halele'a bay in the 1970s, overseen by the area *konohiki 'ohana*. In some Halele'a *ahupua'a*, the species captured through surround net fishing were reserved exclusively for *konohiki* harvest. Through the 1970s, *konohiki* families maintained and deployed the nets, served as *kilo*, and distributed the harvest. Though in current times other area families now also surround in areas formerly reserved for *konohiki*, surround net harvests continue using the same methods in multiple bays each summer in Halele'a. Our analysis uncovered three major themes related to the longevity and perpetuation of surround net fishing: *hō'ihi* (respectful reciprocity), *konohiki* (inviting ability), and *kuleana* (rights based on responsibilities).

Respectful reciprocity: Hō'ihi

Fishing in Halele'a was based on respectful reciprocal relationships between people and their natural environment. In this study, interviewees recalling excellent fishermen and women, including *konohiki* and *kilo*, frequently discussed their relationship with fish. For example, the daughter of one respected Hā'ena *lawai'a* explained that he always released and named the first fish caught in a surround. When it was time to surround the school again, he called that fish by name and it brought the rest of the school to him. Respected *kilo* were described not only observing the movement of schools, but moving these schools towards nets through *oli* (chant) or other manifestations of *mana* (spiritual power). Remembering one area *konohiki*, a community member stated, "He asked the fish to move, they move." The idea that fish were participants in the fishing practice, choosing whether or not to come to the nets of certain *lawai`a*, was common. Some stories described area *lawai`a* working with *'aumakua* (ancestral guardians), departed family members that had taken the shape of particular sharks, who assisted by herding schools of fish into their descend-

THE FOODWAYS OF HAWAI'I

ants' nets. Instead of viewing humans as separate from nature, these accounts exemplify the importance of respectful reciprocal relationships with marine life and the food it provided.

Respectful reciprocal relationships, not only with resources, but also among people, were critical to sustaining surround net fishing in Halele'a. *Konohiki* families helped one another surround in each other's local areas. They also assisted with large tasks, maintenance, and recovery after disasters, including hurricanes and two tsunamis that inundated the area in 1946 and 1957. The 1946 tsunami washed away all but one home in one Halele'a bay, including the area *konohiki's* boathouse and surround nets. The *konohiki* family from another part of Kaua`i came to help dive to retrieve the irreplaceable nets key to providing food for the community. Further, *konohiki* families could not conduct surround net fishing alone. They relied on other area fishing families to fill crucial roles during harvests such as diving to maneuver the nets. Descendants of one fishing family that long served as expert divers for the *konohiki* family in one *ahupua'a* continue to dive for surrounds throughout Halele'a today. Contemporary surround net fishing crews in Halele'a still rely on highly valued relationships of mutual respect and reciprocity, through which area families continue to work together and help one another across generations.

Inviting ability: Konohiki

The word *konohiki* means to invite ability or willingness. This refers to the ability of a *konohiki* to organize people for collective endeavors no one family could achieve alone, such as maintenance of irrigation systems to sustain taro patches or surround net harvests (Andrade 2008). In Hawaiian Kingdom times, the *konohiki* mobilized *hoa`āina* to assist with deploying and pulling in the large nets. Twentieth-century *konohiki* families could not conduct surround net fishing without helpers from the community to provide labor, including expert divers as described earlier. While a few divers might be sufficient to navigate the nets and school safely to shore, many more hands were needed to pull the nets laden with fish to the beach, and then extract the fish, one at a time. In recalling surround net harvests in one Halele'a bay, community members frequently recounted how the area sugar mill rang its bell when the *konohiki* surrounded a school of fish, alerting workers to go to the beach to help pull in the nets.

By organizing and overseeing collective harvests, *konohiki* facilitated community ability to access an important source of protein, targeting schooling species that can only be caught for a few months during the summer. Through surround net fishing, which yields large harvests ranging from 300 to over 1000 lb, *konohiki* "would feed all the families." One respondent whose *'ohana* (family) served as *konohiki* for a coastal area in Halele'a explained, "The people who came to help us … grandpa would give them a share, *mahele*. If you came to work, everyone would get fish."

Equitable and generous distribution of fish, in some cases by large bamboo basketfuls, helped particular *konohiki* and *kilo* to maintain authority and ability

FOOD,
CULTURE &
SOCIETY

101

to mobilize labor. Describing one Hāʻena area *kilo* known for his generosity, a community member recalled, "There was no limit to the *mahele*. His idea was to share his fish with everybody" (Maly and Maly 2003, 404). In interviews with Haleleʻa elders, most say that their families never had to purchase groceries from the store because seafood and other locally produced food was so abundant. Before refrigeration, *akule* from surrounds was dried so that it could be stored and eaten year round. Interviewees recalled fish hanging from sticks stuck in the sand along the length of the beach after a surround, drying in the ocean breeze that kept away flies. One community member recalls a visceral feeling from her childhood of the social process of fishing, fish processing, and sharing:

> But we had enough, or at least enough, and there was a lot of sharing, like most rural communities. There was always the smell of the ocean and fish blood. And I like that because it tells me we are gonna have that kind of fish. It helped us to learn how to process fish as well and how to really enjoy it, and how to eat it, and how to express enjoyment, how to give thanks without saying thank you. How you socialize around food.

Today, Haleleʻa *lawaiʻa* continue to *mahele* shares of fish to helpers and throughout the community. Many *lawaiʻa* share fish with elders who can no longer fish for themselves or assist with pulling in the nets (Vaughan and Vitousek 2013). *Mahele* are now shared by the cooler or in gallon-size Ziploc® bags, instead of bamboo baskets and metal *pākini* (washbasins). Anyone who assists in a surround net effort receives a share of the catch, which they then distribute and share further (Vaughan and Vitousek 2013). All of the *lawaiʻa* in one key area fishery were documented distributing their catch from both throw net and surrounds, among families or friends or for *pāʻina* (large social gatherings; ibid.).

Equitable and generous distribution of fish continues to underpin ability to mobilize labor. Today, *lawaiʻa* communicate via phone or text to quickly organize small groups of eight to ten fishers to assist with deploying and pulling in the monofilament nets. Although the nets are made of different material, labor is gathered via cell phones rather than bells, and authority to surround is no longer limited to *konohiki* families, expert Haleleʻa fishermen maintain ability to mobilize labor for surround net fishing. Through overseeing collective surrounds and sharing *mahele* from the harvest, contemporary *lawaiʻa* continue to feed large segments of the Haleleʻa population, facilitating ongoing community ability to access an important food source.

Responsibility: Kuleana

Today, responsibility to manage near-shore fisheries lies with the State of Hawaiʻi and the Division of Aquatic Resources (DAR). Since management rights formally reside with the DAR, fisheries are open to the public, prohibiting exclusive harvest rights. In Hawaiian Kingdom times, *konohiki* held authority to restrict harvests, rest areas or species in consultation with area *hoaʻāina*, reserve certain species for their exclusive harvest or retain one-third of the catch (Higuchi 2008). However, *konohiki* rights were based upon fulfillment of substantial responsibilities. In addition to feeding the community through *mahele* of catch, these responsibilities included caring for gear required for surrounds, and ensuring resources were managed to assure future harvests. Although *lawaiʻa* today do not retain the same formal rights and authority once given *konohiki*, they maintain many of the same responsibilities.

One responsibility continued over time is maintenance of nets. Historically, nets made of *olonā* fiber were passed down through families. These nets required much care and effort to make, mend, maintain, and dry. *Olonā* left wet would rot and break (Maly and Maly 2003). In the plantation era, nets were transported to nearby beach parks or town baseball fields and spread out to dry before being folded carefully and stored for the next surround. Today, monofilament nets still require cleaning to remove seaweed, coral and debris as well as constant mending, drying, and careful storage. Rowboats are maintained, stored, loaded with heavy nets and towed to the beach for surrounds by *kilo* and their families.

Konohiki responsibilities and authority to make decisions regarding resources also hinged on in-depth knowledge of fish behavior in order to sustain large harvests. In one *ahupuaʻa* within our study area, knowledgeable *konohiki* watched for the changing color of schools of *akule* to signal the fish had finished spawning before deploying their nets. As one area *kupuna* (elder) described *konohiki* management, "The management was in the harvesting, and in respecting the seasons. They knew the spawning cycles. They never took out of season." Some interviewees worried that once community members stopped respecting exclusive *konohiki* rights to oversee surrounds, *lawaiʻa* with less in-depth knowledge began surrounding schools of *akule* before they had a chance to spawn. Multiple interviewees linked termination of exclusive *konohiki* fishing rights to declines in the size and frequency of schools over the past two decades.

Contemporary *lawaiʻa* responsibilities include educational efforts to teach the next generation knowledge they learned from their *kūpuna*. Current educational efforts include *lawaiʻa* camps where elder *lawaiʻa* teach ancestral harvest techniques, and fishing skills such as how to sew and repair nets, how to determine the gender of fish and recognize when they are spawning, how to observe lunar and tidal cycles, and other seasonal changes that affect fish behavior. As important as skills are values, such as *lawa pono* (taking only what you need), values which are also imparted through *lawaiʻa* camps and everyday fishing with area youth.

In these ways, the knowledgeable authority, rights, and ability of head *lawaiʻa* of Haleleʻa to surround fish continue to be based on responsibilities. These responsibilities include caring for, storing and mobilizing gear, fishing in a manner that sustains future harvests, educating future generations, and feeding the community. Social ties within the community are in turn reinforced through *mahele*, as people come together to participate in collective harvests, and to consume fish from surrounds at community *lūʻau* (feasts) and other gatherings. By fulfilling their responsibility to share and feed, Haleleʻa *lawaiʻa* reinforce community relationships that tie people to one another, to their food, and to their home, even in the face of rapid change (Vaughan and Vitousek 2013).

Implications for Access in Near Shore Fisheries

Coastal fisheries are increasingly critical components of food security and healthy communities worldwide (Bell et al. 2009; Béné, Macfadyen, and Allison 2007). There is also a growing awareness of the contribution of coastal fisheries to livelihoods (Allison and Ellis 2001), particularly in coral reef systems (Hicks and Cinner 2014; Kittinger et al. 2012). Access theory is a useful tool for examining the complex array of interactions between people and food systems, particularly for near-shore fisheries (Peluso 1992; Seto et al. Forthcoming; Sikor and Lund 2009). While property rights analysis focuses on formal rights and what resource users are allowed to do, access analysis examines what individuals actually do. Access analysis can explain how and why people benefit even without possessing formal rights. Access analysis is particularly useful for understanding indigenous food systems due to their complexity, the prevalence of informal rights, and the importance of social and power relations. As in similar studies of fishing persistence and motivation (Pollnac, Bavinck, and Monnereau 2012), mechanisms of access are interrelated and difficult to disentangle. In the case of Haleleʻa, Kauaʻi, access analysis revealed three key ways through which community members have maintained a critical local food source: *hōʻihi*, maintaining respectful reciprocal relationships; *konohiki*, inviting ability by mobilizing labor through ancestral knowledge and authority deployed in contemporary ways; and *kuleana*, cultivating balance of rights based on responsibilities. These are all social, rather than economic or technological mechanisms.

Access theory and social relationships

In access theory economic (markets, technology and capital) and social factors (knowledge, authority, identity, ability to mobilize labor) can all mediate benefits people receive from ecosystems (Hicks and Cinner 2014; Seto et al. Forthcoming). In small-scale fisheries, particularly those relied on by indigenous communities, social factors may be more important than economic ones in determining distribution of benefits (Seto et al. Forthcoming). This study highlights how one community's use of a particular fishing method is embedded in and helps to reinforce complex social relationships, knowledge, and values systems. Customary norms that continue to govern behavior are crucial to maintaining local control over an important aspect of the community food system. Fish are seen as food, but *lawaiʻa* also feel responsibility to care for and maintain respectful balanced relationships with them. In this case, viewing fishery resources not just as food but also, in some cases, as family has helped to sustain resources over time. While access theory often categorizes benefits in terms of social relationships (Ribot and Peluso 2003), this case demonstrates that relationships can extend beyond human interactions to include respectful relationships between people and the environment. In this case, as in other indigenous communities, reciprocity and responsibility govern complex human–environmental interactions (Garibaldi and Turner 2004).

This study supports past literature suggesting the need to amend access theory to account for sociocultural perspectives (Scholte, van Teeffelen, and Verburg 2015), cultural bequest values (Oleson et al. 2015) and cultural ecosystem services (Plieninger, Dijks, Oteros-Rozas, and Bieling 2013). Our study illuminates multiple "immaterial benefits," such as perpetuation of ancestral roles and authority, respectful relationships, social cohesion, and balance of rights and responsibilities, all provided by surround net fisheries, that are not captured by mainstream ecosystem services accounting methods (Chiesura and de Groot 2003; Vaughan and Vitousek 2013). Other study locations, resources, and food systems may offer many others.

Access, planning, and policy change

Much of this study was undertaken during one Halele'a *ahupua'a*'s decade-long effort to restore local-level management of their near-shore fishery by developing state law to govern coastal use based on customary practices for the area. Legislation passed in 2006 designated Hā'ena as a community-based subsistence fishing area (CBSFA), recognizing the importance of the fishery for "reaffirming and protecting fishing practices customarily exercised for purposes of Native Hawaiian subsistence, culture, and religion" (Hawai'i Revised Statutes, Chapter 188, Section 22.6). Although legislation designated the area for local-level management, the community still had to work with the state resource management agency to co-develop fishing regulations, and secure their approval through the same onerous public process as any administrative rules promulgated by state government agencies. These rules became law in August 2015 after nearly ten years of planning and negotiation, over seventy meetings, fifteen rules drafts, three public hearings, and multiple studies undertaken to document visitor impacts, user groups, fishery health and the importance of locally caught fish within and beyond the Hā'ena community (Vaughan and Vitousek 2013). Ancestral norms guided the creation of rules (Vaughan et al. Forthcoming) and three of these norms: *hō'ihi*, respectful reciprocity; *konohiki*, inviting ability; and *kuleana*, rights based on responsibilities, were based on indigenous access mechanisms. These indigenous access mechanisms were an integral component of the creation of new law. Passage of these rules made Hā'ena only the second active CBSFA in the state of Hawai'i and the first coastal area in Hawai'i to be permanently governed by community developed, local-level rules based on ancestral knowledge and practice. Many communities across Hawai'i view this effort as the cusp of a larger community movement to increase self-sufficiency and reestablish formal local-level control over ocean resources as a food source. This case illustrates how perpetuation of customary mechanisms of access can provide a powerful foundation for policy change and restoration of local control of food systems.

Importance of perpetuating ancestral practices for local control of Hawai`i food systems

The continued importance of surround net fishing across three centuries in the Halele`a *moku* on Kaua'i Island demonstrates the value of preserving ancestral, place-based knowledge and practices in maintaining local control over food systems. Much work has documented the importance of *kua`āina* (those living and embodying Native Hawaiian culture, particularly in rural areas of Hawai'i) in perpetuating cultural practices related to food and resource harvest (McGregor 2007). It is important for communities seeking to enhance food sovereignty to maintain communal, intergenerational, cultural harvest, distribution, and consumption practices because they create "a social environment that cultivates community and kinship ties, emotional interdependency and support" (McGregor 2007, 17). Perpetuating ancestral practices related to food provides roles for individuals of all ages within a society, while maintaining relationships and balance with the natural world in specific areas (McGregor 2007; Turner et al. 2013). Customary food systems continue through formal education programs and camps but also through daily perpetuation of cultivation and harvest practices (Vaughan and Caldwell 2015).

As important as maintaining ancestral practices such as communal surround net fishing may be, global environmental changes beyond the scale of local control will likely require future adaptation. Research has documented the effectiveness of ancestral knowledge and Hawaiian near-shore marine management approaches in increasing fishery health. Traditionally managed community fisheries have exhibited higher biomass than even no-take marine protected areas (Poepoe et al. 2003; Friedlander et al. 2013). However, past management practices and levels of sustainable harvest may not be effective in future near-shore fisheries impacted by ocean acidification, decreased fresh water flow, changing wind patterns and currents, coral bleaching, sea-level rise, and increases in temperature (Mora et al. 2013). Historically, Native Hawaiians have been quick to adopt useful innovations in governance, technology and society (Beamer 2014). Future innovation will continue to be necessary as climate change increasingly impacts Hawai'i (Anderson et al. 2015; Keener 2013). Local-level governance and decision-making offers potential to observe and adapt effectively to future changes in fisheries. If existing harvesting practices become unsustainable (Turner et al. 2013), local communities will need to use the ancestral values underlying these older practices to guide development of new ones. Engaging communities to perpetuate the values, relationships and responsibilities underlying food systems is crucial to long-term food security and resilience.

Acknowledgements

The authors would like to thank Malia and Victor Nobrega-Olivera, Malia Akutagawa, Kaui Fu, Billy Kinney, Kamealoha Forrest, Bethany Wylie, the students of Kaiaulu, transcriptionists of Stanford's Hui o Hawai'i and LAMA, for helping to bring these interviews to life. Mahalo to Hi`ilei Hobart for her patience and insights throughout the editorial process, to all reviewers; to funders NSF SEES (1216109), Emmett Interdisciplinary Program for Environment and Resources, Community Forestry and Environmental Research Partnerships, Heinz, and Switzer fellowships; Peter Vitousek, Barton Thompson, Meg Caldwell, Nicole Ardoin, Jack Kittenger, Louise Fortmann and lab members. Mahalo to KUA, HCSN, and E Alu Pū, Waipā Foundation, Limahuli Gardens, Hā`ena Community Members, Hui Maka'ainana o Makana, our families, and everyone who helped to contribute to this article and effort. Thank you especially to the fishing families and kūpuna (elders) of Ko'olau and Halele'a: Hā'ena, Wainiha, Hanalei, Wanini, Kalihikai, and Kalihiwai for your generous sharing and aloha for your 'āina, your home.

Disclosure statement

No potential conflict of interest was reported by the authors.

Notes

1. This article makes extensive use of Hawaiian terms to describe Native Hawaiian culture and practices. We define and italicize each term the first time it is introduced.
2. Newer research suggests that the actual number of *konohiki* fisheries was far higher than 400 (Akutagawa Forthcoming), with one map from 1923 delineating close to 100 *ahupua'a* fisheries on the island of O'ahu alone (Friedlander, Shackeroff and Kittinger, 2013; Murakami and Tanaka, 2015).
3. The name may also refer to the many (*lau*) people needed to pull the catch to shore.

References

Akutagawa, Malia. *The Return of the Konohiki*. Forthcoming.

Allison, E. H., and F. Ellis. 2001. "The Livelihoods Approach and Management of Small-scale Fisheries." *Marine Policy* 25 (5): 377–388.

Anderson, T., C. Fletcher, M. Barbee, L. N. Frazer, and B. Romine. 2015. "Doubling of Coastal Erosion under Rising Sea Level by Mid-century in Hawaii." *Natural Hazards* 78 (1): 75–103. http://doi.org/10.1007/s11069-015-1698-6.

Andrade, C. 2008. *Haena: Through the Eyes of the Ancestors*. Honolulu: University of Hawai'i Press.

Ayers, A. L., and J. N. Kittinger. 2014. "Emergence of Co-management Governance for Hawai'i Coral Reef Fisheries." *Global Environmental Change* 28: 251–262. http://doi.org/10.1016/j.gloenvcha.2014.07.006.

Beamer, K. 2014. *No Mākou ka Mana: Liberating the Nation*. Honolulu: Kamehameha Publishing. Accessed 20 July 2016. http://kpstore.deliveryhawaii.com/KS/product/978-0-87336-293-1.html.

Bell, J. D., M. Kronen, A. Vunisea, Nash W. J., G. Keeble, A. Demmke, S. Pontifex, and S. Andréfouët. 2009. "Planning the Use of Fish for Food Security in the Pacific." *Marine Policy* 33 (1): 64–76. http://doi.org/doi: DOI: 10.1016/j.marpol.2008.04.002.

Béné, C., G. Macfadyen, and E. H. Allison. 2007. *Increasing the Contribution of Small-scale Disheries to Poverty Alleviation and Food Security*. Rome: Food and Agriculture Organization of the United Nations.

Born, B., and M. Purcell. 2006. "Avoiding the Local Trap: Scale and Food Systems in Planning Research." *Journal of Planning Education and Research* 26 (2): 195–207. http://doi.org/10.1177/0739456X06291389.

Boyle, F. A. 1994. "Restoration of the Independent Nation State of Hawaii Under International Law: Back to the Future." *St. Thomas Law Rev.* 7: 723–756.

Brown, L. R. 2012. *Outgrowing the Earth: The Food Security Challenge in an Age of Falling Water Tables and Rising Temperatures*. Florence, KY: Taylor & Francis.

Chiesura, A., and R. de Groot. 2003. "Critical Natural Capital: A Socio-Cultural Perspective." *Identifying Critical Natural Capital* 44 (2–3): 219–231. http://doi.org/10.1016/S0921-8009(02)00275-6.

Chock, J. M. 1995. "One Hundred Years of Illegitimacy: International Legal Analysis of the Illegal Overthrow of the Hawaiian Monarchy, Hawai'i's Annexation, and Possible Reparations." *University of Hawaii Law Review* 17: 463–512.

Cox, M. 2015. "A Basic Guide for Empirical Environmental Social Science." *Ecology and Society* 20 (1). http://doi.org/10.5751/ES-07400-200163.

Dye, T. 1994. "Population Trends in Hawai'i before 1778." *Hawaiian Journal of History* 28: 1–20.

Ericksen, P. J. 2008. "Conceptualizing Food Systems for Global Environmental Change Research." *Global Environmental Change* 18 (1): 234–245.

Finkbeiner, E., A. Ayers, J. N. Kittinger, and L. Crowder. 2015. "A comparison of small-scale fisheries governability: Baja California Sur, Mexico and the Hawaiian Islands." In *Interactive Governance for Small-Scale Fisheries: Global Reflections*, edited by Svein Jentoft and Ratana Chuenpagdee, 199–221. Cham, Switzerland: Springer.

Friedlander, A., G. Aeby, R. Brainard, E. Brown, K. Chaston, A. Clark, P. McGowan, T. Montgomery, W. Walsh, and I. Williams. 2008. "The State of Coral Reef Ecosystems of the Main Hawaiian Islands." NOAA Technical Memorandum NOS NCCOS 73. Silver Spring, MD: NOAA/NCCOS Center for Coastal Monitoring and Assessment's Biogeography Team. https://coastalscience.noaa.gov/research/docs/CoralReport2008.pdf.

Friedlander, A., E. Brown, and M. Monaco. 2007. "Defining Reef Fish Habitat Utilization Patterns in Hawaii: Comparisons between Marine Protected Areas and Areas open tyo Fishing." *Marine Ecology Progress Series* 351 (December): 221–233. http://doi.org/10.3354/meps07112.

Friedlander, A. M., and J. D. Parrish. 1997. "Fisheries harvest and standing stock in a Hawaiian Bay." *Fisheries Research* 32 (1): 33–50. http://doi.org/10.1016/S0165-7836(97)00038-6.

Friedlander, A. M., E. K. Brown, P. L. Jokiel, W. R. Smith, and K. S. Rodgers. 2003. "Effects of Habitat, Wave Exposure, and Marine Protected Area Status on Coral Reef Fish Assemblages in the Hawaiian Archipelago." *Coral Reefs* 22 (3): 291–305. http://doi.org/10.1007/s00338-003-0317-2.

Friedlander, A. M., and E. E. DeMartini. 2002. "Contrasts in Density, Size, and Biomass of Reef Fishes between the Northwestern and the Main Hawaiian Islands: The Effects of Fishing Down Apex Predators." *Marine Ecology Progress Series* 230: 253–264.

Friedlander, A. M., J. M. Shackeroff, and J. N. Kittinger. 2013. "Customary Marine Resource Knowledge and Use in Contemporary Hawai'i 1." *Pacific Science* 67 (3): 441–460. http://doi.org/10.2984/67.3.10.

Garibaldi, A., and N. Turner. 2004. "Cultural Keystone Species: Implications for Ecological Conservation and Restoration." *Ecology and Society* 9 (3). http://www.ecologyandsociety.org/vol9/iss3/art1/.

Geslani, Cheryl, Matthew Loke, Brooks Takenaka, and PingSun Leung. 2012. "Hawaii's Seafood Consumption and its Supply Sources." SOEST 12-01. JIMAR 12-0379. Honolulu: University of Hawaii at Manoa. http://www2.hawaii.edu/~geslani/files/Leung_HIseafood.final.pdf.

Godfray, H. C. J., J. R. Beddington, I. R. Crute, L. Haddad, D. Lawrence, J. F. Muir, J. Pretty, S. Robinson, S. M. Thomas, and C. Toulmin, 2010. "Food Security: The Challenge of Feeding 9 Billion People." *Science* 327 (5967): 812–818. http://doi.org/10.1126/science.1185383.

Gonschor, L., and K. Beamer. 2014. "Toward an Inventory of Ahupua'a in the Hawaiian Kingdom: A Survey of Nineteenth- and Early Twentieth-century Cartographic and Archival Records of the Island of Hawai'i." *Hawaiian Journal of History* 48: 53–87.

Gopalakrishnan, C., J. Levy, K. W. Li, and K. W. Hipel. 2005. "Water Allocation among Multiple Stakeholders: Conflict Analysis of the Waiahole Water Project, Hawaii." *International Journal of Water Resources Development* 21 (2): 283–295.

Hicks, C. C., and J. E. Cinner. 2014. "Social, Institutional, and Knowledge Mechanisms Mediate Diverse Ecosystem Service Benefits from Coral Reefs." *Proceedings of the National Academy of Sciences* 111 (50): 17791–17796. http://doi.org/10.1073/pnas.1413473111.

Higuchi, J. 2008. "Propogating Cultural Kipuka." *University of Hawaii Law Review* 31: 193–224.

Jarman, M. C., and R. R. M. Verchick. 2002. "Beyond the Courts of the Conqueror: Balancing Private and Cultural Property Rights under Hawai'i Law." *Scholar: St. Mary's Law Review on Minority Issues* 5: 201.

Jerardo, A. 2008. "What Share of U.S. Consumed Food Is Imported?" *Amber Waves* 6 (1): 36–37.

Jokiel, P. L., K. S. Rodgers, and D Kahaulelio. 2011. "Marine Resource Management in the Hawaiian Archipelago: The Traditional Hawaiian System in Relation to the Western Approach." *Journal of Marine Biology* 2011: 1–16. http://doi.org/10.1155/2011/151682.

Kahaulelio, A. D., P. Nogelmeier, and D. Kahaulelio. 2005. *Ka Oihana Lawaia: Hawaiian Fishing Traditions*. Honolulu: Bishop Museum Press.

Kahaulelio, A. D., P. Nogelmeier, W. J. Walsh, D. A. Polhemus, and T. A. Wilhelm. 2005. *Ka Oihana Lawaia: Hawaiian Fishing Traditions*. Honolulu: Bishop Museum Pr.

Keener, V. 2013. *Climate Change and Pacific Islands: Indicators and Impacts: Report for the 2012 Pacific Islands Regional Climate Assessment*. Island Press.

Kirch, P. V. 1990. "Monumental Architecture and Power in Polynesian Chiefdoms: A Comparison of Tonga and Hawaii." *World Archaeology* 22 (2): 206–222.

Kirch, P. V., and Rallu, J. L. 2007. *The Growth and Collapse of Pacific Island Societies: Archaeological and Demographic Perspectives*. University of Hawaii Press.

Kittinger, J. N., E. M. Finkbeiner, E. W. Glazier, and L. B. Crowder. 2012. "Human Dimensions of Coral Reef Social-ecological Systems." *Ecology and Society* 17 (4): 17.

Kittinger, J. N., J. M. Pandolfi, J. H. Blodgett, T. L. Hunt, H. Jiang, and K. Maly, L. E. McClenachan, J. K. Schultz, and B. A. Wilcox. 2011. Historical Reconstruction Reveals Recovery in Hawaiian Coral Reefs. *PLoS ONE* 6 (10): e25460. http://doi.org/10.1371/journal.pone.0025460.

Kittinger, J. N., L. T. Teneva, H. Koike, K. A. Stamoulis, D. S. Kittinger, and K. L. L. Oleson, and A. M. Friedlander. 2015. "From Reef to Table: Social and Ecological Factors Affecting Coral Reef Fisheries, Artisanal Seafood Supply Chains, and Seafood Security." *PLoS ONE* 10 (8): e0123856. http://doi.org/10.1371/journal.pone.0123856.

Kosaki, R. 1954. *Konohiki Fishing Rights, Hawaii Legislature*. Honolulu: Legislative Reference Bureau.

Kuhnlein, H. V., B. Erasmus, and D. Spigelski. 2009. *Indigenous Peoples' Food Systems: The Many Dimensions of Culture*. Rome: Food and Agriculture Organization of the United Nations Centre for Indigenous Peoples' Nutrition and Environment.

Leunga, PingSun, and Matthew Lokeb 2008. "Economic Impacts of Increasing Hawaii's Food Self Sufficiency." EI-16. Economic Issues. Honolulu: Cooperative Extension Service, College of Tropical Agriculture and Human Resources, University of Hawaii at Manoa. http://www.ctahr.hawaii.edu/oc/freepubs/pdf/EI-16.pdf.

Maly, Kepa, and O. Maly. 2003. "'Hana Ka Lima, Ai Ka Waha' a Collection of Historical Accounts and Oral History Interviews with Kama'Aina Residents and Fisher-People of Lands in the Halele'A-Napali Region." Prepared for the Nature Conservancy and The National Tropical Botanical Gardens - Limahuli Gardens. Hilo, HI: Kumu Pono Associates LLC. http://www.ulukau.org/elib/collect/maly4/index/assoc/D0.dir/book.pdf.

McCoy, K. 2015. "Estimating nearshore fisheries catch for the main Hawaiian Islands." Master's thesis, University of Hawai'i at Manoa.

McGregor, A., R. M. Bourke, M. Manley, S. Tubuna, and R. Deo. 2009. "Pacific Island Food Security: Situation, Challenges and Opportunities." *Pacific Economic Bulletin* 24 (2): 24–42.

McGregor, D. P. 2007. *Na Kua'aina: Living Hawaiian Culture*. Honolulu: University of Hawaii Press.

McGregor, D. P. 1996. "An Introduction to the Hoa'aina and Their Rights." *Hawaiian Journal of History* 30: 1–27.

Mora, C., A. G. Frazier, R. J. Longman, R. S. Dacks, M. M. Walton, E. J. Tong, J. J. Sanchez, et al. 2013. "The Projected Timing of Climate Departure from Recent Variability." *Nature* 502 (7470): 183–187.

Murakami, A. T. and W. C. Tanaka. 2015. *Native Hawaiian Law—A Treatise, Chapter 10: Konohiki Fishing Rights*. Honolulu: Kamehameha Publishing.

Oleson, K. L. L., M. Barnes, L. M. Brander, T. A. Oliver, van I. Beek, B. Zafindrasilivonona, and P. Van Beukering. 2015. "Cultural Bequest Values for Ecosystem Service Flows among Indigenous Fishers: A Discrete Choice Experiment Validated with Mixed Methods." *Ecological Economics* 114 (June): 104–116. http://doi.org/10.1016/j.ecolecon.2015.02.028.

Peluso, N. L. 1992. "Teak and Temptation on the Extreme Periphery: Cultural Perspectives on Forest Crime." *Rich Forests, Poor People: Resource Control and Resistance in Java*, 201–232. Berkeley: University of California Press.

Perkins, M. U. 2013. "Kuleana: A Genealogy of Native Tenant Rights." PhD diss., University of Hawai'i at Manoa.

Plieninger, T., S. Dijks, E. Oteros-Rozas, and C. Bieling. 2013. "Assessing, Mapping, and Quantifying Cultural Ecosystem Services at Community Level." *Land Use Policy* 33 (July): 118–129. http://doi.org/10.1016/j.landusepol.2012.12.013.

Poepoe, K., P. K. Bartram, and A. M. Friedlander. 2003. "The Use of Traditional Hawaiian Knowledge in the Contemporary Management of Marine Resources". In *Fisher's Knowledge in Fisheries Science and Management*, edited by N. Haggan, C. Brignall, and L. Wood, 328–339. Vancouver: Fisheries Centre, University of British Columbia.

Pollnac, R., M. Bavinck, and I. Monnereau. 2012. "Job Satisfaction in Fisheries Compared." *Social Indicators Research* 109 (1): 119–133.

Ribot, J. C., and N. L. Peluso. 2003. "A Theory of Access." *Rural Sociology* 68 (2): 153–181.

Schemmel, E. 2014. "Integrating Local Ecological Knowledge with Novel Scientific Tools to Refine Traditional Community Based Fishing Moon Calendars." Hawaii Department of Land and Natural Resources. Accessed 13 July 2016. http://dlnr.hawaii.gov/coralreefs/files/2014/11/HCRS_2pager_Moon-calendar_2014.pdf.

Schlager, E., and E. Ostrom. 1992. "Property-Rights Regimes and Natural Resources: A Conceptual Analysis." *Land Economics* 68 (3): 249–262.

Scholte, Samantha S. K. Astrid J. A. van Teeffelen, and Peter H. Verburg. 2015. "Integrating Socio-cultural Perspectives into Ecosystem Service Valuation: A Review of Concepts and Methods." *Ecological Economics* 114 (June): 67–78. http://doi.org/10.1016/j.ecolecon.2015.03.007.

Seto, Katherine Adam Ayers, Merrill Baker-Medard, Clare Fitzsimmons, Christina Hicks, Kirsten Oleson, Rachel Turner, and Mehana Blaich Vaughan. Forthcoming. *Sustaining Small-scale Fisheries: A Multi-country Comparison of Fisheries Access*.

Sikor, T., and C. Lund. 2009. "Access and Property: A Question of Power and Authority." *Development and Change* 40 (1): 1–22. http://doi.org/10.1111/j.1467-7660.2009.01503.x.

Stannard, D. E. 1989. *Before the Horror: The Population of Hawaii on the Eve of Western Contact.* Honolulu: University of Hawaii Press.

Tashakkori, A., and C. Teddlie. 2003. *Handbook of Mixed Methods in Social & Behavioral Research.* Thousand Oaks, CA: SAGE.

Turner, N., F. Berkes, J. Stephenson, and J. Dick. 2013. "Blundering Intruders: Extraneous Impacts on Two Indigenous Food Systems." *Human Ecology* 41 (4): 563–574. http://doi.org/10.1007/s10745-013-9591-y.

United States Department of Agriculture Farm Service Agency. 2014. p. 2. https://www.fsa.usda.gov/Internet/FSA_File/hi_facts_v6.pdf.

US Census Bureau. 2010. *Hā'ena CDP, Hawai'i: Profile of General Population and 2010 Demographic Profile Data.* Accessed 13 July 2016. http://files.hawaii.gov/dbedt/census/Census_2010/demographic/demo_profile_cdp_NI/Haena.pdf.

US Census Bureau. 2015. Quickfacts: Hawaii, July 1. Accessed 13 July 2016. http://www.census.gov/quickfacts/table/PST045215/15.

Van Houtan, K. S., L. McClenachan, and J. N. Kittinger. 2013. "Seafood menus reflect long-term ocean changes." *Frontiers in Ecology and the Environment* 11 (6): 289–290.

Vaughan, M. B. 2014. "'Āina (Land), That Which Feeds: Researching Community Based Natural Resource Management at Home." *Journal of Research Practice* 10 (2): 1–5.

Vaughan, M. B., and N. M. Ardoin. 2014. "The Implications of Differing Tourist/Resident Perceptions for Community-Based Resource Management: A Hawaiian Coastal Resource Area Study." *Journal of Sustainable Tourism* 22 (1): 50–68. http://doi.org/10.1080/09669582.2013.802326.

Vaughan, M. B., and M. R. Caldwell. 2015. "Hana Pa'a: Challenges and Lessons for Early Phases of Co-management." *Marine Policy* 62: 51–62. http://doi.org/10.1016/j.marpol.2015.07.005.

Vaughan, M. B., B. Thompson, and A. Ayers. Forthcoming. "Pāwehe ke kai a'o Hā'ena: Integrating Informal Local Norms of Coastal Management into Law." *Society and Natural Resources.*

Vaughan, M. B., and P. M. Vitousek. 2013. "Mahele: Sustaining Communities through Small-scale Inshore Fishery Catch and Sharing Networks." *Pacific Science* 67 (3): 33.

Vitousek, P. M., T. N. Ladefoged, P. V. Kirch, A. S. Hartshorn, M. W. Graves, S. C. Hotchkiss, S. Tuljapurkar, and O. A. Chadwick. 2004. "Soils, Agriculture, and Society in Precontact Hawai`i." *Science* 304 (5677): 1665–1669. doi:10.1126/science.1099619.

World Health Organization. 2015. Food Security. Accessed 1 October 2015. http://www.who.int/trade/glossary/story028/en/.

Cultural Traditions and Food: Kānaka Maoli and the Production of Poi in the He'e'ia Wetland

Hōkūlani K. Aikau and Donna Ann Kameha'ikū Camvel

Abstract

For five years, a Native Hawaiian non-profit organization has been working to restore wetland taro farming in the ahupua'a of Hee'ia. This article argues that the cultivation of taro and the production of poi are critical means of resilience and Indigenous resurgence for Kānaka Maoli. Participant observations indicate that the modern-day farming of taro for poi is a struggling and backbreaking enterprise often hampered by funding shortages, lack of infrastructure, management challenges, an insufficient supply of taro and, more critically, access to fresh clean water. The primary objective of this article is to articulate how the agronomics of taro farming and poi milling manifests as resilience in and through the kanaka 'ōiwi body. What drives this kind of commitment to such an arduous undertaking? Through ethnographic field observations, field notes, surveys, and interviews the authors show how resilience is an embodied and regenerative experience; one that transforms both kalo and kanaka. The obstacles and grueling realities in the cultivation of kalo and the production of poi are highlighted from an Indigenous perspective, one that articulates the daily difficulties and successes in integrating Kānaka 'Ōiwi customary traditions or practices with modern-day management strategies but, more critically, identifies as cognate the relationship between kalo and kanaka.

Introduction

Located on the windward side of the island of Oʻahu lies a wide expanse of wetland in Heʻeʻia Uli, an ʻili (smaller land section) in the ahupuaʻa of Heʻeʻia.[1] Consisting of an expansive 405 acres of ʻāina or land, the waters of this fertile marshland meet, at the end of their downstream course, the coastal shoreline where the infusion of salty ocean water mixes with the wetlands' sweet, fresh water, creating the muliwai or estuarine brackish waters that were essential spawning grounds for Native Hawaiian species of fish and shrimp. These waters then flow into an eighty-acre fishpond, Kāneʻohe Bay and out to the near-shore fisheries. In the late eighteenth and early nineteenth centuries, this lush and fertile wetland was completely used to grow kalo (taro, *Colocasia esculenta*) using traditional cultivation practices that required channeling wai (fresh water) into and through ʻauwai (ditch system). These loʻi (irrigated taro fields) were banked by pōhaku (stone) revetments that were fitted precisely so as not to allow leakage of water from the loʻi. The Heʻeiʻia community hāpai pōhaku (passed each rock hand to hand) to build these compact and tight walls. The ʻauwai brought water down from the springs and streams in the mauka (forested upland) sections of the ʻili into the loʻi allowing for the life-giving waters to flow through each pond field before returning to its original source, the stream. These loʻI, in conjunction with walled fishponds and systematic dry-land cultivation, contributed to what anthropologist Marion Kelly refers to as "the dynamics of production intensification in pre-contact Hawaiʻi" (Kelly 1989, 83).

Although it is clear that our Hawaiian ancestors were able to efficiently and successfully cultivate and manage 405 acres of loʻi kalo to produce poi (cooked and mashed taro mixed with water), duplicating that effort in today's drastically altered cultural, social, economic and political environment presents a most challenging front. Drawing on ethnographic research conducted between July 2013 and March 2015 the authors argue that, despite the dramatic differences between historical and contemporary contexts, the process of producing poi continues to be critical to a Kanaka Maoli consciousness and an important benchmark toward sustainable self-determination (Corntassel 2008);[2] planting kalo and making poi returns Kanaka ʻŌiwi to the ʻāina and to the life-giving properties found therein.[3] It also breathes new life into, as Kānaka geographer Kapā Oliviera suggests, "our deep consciousness and appreciation for the natural environment." We developed such a keen understanding of our environment, she argues, through a generations-long, sustained interaction with ʻāina, which produced a distinct "sense ability." "In this context," she writes, "'sense ability' is the capacity to receive and perceive stimuli from our oceanscapes, landscapes, and heavenscapes and to respond to these sensory stimuli in ways that contribute to our overall understanding of the world"(Oliveira and Nakoa, 2014, 94). We argue that when kānaka work in the loʻi and make poi we begin the process of re-enlivening our sense abilities by restoring the physical, genealogical, and sensual relationship that connects kanaka (a person), ʻāina and kalo.

THE FOODWAYS OF HAWAI'I

The Ahupua'a System of Hawai'i

Kanaka 'Ōiwi scholar, Dr. Kamanamaikalani Beamer, describes an ahupua'a system as "a contemporary phrase used to describe 'Ōyst resource management in ancient times" (Beamer 2014, 33). Paul F. Nahoa Lucas, a Kanaka 'Ōiwi attorney, defines ahupua'a as a "unit of land" or "a land division usually extending from the uplands to the sea" (Lucas 1995, 4). The ahupua'a has also been described geographically as a wedge-shaped section of land, running from the ridgeline of the mountain to the near-shore fisheries, often the first reef beyond the shoreline. While all of these definitions are correct, missing from them are the spiritual and culturally complex relationships that exist between the 'āore (land) and the kupa (those people well acquainted with the land). It was here, in the ahupua'a, that the maka'āinana (people of the land) lived; those who made up the ranks of farmers, fishermen, gatherers, kapa or bark cloth beaters, wood carvers, adze makers and others whose stewardship of the 'āina, along with the production of food crops, was essential in both mālama 'āina (to care for the land) and aloha 'āina (having a deep love for the land).

This relationship was expressed through mo'okū'auhau (genealogy), mo'olelo (stories and histories) and ka'ao (traditional literature and legends) that were specific to particular places and remembered by the people who were from there. Additionally, each place had a special significance or connection to certain akua (religious deities). To know a place was to know the names of the akua, winds, rains, and clouds, and to be able to recite the mo'okū'auhau and mo'olelo of a place.

The relationship of kanaka to 'āina was personal and continues to persist through the cultural practices performed on the land in places across Hawai'i. As we describe below, the story of Hāloanakalaukapalili (the first-born son of Wākea and Ho'ohōkūkalani) and his younger brother, Hāloa, serves as a cultural and practical guide for contemporary Hawaiians working to restore our personal and familial relationship to 'āina. The story of Hāloa motivates and frames the work Kāko'o 'ōiwi is doing in the lo'i to grow kalo and produce poi, to manage the flow of water, and to mitigate the impacts of climate change. The story of Hāloa motivates volunteers to work until muscles ache and sweat runs down like rivers on their backs. The story of Hāloa motivates us to be Hawaiian scholars who work to restore our lāhui (nation and People).

He'e'ia Uli Transformed

The lo'i system in He'e'ia was highly productive and has been described as the calabash (poi bowl) for O'ahu because of the many acres of kalo grown here. However, over the past 165 years the engineering success of the irrigated pond system has been severely compromised. Three historical events, the Māhele in the 1850s, the plantation economy during the territorial period of 1900–1959, and suburban development combined with the flood of 1969, capture the transformation of the 'āina in the He'e'ia ahupua'a from a source of physical and spiritual nourishment to land as property with economic value.

In what is referred to as the Māhele, a systematic process of land privatization, the collective interest in land was divided amongst the aliʻi (chiefly class), the makaʻāina, and the ʻaupuni (the government).

Although the entire ahupuaʻa was awarded to Abner Kahoʻoheiheipahu Pākī through the Māhele process many government remnants and small pieces of land were claimed by those families who had already been cultivating the land. Prior to the Māhele the konohiki (the representative of the aliʻi and resource manager of an ahupuaʻa) changed when a new aliʻi came into power; it was common practice for makaʻāinana, who had been on the land for generations, to remain. Under the privatization of land, makaʻāinana families could apply for a Kuleana award or purchase parcels in fee simple. Those families who were not awarded or did not purchase land became landless.[4]

In 1871, Bernice Pauahi Bishop, Pākī's daughter who inherited her father's lands after his death, began leasing land in Heʻeʻia to Chinese planters, where rice replaced most of the kalo grown in the wetland.[5] The transition from taro to rice had very little impact on the overall system. Indeed, interviews with kūpuna (elders) suggest that although Chinese planters moved into predominantly Hawaiian communities, Hawaiian values and practices were pervasive. They describe growing up in a multi-ethnic community where Hawaiian, Chinese, and Japanese families shared resources from the loʻi and from the sea.

At the turn of the twentieth century, agricultural interests in Heʻeʻia's lands escalated and KSBE leased lands for the production of sugarcane and pineapple. These endeavors dramatically modified the land causing ecological and cultural damage to the wetland, the muliwai (estuary), and the adjoining fishpond. One of the most significant impacts was topsoil erosion. The solution? To plant mangrove trees in the muliwai. Although mangroves were marginally successful in trapping downstream sediment, their planting also had a severe impact on the estuary, which formed a natural fish nursery for native fish. Today, the mangrove trees have completely inundated the stream and fishpond transforming the water quality and preventing native vertebrates and invertebrates from living in the stream.

Between 1900s and 1959, the territorial period, many makaʻāinana left the farming of fields and loʻi kalo to work in Honolulu. According to Kanaka ʻŌiwi scholar Davianna Pōmaikaʻi McGregor, the growth of the sugar planation economy correlated with the ever-increasing need for fresh water, which led to the construction of an elaborate irrigation system. "The impact of these irrigation systems upon rural Hawaiian taro farmers," she explains, "reverberated throughout the twentieth century. Cut off from the free flow of stream waters into their loʻi kalo or taro pond fields, many kuaʻāina [rural people who were considered the backbone of the land] gave up taro farming and moved into the city to find new livelihoods" (McGregor 2007, 43). McGregor traces the migration of kānaka from rural communities into the city as well as those families that remained on the land creating cultural kīpuka (oases) where the land- and water-based practices of our ancestors were maintained. Heʻeʻia Kūpuna (elders) born and raised during the territorial period describe a multi-racial community where rice and kalo continued to be cultivated in the terraced water ponds. They told stories about running along the kuāuna, of the poi mill, and of the uncle who still took care of the loʻi. But they also remember the new housing development projects that began in the 1950s that required the evictions of Hawaiian families and local farmers. Along with suburban development, the most severe impact to this once productive kalo land was the devastating flood in 1969 and resulting fallow condition over the next several decades. The effect of both non-use and misuse in the wetland of Heʻeʻia has been the extensive proliferation of non-native plant species, the dominant one being California grass (*Brachiaria mutica*), which was probably introduced as a feed grass for cattle. The inundation of non-native plants and the lack of management of feral pigs and cattle severely damaged the ʻauwai, destroyed kuāuna, polluted the streams, slowed water flow, and reduced water quality.

In 2008 lineal descendants of the Kānaka Maoli who had once labored in the loʻi kalo of Heʻeʻia Uli began to talk about restoring the wetland to kalo production. The kūpuna (grandparent generation) and mākua (parent generation) of Heʻeʻia provided moʻolelo (stories and histories) and precious memories about the "good old days" of kalo, poi, fish, rice, and the families who made up the community of Heʻeʻia. The Koʻolaupoko Hawaiian Civic Club, whose membership includes many of the lineal descendant families of Heʻeʻia, began an earnest effort to bring kalo cultivation back to the wetland with the intention of producing poi. Galvanized by the interest of the Nature Conservancy of Hawaiʻi and the landowner, Hawaiʻi Community Development Authority (a state entity),[6] all three became collaborative partners in a community effort to restore the Heʻeʻia Uli to kalo cultivation in order to make poi.

Embodying the Hāloa Triad

Na aliʻi o ke kuamoʻo o Hāloa

(Chiefs from the lineage of Hāloa)

"Said of chiefs whose lineage goes back to ancient times—to Hāloa, son of Wākea.

FOOD, CULTURE & SOCIETY

Wākea mated with Hoʻohōkūkalani who had two sons, both named Hāloa.

The older Hāloa was born a taro, the younger one a man.

It was this younger brother that the high chiefs name with pride as their ancestor." (Pukui, 1983, 241)

The primary objective of this article is to explain how the agronomics of kalo farming and poi milling contributes to resilience in the kanaka ʻōiwi body. The process of removing California grass and digging out loʻi that are undetectable on the land due to lack of use and misuse, planting and tending to kalo once lo'i are restored, and producing poi by hand is a labor-intensive process (which we describe in detail below). What drives this kind of commitment to such an arduous undertaking? We highlight here the Hāloa Triad, a descriptor that explains the consanguineous relationship between Kānaka 'Ōiwi, 'āina and kalo.

The mo'olelo of Papahānaumoku (earth mother—she who births islands) and Wākea (sky father) establishes the foundations for the Hāloa triad, where the genealogical connections between the 'āina (Papahānaumoku), kalo (Hāloanakalaukapalili), and the first human ancestor and Ali'i Nui (Hāloa) are set forth. The mo'olelo of Papahānaumoku, Wākea and their daughter, Ho'ohōkūkalani is established in the Kumulipo, a cosmogonic chant or mele ko'ihonua. Papa and Wākea have a daughter, Ho'ohōkūkalanai, who later mates with her father and miscarries the fetus. In this instance Papahānaumoku is Haumea, the essence of the procreant, or the goddess of birthing, bearing all fecund elements associated with the bringing forth of life. Hāloanakalaukapalili, prematurely delivered from the pū'ao or womb of Papahānaumoku (the 'āina, earth), is born of a sacred lineage, that of father and daughter. The fetus is miscarried, wrapped in his mother's walewale (slime, mucus), that biological procreative slime teeming with life-giving elements. It is then buried in the earth, mixing with the lepo momona (ancient dark rich soil) that is infused with mana (spiritual power), biological and decomposed matter and DNA, the essence of life. Hence the regenerative powers of Haumea are activated in the *planting back* of the agglutinated keiki 'alu'alu (premature baby) into the rich soil from which the kalo plant thrusts forth from the ground becoming the living metaphor for 'āina or what Pukui defines as "that which feeds." When Hāloa, the second child, is born from this sacred lineage, he is the younger sibling to Hāloanakalaukapalili and becomes the first chief among Kānaka 'Ōiwi.

The Hāloa triad represents the cognate relationship between 'āina as that which feeds, kalo as 'ai (a staple food or poi) and Hāloa as kanaka. It is important to understand how this triad functions as an analogy for the contemporary restoration of kalo. The embodiment of that reclamation by the kanaka body as kalo mahi'ai (taro farmer) signals and restores the regenerative powers of Haumea that are enacted and made tangible with the cultivation or planting, birth and delivery of kalo (Hāloanakalaukapalili), by kanaka (Hāloa), into the rich and proliferant 'āina (Papahānaumoku/Haumea). This *is* the cycle of metamorphosis or, as the Haumea mo'olelo tells us, she is reborn in this and all prior and following generations and the ancestral foundation for Kānaka Maoli. Hence, kanaka re-enact the Hāloa triad—re-immersion, re-generation and re-birth of 'āina—each time kalo is cultivated and poi pounded for food.

When the mo'olelo of Papahānaumoku and Wākea, Ho'ohōkūkalani and her sons Hāloanakalaukapalili and Hāloa is told at the lo'i, visitors are provided with a rationale for the need to restore kalo culitvation and an explanation of how this place-based practice connects to the health and well-being of Kākanka 'Ōiwi. This mo'olelo in particular offers specific insight into how kalo fits within a Hawaiian worldview. The story highlights the reciprocal and interdependent relationship between ʻād i, kalo and kānaka whereby kānaka, as the younger sibling of kalo, has the kuleana (responsibility and obligation) to plant and mā lama (care for) our elder sibling kalo and provides the ontological basis for the ethical practice and principle of mālama ʻāina (to care for the land; that which feeds). When kānaka mālama ʻāina, āina can achieve its reciprocal kuleana, which is to mālama and feed kānaka. The history of changes in land-use practices in Heʻeʻia reveals what happens when this interdependent relationship is disrupted or severed. The Māhuahua ʻAi o Hoi project, which translates to "re-planting the fruit of Hoi,"[7] strives to restore this relationship by providing the larger community with opportunities to volunteer at the loʻi on community workdays. An invaluable aspect of the experience of volunteers is the orientation.[8] More importantly, these events offer volunteers and staff the experience to connect with Hāloa, to enter into the lepo of Papa with hands, feet, body and mind, to plant, or weed kalo, to sink into the walewale of the ʻāina momona. For Kānaka Maoli, this is the embodiment of Hāloa on the ʻōiwi body.

Theory and Methods

Our ethnographic findings indicate that the restoration of kalo farming and the production of poi in Heʻeʻia Uli has renewed ancestral, cultural and political pride for Kānaka Maoli in the Heʻeʻia community. The critical condition of the wetland requires more integrative and adaptive management strategies in which cultural and organizational values inform administrative decisions as opposed to a centralized management regime in which management standards are more aligned with harvested yield as a commercial commodity. In this way, the growing of kalo is an everyday act of "resistance." For settler ecologist Fikret Berkes, the goal is the "generation of new knowledge through the synergy of combining what is already known to science and to local tradition" (Berkes 2012, xxiv). It is this kind of propagated management, to hoʻoulu (to grow, to sprout, to cause to increase) that is in alignment with traditional values. Tsalagi scholar Jeff Corntassel refers to Indigenous efforts to restore our land- and water-based practices as "the engagement of everyday acts of resurgence" (Corntassel, 2012). In this way, the planting of kalo *is* an act of resistance, a way for Kānaka ʻŌiwi to recall, re-immerse and revive the pathways of their ancestors not only in the cultivation and harvesting of kalo for poi, but as a tangible and cultural provision in the quest for food security, food sovereignty, and resilience.

FOOD,
CULTURE &
SOCIETY

In 2010, Kākoʻo ʻŌiwi, a 501 (c) (3) nonprofit corporation, acquired a 38-year lease agreement with the State of Hawaiʻi Community Development Authority (HCDA) for the wetland to implement a long-range agricultural and ecological restoration plan, one that would promote the social and economic advancement of the local community using cultural, educational and ecosystem restoration programs as the framework for resource management and sustainability.[9] While the Māhuahua ʻAi o Hoi project commenced in 2010, the ethnographic data gathered for this article were collected from August of 2013 to March of 2015.[10] Our approach is grounded in an understanding that "being

Indigenous today means engaging in a struggle to reclaim and regenerate one's relational, place-based existence as a continuously renewing relationship to each other and to 'āina" (Alfred and Corntassel 2005). We understand the restoration and regeneration of Indigenous place-based existence as the necessary preconditions for doing Indigenous research (Goodyear-Kaʻōpua 2009). Our approach posits customary and contemporary knowledge as the Indigenous/Kānaka Maoli centerpiece from which Māhuahua ʻAi o Hoi's ontological and pragmatic strategies are incorporated in the re-cultivation of kalo and the reproduction of poi in Heʻeʻia Uli.

We used a multi-methods approach to understand how and where Kākoʻo ʻŌiwi uses kanaka protocol and practices in its restoration process. We conducted participant observations of community workdays at Māhuahua ʻAi o Hoi. Kākoʻo ʻŌiwi hosts these community workdays on the second Saturday of every month. Participation in the workday involves interfacing with community volunteers, Kākoʻo ʻŌiwi staff and interns as well as working on the farm in a variety of capacities: clearing fields, restoring loʻi kalo, removing trash, clearing brush, etc. At each community workday, we used field notes to record the information presented to volunteers during the orientation, paying particular attention to how staff and interns describe the cultural importance of restoring loʻi kalo, the eco-system services from restoration work, and the role of native species, healthy wetlands, and clean, accessible water in the ahupuaʻa.

We conducted semi-structured interviews with Kākoʻo ʻŌiwi staff, which were audio-recorded and transcribed. The interviews provided information regarding the goals of community workdays, asked staff how they came to be associated with the Māhuahua ʻAi o Hoi project, and inquired about the Hawaiian cultural and environmental impact of the restoration on the wetland, the fishpond and coral reefs. In August 2013, we documented the poi production process through participant observations recorded in field notes and through informal "talk story" with staff and community volunteers who participated in cleaning kalo. These talk story sessions were also recorded in field notes. We now turn to two vignettes, one by each author. The first reflects on the process of clearing non-native invasive grasses from the freshwater ponds so that kalo can be planted. The second vignette recounts the process of producing poi without proper resources. We use the first-person narrative voice in order to remind the reader that moʻolelo (stories) are repositories of Indigenous knowledge. Stories about people and places provide the original instructions for how best to live in a relational and reciprocal way in specific places (Nelson 2008).

Clearing Space, Growing Kalo: Reflections from the Field

Any romantic notions of farming and the agronomics of kalo cultivation quickly crumble as one steps into the wet, slimy, muddy terraces, sometimes waist high, to pull out stubborn weeds, collect kalo corms, plant huli (taro tops) or clear auwai (waterways) in prepared loʻi (irrigated terraces). Clearing

Fig 1: Volunteers working in loʻi ʻeha clearing California grass. Photograph by author.

California grasses from loʻi is not a job done once (see Figure 1). It grows and spreads so quickly it seems as though we will never get rid of it.

I have cleared California grass from loʻi ʻeha (the fourth loʻi) too many times to count. Today was no exception. We had a small group of volunteers and our goal was to finish clearing California grass from the back half of the loʻi. Last month the volunteers started working on the front half of the loʻi. I get to the loʻi after the rest of the group has already started working. I see they are nearly waist deep in water. I worry the loʻi might be too deep for my five-year-old daughter who is with me today. Although she has been coming with me to the loʻi since she was 2 years old, I still worry she could get hurt.

We make our way to the edge of the loʻi. I slide in first, testing my footing. The ground seems firm, solid near the edge but as I slowly take a few steps away from the bank the ground drops off and I sink to my thighs in the cool muddy water. I realize it might in fact be too deep for my daughter but she is begging me to get in. I reach my hand out to help her slide from the kuāuna into the loʻi. She loves to be in the muddy water. She releases my hand and moves expertly through the watery mud even though its up to her waist.

Fig 2: Volunteers cleared all of the California grass in the right corner of the loʻi. Volunteers scheduled for the next week will remove the grasses piled on the kuāuna and in the loʻi. Photograph by author.

Fig 3: On the left is kalo being milled in the meat grinder. On the right are bowls of paʻiʻai ready for distribution. Photograph by author.

THE FOODWAYS OF HAWAI'I

Immersed in the cool thick mud of the lo'i I am reminded of the insights of kanaka 'ōiwi geographer Kapā Oliveira who details how "Kānaka developed keen intellectual perception informed by our interactions with our environment and our kūpuna"(Oliveira and Nakoa, 2014, 94). My daughter already exhibits a "sense ability" that comes from having grown up working in the lo'i.

I realize almost immediately that I forgot to get a sickle from the shed so I cannot help cut the California grass. I decide to move around to the far side of the lo'i and help drag the cut grasses to the kuāuna. I partner with the newest member of the staff. Although he is new to Kāko'o 'Ōiwi, he is not new to farming kalo. He grew up growing kalo with his family in their lo'i two ahupua'a north of He'e'ia. He uses the sickle to cut the hollow stocks of the grasses in order to clear a little space to reach the roots that feel like carpet soaked in mud. He floats bundles of grass to me and I drag them towards the sides and push them up onto the banks. We repeat this process until we get to the roots. The root bunches are thick and heavy with mud, centipedes, crawfish (and these are only the critters we see). It takes the two of us to roll the three-feet long mass of mud-encrusted roots out of the water and onto the bank of the lo'i. The eighteen-inch to three-feet deep dense thick root system traps the muddy soil making them very heavy and difficult to remove. It is not enough to pull the grasses up by the tops, which is also difficult due to the prickly fine "hairs" that cover the leaves; we have to remove the roots. We are struggling; it is heavy. We make one more strenuous effort and finally get it onto the bank. We rest on the edges of the lo'i, taking a breath before getting back to work. We have almost met our initial goal of breaking through the mass to meet up with the group on the other side of this island of grass.

As we work we talk story. My daughter helps to drag smaller bundles to the sides. She is most interested in catching crawfish and toads with her small net. We are making progress. We meet up with the other group, which inspires us to work harder to get this last mound of weeds out of the lo'i. It feels like this last bunch is the most persistent but we clear it one mass at a time. I look at my watch and realize it's time for my daughter and me to leave. We finish helping to clear this last bunch and then we prepare to leave. The rest of the group will spend another thirty minutes or so clearing the grasses from the other side of the lo'i. As we walk away, my daughter, disappointed we have to leave so early, and I look back at what we accomplished in the 90 minutes while we worked. I feel really good; my arm muscles ache but I feel good. (See Figure 2)

The authors have often wondered if volunteers know what they are getting into when they show up at 8:00 a.m. on these Saturday mornings. Do volunteers have any idea about the kind of effort that is required for those pristinely sealed and stacked bags of poi to be available on supermarket shelves? For first-time volunteers, working in the loʻi can be a very dramatic change from their other life experiences. I am reminded of one young man who volunteered at the loʻi a few years ago who was visiting from Virginia and grew up farming tobacco with his family. When he was told he would be working at a farm he had very different expectations, which was evident in his attire: Wrangler™ jeans, work boots, and a utility knife on his belt. When he stepped into the loʻi he sunk thigh deep into the mud and had to be pulled out. Despite getting stuck, he got back into the loʻi and worked for the next two hours to dig out five-feet-high weeds. Afterwards, during lunch, he expressed a sense of gratitude for having had an opportunity to work with his hands in the soil again. Yes, it was unlike anything he had experienced growing up but it was deeply satisfying.

The farming of kalo is intensely strenuous but there is something quite satisfying for having worked that hard with others working equally hard. Just as Oliveira's theory of a kānaka "sense ability" incorporates our bodies and our relationships with the elements that surround us, Leanne Simpson explains in *Dancing on Our Turtle's Back* that the process of resurgence must also be fully embodied. In order to access the knowledge needed for Indigenous resurgence, she writes, "we have to engage our entire bodies: our physical beings, emotional self, our spiritual energy and our intellect. Our methodologies, our lifeways must reflect those components of our being and the integration of those four components into a whole" (Simpson 2011, 42). Working in the loʻi provides volunteers with an opportunity to bring their physical, emotional, spiritual and intellectual selves to the work. We do not presume to suggest that the young haole (white) man from Virginia experienced the work at the loʻi in the same way as Kanaka ʻŌiwi whose work rebuilds their relationship with Hāloa. But the embodied nature of the work creates a space where volunteers can leave feeling a sense of satisfaction; a sense that their labor has contributed to something meaningful. For some Kanaka Maoli, the experience at the loʻi restores or strengthens a connection that has been stretched and sometimes severed due to colonialism, development, militarism, and capitalism to name only a few of the structural forces that impact our ability to live authentic Indigenous lives in our homeland. The embodied practice of pulling weeds to clear space for kalo to be planted and grow is a powerful metaphor for and a material manifestation of the decolonial possibilities that emerge when Indigenous peoples restore our land-based practices.

Preparing Kalo for Poi: Reflections from the Field

The milling of cooked taro into poi is complicated at Hoi by limited access to fresh, clean water, lack of infrastructure, and tension amongst the staff and management. Workers also have to be conscious of a very short turn-around time in which to retain the poi's freshness so that it does not go sour. We examine notions of growing kalo and producing poi in the face of a drastically changed landscape. We argue that in spite of these challenges, the very act of cultivating taro and producing poi is, in and of itself, an act of resurgence that provides an Indigenous pathway to food sovereignty and food security in the form of resilience. It is a reminder of the connection to Hāloa, the elder sibling, culturally, physically, and mentally.

During the summer of 2013, we found that we were not getting new information from our observations of the regular community workdays so we asked a staff member if there was any other aspects of their work that they would like us to document. The staff member suggested we take a look at their poi production process.[12] At that time they had been milling and selling poi for about a year and she thought it might be a good way for us to see how the kalo grown in the fields contributes to food sovereignty. We loved this idea and over three weeks in August 2013 we observed and recorded the poi production process. At that time, Mahuahua 'Ai o Hoi did not grow enough kalo on site to meet their orders so they procured additional kalo from a family on Māui Island. The raw kalo was usually delivered on Wednesday afternoon and the poi production process would commence.

I arrive to He'e'ia Uli about 5:00 a.m. Kānehoalani (sun) has yet to rise so it is cool and dark. I sit down on the bench of a wooden picnic table with my steaming mug of hot coffee. Nalani, who came in at 4:30 a.m., already had the kalo in the large stainless steel pot, submerged in water and cooking. They use propane stoves to boil the huge pots of kalo. I look around me, taking in the lush landscape as the sky begins to lighten. Nalani had already gotten situated and had eaten her breakfast by flashlight. We talk story a bit. I did not sense a feeling of 'ohana or kinship between the hui or core workers with their management team. Nalani tells me that another staff member, Sista, was now in charge of getting the provision needed for cleaning and milling the kalo. Things such as water, ice, bags and ties, scale, gloves were now her responsibility. Sista and Ioane arrive at 6:00 a.m. and begin to prepare the area for peeling the kalo and the arrival of volunteers from a local company. I learn that prior to cooking the taro, the corms are checked for pocket rot, a metal screen placed on the bottom of the pot to avoid sticking and burning, and the corms are layered in the pot (biggest to smallest). A second pot is on another burner with boiling water, which will be poured over the prepared corms. Once the water is ready, the corms are covered with the boiling water, burlap bags are arranged on the top of the pot, and covered with the lid, then made secure by heavy pōhaku and/or stone dowels. Nalani estimates the cooking time will be four to six hours. After about an hour and every half-hour after that, the kalo is checked for readiness until it no longer "itches" the throat when eaten.

Nalani checks the kalo, re-arranges the thick brown burlap bags covering the kalo at the top of the pot while explaining that the bags help to hold in the heat. She estimates the cooking time to be another four hours. She inputs this data into her computer. It is now 7:30 a.m. and the sun has risen. Jensen, a volunteer, arrives and both he and Ioane leave to weed-whack an

overgrown loʻi in preparation of the volunteers. The kalo is still cooking and Nalani checks it once more at 8:00 a.m. A half hour later, she checks again and takes a piece of kalo from the pot to test for doneness, cutting pieces for sampling and she explains, "if the mouth gets itchy, it means the kalo is not done." We take a taste finding its flavor exceptional. The texture was moist but not sticky and the sweetness a characteristic of the type of kalo. The taro was almost ready for peeling and rinsing. Sista left Hoi to buy water and ice in order to soak the now fully cooked taro so as to be able to cool it before peeling the skin from the corm. The process seemed rather chaotic, but managed well by the workers. When Sista returns with the ice and water the cooked taro is placed in an ice bath in a very large cooler.

At about 8:30 Luana, the liaison from the local company, has arrived with employee volunteers. Things begin to move quickly once volunteers arrive.

8:40 the smaller pot of kalo was turned off.

8:42 Nalani checks the large pot but the kalo is not quite done.

8:52 the larger pot is turned off, the kalo finally cooked. Sista and Nalani realize they still do not have enough ice so they text Lyla to ask her to pick up ice at the pier where Māhuahua ʻAi o Hoi has an account.

9:10 and Nalani adds water from the hose into the smaller pot to boil it.

9:28 Lyla gives the volunteers an orientation to Heʻeʻia Uli, its use, land history, and site for restoration. She tells them that they will be weeding one of the loʻi but does not include any other information about the places. I wonder about the lack of a cultural orientation; these volunteers will not learn the moʻolelo, names of the akua (gods), the place names or landscape associations relevant to this place. I'm a bit bothered by this because I am from Heʻeʻia and there is much to know about it. Meanwhile Sista is rinsing and preparing the pots needed for the ice bath for the kalo. She then washes the white coolers and red buckets, which will be used for packing the cleaned kalo. Nalani shoots down the burlap bags used in the cooking process.

9:55 the smaller pot is turned off.

10:10 Ioane and Jensen return from the loʻi and help to finalize preparations for peeling the kalo.

Although the plan for the day for the volunteers is to have them work in the loʻi, Lyla offers the opportunity for anyone interested to work back in the tented area cleaning kalo. The volunteers, who opt out of the loʻi, all women, come into the tented area where Nalani, Sista and Ioane explain the process for peeling and cleaning the kalo.

THE FOODWAYS OF HAWAI'I

At 10:33 a.m. Ioane and Sista leave to get more purified water. Upon their return with the water, another ice bath is prepared and the instructions on how to peel and clean the kalo is shared once more as the volunteers sit down, placing transparent gloves on their hands to begin the work. Using gloved hands and spoons, the kalo seems slippery at first, but we get used to it. We remove the skin and dark spots from the kalo, scraping and digging while trying to leave as much of the corm as intact as possible.

While we did not get as muddy and wet as the other volunteers in the lo'i, there were some of us who did not leave completely dry when we were finished. Every once in a while one of the corms would be real hot and someone would quickly drop the kalo back into the pot of cool water with a slight splatter coming out of the pot once the corm splashed into it. It was an assembly line of sorts, everyone sitting in a circle on metal folding chairs, laughing, talking story, sharing responses on the art of taro cleaning and how not to get wet in the process. Hot corms were placed in two large metal pots of purified water steeped in ice. Another large pot with purified water was where the cleaned corms were placed. From there Nalani and Sista provided quality control by checking the corm a final time for any discoloration, rot, or other blemishes we might have missed.

There were six of us working and it was a pleasant experience, a transformative one for all in different ways. I shared a little bit of the Hāloa mo'olelo and the volunteers were happy to hear its tangible connection to the kalo they were physically cleaning that would become poi. Much laughter took place as the ladies were far haappier cleaning the kalo than being in the wet, muddy, lo'i and in no time at all the kalo was cleaned. Nalani and Sista took the corms and cut them into cubes then the kalo was then placed in clear plastic bags, the coolers filled with the prepared kalo and covered completely in ice to prohibit spoilage. All tubs, pots, spoons, screens are thoroughly washed, area cleaned. Nearly eight hours from our arrival to the wetland the kalo is packed and ready for the next day's milling.

Grinding and Milling Kalo: Reflections from the Field

Ke hō'ole mai nei o Hāloa.

Hāloa denies that.

Hāloa is the god of taro.

It was said that whatever business was discussed before an open bowl of poi was denied by Hāloa. (Pukui, 1983, 183)

THE FOODWAYS OF HAWAI'I

I arrive to Heʻeʻia Uli at 6:00 a.m. the following day. Ioane loads the coolers filled with kalo onto Jensen's truck for transport to Aunty Pua's house, the place where the poi will be milled about three-quarters of a mile down the road from the wetland. Jensen, a good friend of Ioane's and a dedicated volunteer, started loading the coolers onto the truck. Sista had just returned to Aunty Pua's house with purified water, which they will use to mix the poi. She has had to use her own money to buy water and ice for yesterday's cleaning and today's milling. "Why?" I ask, "No petty cash on hand for stuff like that?" "No" she replies, "and every time we ask upper management they keep forgetting! It's not like we don't need water!" Nalani arrives to Aunty Pua's with the supplies needed for bagging the poi. Ioane and Jensen roll out a large machine on wheels, an old meat grinder. They hose it down and once thoroughly cleaned, the machine is rolled to the middle of the area. I watch them put it together and turn it on. In their gloved hands they place the cut kalo pieces onto the plate and then push it into the grinder with the aid of a plastic water bottle. I smile inside thinking "reduce, reuse, recycling at it's best." I watch the grounded mass being pressed through tiny holes and come out looking like pasta only thicker and bulkier. I want to take my finger and scoop up a glob and eat it already! It looks so amazingly delicious! I take pictures of it. The process of kalo milled through the grinder again and again mesmerizes me. I feel like this is an important moment. I keep staring at the kalo as it comes out. I laugh to myself thinking it looks like pasta, but oh no, this is better than pasta. It is the perfect food and it's filled with mana (divine power) because ... yes that's it! It is the tangible connection to Hā loa. I am reminded that just as Haumea is being reborn in every generation, so too is Hāloa being reclaimed with every planting, every harvest, with each cooking, milling and preparation of the kalo into poi. Hāloa feeds us literally, spiritually and culturally. Because of Hāloa, we are resilient! Because of Hāloa we are alive. Hāloa is the literal and symbolic foundation behind the resurgence efforts of Kānaka Maoli returning to the ʻāina, the reason why against all the odds, the challenges, the hardships, the frustrations and back-breaking hard work, we continue. This is an epiphany! I come back to the present and remember where I am. (See Figure 3)

The poi is placed in a large clean pot and taken to Nalani and Sista who will weigh and process the paʻiʻai (kalo that has been milled with very little water) orders. The 106 orders of Paʻiai are processed first. The remaining ground kalo is placed in a huge pot, purified water added, and a handheld commercial mixer is used to turn the paʻiʻai into poi. As the poi was being ground and processed, Sista and Nalani, in gloved hands, are weighing paʻiʻai (1 lb each) and placing them into containers, lidding and then putting them into iced coolers for delivery to customers. Lyla arrives with the confirmed orders in hand, hurriedly checking the numbers to make sure there is enough paʻiʻai and poi for the orders as Jensen begins to wash the grinding machine down.

THE FOODWAYS OF HAWAI'I

They are three hours into this process and while I am amazed at how it seems to flow, I am also privy to critical conversations taking place around me of how the workers feel regarding management, personnel and workplace issues. Peter and John, who will deliver the orders, arrive at the milling site as Lyla tastes the poi. She then voices concern about the ability to fill all of the orders. As it turned out, she was right to be concerned. There were only 135 bags for 156 orders of poi. Some of the workers including management gave up their own orders of poi in order to complete customer orders. At 11:05 a.m., Nalani and Sista left. We talk story a little longer and leave at 11:30 a.m.

We learned more from our fieldwork than just how Kāko'o mills poi. Our observations and talk stories reveal tensions between the core workers (Sista, Nalani and Ioane) and their managers. Workers do not feel empowered, and say they are marginalized within the management structure that appears to be hierarchal and where decisions are made without the workers' input. In spite of these issues, Sista, Nalani and Ioanea, who are Kānaka Maoli, are committed to the cultivation of kalo and the production of poi and will stay unless they resign or are terminated. I ask why? They tell me because we want to see this 'āina restored, we want to see more kalo growing, more poi made. What is it that keeps them there? Hāloa.

Management Strategies for Mahuahua 'Ai o Hoi

"Maika'i ka hana a ka lima, 'ono nō ka 'ai a ka waha!"

(Good work with the hands, very delicious the food in the mouth.) (Samuel Kamuela Waha Pōhaku Grace, interview with Kepā Maly and Gilbert Kahele, Miloli'i, 2003)

Restoration projects such as this one are often burdened with contemporary governance structures, land-use issues, bureaucratic oversight, lack of funding, and the delicate management of employees. Due to the lack of consistency in the procurement of funds, the organization must constantly re-adjust its work plans in order to fulfill their funded objectives, which can include the cultivation of kalo but not always. The organization struggles with basic needs such as machinery breaking down and equipment being stolen, to challenges more structural in nature such as changing production goals and timelines, and workers who leave or are terminated and high turnover in farm managers. In interviewing both former and current staff, one of the things that was glaringly evident is the lack of consistent and committed help. We heard the phrase "We could use more hands" many times in our interviews and during our many hours of talk story. This refers not only to more volunteers, but the He'e'ia community as well.

One reason for the lack of enough hands is the lack of infrastructure on site. As an example, at the start of our observations there were three showers that could be used to rinse off after getting very wet, muddy, dirty, and sweaty. This water was not potable but was clean enough for volunteers to wash off the mud at the end of the day. This complicated not only the volunteers' efforts to get all that mud off after spending hours in the loʻi but on any given community workday there could be more than fifty volunteers waiting for the showers. Presently, the site has a dedicated water line and rinsing off is much easier; however, infrastructure or rather the lack of it (electricity and plumbing) is still problematic.

While not a published ʻōlelo noʻeau, we have heard kūpuna say some of the following phrases, which in our observations function as such. First, "If the hand good, then the poi going be good, but if the hand no good, the poi going sour." This translates to, "if you have thoughts and behaviors that are not conducive to being pono (being in the right balance), you have no business mixing poi because it will be sour." Second, "Do not fight in front of the poi bowl, it is disrespectful to Hāloa." This ʻōlelo noʻeau instructs us that "If there is negativity around the poi bowl, those who are projecting it should not eat from the bowl for the kalo is Hāloa." What the authors find striking is the way these words of wisdom move through time to align and make more meaningful the contemporary production of poi at Māhuahua ʻAi o Hoi. There have been times when, in fact, the poi has been reported as sour after delivery, or after being bought at the farmers' market. Considering the stressful environment in which it was produced, perhaps indeed the disposition of both the hands and the minds of those preparing the poi was not pono. However, there are many more times when the kalo planted in Heʻeʻia Uli has been harvested, prepared, and milled to produce the sweetest poi, filling many ōpū (stomachs) to satisfaction in the Heʻeʻia ahupuaʻa, sold at the farmers' market and to those who ordered and purchased poi. This is no small feat, and to be sure organizational growing pains are part of the process.

In terms of day-to-day management, we observed a very real disconnect between management, supervisors, and core workers. Lack of communication, decision-making, daily needs, administrative and overall dissatisfaction manifested in low morale and ideas of transitioning elsewhere in spite of their very real and culturally appropriate attachment to this ʻāina. Management that is pono (balanced) is paramount to the success of producing taro and poi. In this case, the resilience of Kānaka Maoli is predicated on the connection to Hāloa through the fostering of ʻohana and reciprocity. Let us investigate this word ʻohana.

The word ʻohana means family, kin, group or related. Oha means to spread, thrive, to grow lush. ʻOhā describes a taro corm growing from the older root, especially from the stalk of the kalo. It figuratively means offspring, youngsters, (Pukui 1983, 276). From Hāloa, our elder sibling, we are nourished and fed, spiritually and physically. When we put cooked kalo into our mouths, or taste the cool texture of freshly mixed poi, we are being fed by Hāloa. When we think about the ʻāina, that which feeds us, that which sustains us, and that from which we are connected by genealogy, how can we not embody Hāloa? We are the land and the land is us.

In tandem with the foundation of the Hāloa triad, the sustainable growth of kalo or Hāloa and its offshoots, Kākoʻo ʻŌiwi's upper management and core workers must be mediated by meaningful relationships which are socially or culturally appropriate, recognizes and incorporates economic strategies that sees humans as capital and perhaps the most critical, honors the 'āina. Indicative of the difficulty in executing a more adaptive and sustainable management strategies, Kāko'o 'Ōiwi is, nonetheless, attempting to integrate traditional customary values into the framework of triple bottom-line organizational tenets; one that seeks to make sustainability a form of environmental resilience.

Planting back is tantamount to returning to or engendering kalo as Hāloa, that is, the genealogical link between 'āina as Papahānaumoku and Kānaka Maoli. In other words, replanting both kanaka and kalo serves as a spiritual and practical guide for contemporary Kānaka 'Ōiwi working to restore personal and familial relationships to 'āina. The cultural construct of kalo as Hāloa who are rooted to the land is the piko (umbilical cord) that attaches Māhuahua 'Ai o Hoi to the 'āina. In this way, both kalo and kānaka are re-planted and re-generated, literally, physically and spiritually, into the lepo and the cultural landscape. Hence, the propagation of kalo and the making and production of poi serve as acts of resurgence, which resist settler colonial and capitalist paradigms and definitions of economic success. The restoration of these land-based practices brings to the forefront an irrepressible resistance, determined resilience, and a cultural resurgence that allows the Kānaka Maoli body, spirit, and intellect to return to Hāloa.

Conclusions

Our ethnographic experiences indicate that the restoration of kalo farming and the production of poi by Māhuahua 'Ai o Hoi in the He'e'ia wetland is, in and of itself, a planting back of all things Indigenous, physical and spiritual, seen and unseen. Are there challenges? Yes, the difficulties are many and complex, but those hardships test our resilience. Despite attempts to eradicate Kānaka Maoli customary practices, the growing of kalo and of kanaka in the He'e'ia wetland is not only an embodied and regenerative experience for the kānaka body and kalo, it is also the ho'oulu (re-propagation) of resource management framed by Indigenous values that help us to achieve those critical benchmarks toward sustainable self-determination (Corntassel 2008).

Our approach posits customary and contemporary knowledge as the Indigenous/Kānaka Maoli centerpiece from which Māhuahua 'Ai o Hoi's ontological and pragmatic strategies might be incorporated in the re-cultivation of kalo and the reproduction of poi more broadly. We also acknowledge that landscape degradation, deterioration of the 'adati, a serious lack of funding for various kinds of material and human resources, and management challenges are indicative of the struggles that Indigenous community-driven efforts such as Māhuahua 'Ai o Hoi experience. Yet for all of the trials and tribulations one thing remains clear: there is a resolute persistence, dedication, and commitment to the agricultural restoration of the He'e'ia wetland. The steep learning curve is part of the process of becoming resilient and resurgent once again. What the He'e'ia wetland offers is an optimal location for reclaiming and restoring Indigenous presence, one that generates traditional foods (kalo, poi, banana, breadfruit, sweet potato) for a healthy diet and a pathway to resilience. Confirmed in the analysis of our ethnographic field notes, observations, surveys and interviews, is that Native Hawaiian cultural knowledge and contemporary systems used at Māhuahua 'Ai o Hoi in the production of kalo and making of poi, while challenging, continues. The hardships in the milling of poi, meeting orders, having enough kalo for poi continue but while success may seem daunting, positive achievements have been made. Poi is available to the community at an affordable price. Additionally, Kāko'o 'Ōiwi staff have planted more than twenty rows of mixed greens and other vegetables, which are then sold to local restaurants. Diversification is adaptation, but the production of poi and the cultivation of kalo are a key mechanism for restoring Kānaka Maoli sense abilities born of our genealogical relation to 'āina and kalo. In this way the planting of kalo is an act of resistance, a way to recall, re-immerse and revive the pathways of the ancestors not only in the cultivation and harvesting of kalo for poi, but as a tangible and cultural provision in the quest for food security, food sovereignty and resilience.

Acknowledgements

We want to thank the Kāko'o 'Ōiwi staff for sharing their time with us and for trusting us with their mana'o (thoughts insights).

Disclosure statement

No potential conflict of interest was reported by the authors.

Funding

This paper is funded by a grant/cooperative agreement from the National Oceanic and Atmospheric Administration, Project R/SB-4, which is sponsored by the University of Hawai'i Sea Grant College Program, SOEST, under Institutional Grant No. NA09OAR4170060, NA14OAR4170071 from NOAA Office of Sea Grant, Department of Commerce. The views expressed herein are those of the authors and do not necessarily reflect the views of NOAA or any of its subagencies. UNIHI-SEAGRANT-JC-12-37.

THE FOODWAYS OF HAWAI'I

Notes

1. The associative meanings and spellings of Heeia, He'eia, He'e'ia reflectâ the orthography of the Hawaiian language. In this essay we use He'e'ia because it reflects the geographical, topographical, and cultural significance of this place. The word he'e is commonly known as octopus and also means to slide, surf, slip or flee (Pukui 1983, 63). 'Ia is a particle marking passive/imperative and eia is an idiom that means here, here is, here are, this place. As such, it is understood that the He'e'ia is a place with abundant he'e and a place that is slippery from the numerous streams and springs
2. In this essay we use Kānaka Maoli and Kānaka 'Ōiwi interchangably to refer to the Indigenous peoples of Hawai'i. Kanaka, when used as a noun, refers to person; kā naka is the plural form. Moali and 'ōiwi are adjectives that refer to the real or true people of this place.
3. For a discussion of Indigenous resurgence as a new paradigm in Indigenous politics see Alfred (2005); Simpson (2011); Corntassel (2012).
4. For an extended discussion of the Māhele see Kame'eleihiwa (1992); Preza (2010); (Perkins 2013); Beamer (2014).
5. All of Pauahi's lands were transferred to Kamehameha Schools Bishop Estate Trust (KSBE) after her death in 1884. The KSBE Trust managed all of Pauahi's lands (King and Roth 2006).
6. In 1991, Governor John Waihe'e, on behalf of the state of Hawai'i, entered into an agreement with the landowners Kamehameha Schools-Bishop Estate to swap state-owned land in Kaka'ako, a neighborhood in Honolulu adjacent to Waikīkī, with the 400 acres of wetland. The land swap was in response to community opposition against KSBE's plans to dredge the wetland in order to develop luxury condomiums, harbors, and a golf course. Although there were efforts to turn the wetland into a public park or to restore the lo'i, they were not successful.
7. The name Māhuahua 'Ai o Hoi was given to the project area by Kumu Hula Kawaikapuokalani Hewett, a lineal descendant, Native Hawaiian language expert and noted loea from the He'e'ia ahupua'a.
8. We argue that the orientation for community workday volunteers is a critical piece in the introduction of He'e'ia Uli or Hoi to those who come there to work and to learn. Given the familial relationship between kānaka and place it is important for visitors to be properly introduced to the 'āina. Who you are and where you come from is particularly significant and, as such, protocols for entering a place are paramount because it is respectful of the 'āina. The simplest or basic forms of protocol should consist of a kāhea (a recited greeting) from the visitor, a pane (response or answer) from the host, noi (asking permission from the 'āina, the gods, as particularly associated with He'e'ia Uli), all done with ho'ihi (reverence and respect).
9. Kāko'o 'Ōiwi's mission is to perpetuate the cultural and spiritual practices of Native Hawaiians. The family of descendants of the 'āiss and the community at large stressed the need for the project to grow kalo and make poi once again in He'e'ia Uli. The kūpuna or elders of the community who have the most ancestral ties to He'e'ia are guiding the project using integrated resource management and place-based approaches. This includes the use of science, collaborative partnerships with educational institutions, community organizations, and volunteers and preserving the cultural landscape by keeping as much open space as possible.

FOOD, CULTURE & SOCIETY

10. This research was funded in part by a grant from the University of Hawai'i Sea Grant Program.
11. Where possible we omit names of Kāko'o 'Ōiwi staff members. When the narrative suffers for lack of clarity pseudonyms are used.

References

Alfred, Taiaiake. 2005. *Wasáse : Indigenous Pathways of Action and Freedom*. Peterborough, Canada: Broadview Press.

Alfred, Taiaiake, and Jeff Corntassel. 2005. "Being Indigenous: Resurgences against Contemporary Colonialism." *Government and Opposition* 40 (4): 597–614.

Beamer, Kamanamaikalani. 2014. *No Makou Ka Mana: Liberating the Nation*. Honolulu: Kamehameha Publishing.

Berkes, Fikret. 2012. *Sacred Ecology*. 3rd ed. New York: Routledge.

Corntassel, Jeff. 2008. "Toward Sustainable Self-Determination: Rethinking the Contemporary Indigenous-Rights Discourse." *Alternatives* 33 (1): 105.

Corntassel, Jeff. 2012. "Re-Envisioning Resurgence: Indigenous Pathways to Decolonization and Sustainable Self-Determination." *Decolonization: Indigeneity, Education & Society* 1 (1). http://decolonization.org/index.php/des/article/view/18627.

Fa'anunu, Angela, Brian Cruz, and Hallet H. Hammet. 2009. *Cultural Impact Assessment for King Intermediate School at Kalimaloa, He'eia Ahupua'a, Ko'olaupoko District, O'ahu Island, TMK: [1] 4-6-004:002 (por)*. Kailua: Cultural Surveys Hawai'i.

Goodyear-Ka'ōpua, Noelani. 2009. Rebuilding the 'Auwai: Connecting Ecology, Economy and Education in Hawaiian Schools. *AlterNative: An International Journal of Indigenous Scholarship* 5 (2): 46–47.

Kāko'o 'Ōiwi. 2010. *Māhuahua 'Ai o Hoi, He'eia Wetland Restoration, Strategic Plan 2010–2015*. Kāne'ohe: Kāko'o 'Ōiwi.

Kame'eleihiwa, Lilikalā. 1992. *Native Land and Foreign Desires: Pehea La E Pono Ai?*. Honolulu: Bishop Museum Press.

Kelly, Marion. 1989. "Dynamics of Production Intensification in Precontact Hawai'i." In *What's New? A Closer Look at the Process of Innovation*, edited by Sander Van der Leeuw and Robin Torrence, 82–106. London: Unwin Hyman.

King, Samuel P., and Randall W. Roth. 2006. *Broken Trust: Greed, Mismangagement and Political Manipulation at America's Largest Charitable Trust*. Honolulu: University of Hawai'i Press.

Lucas, Paul F. Nahoa. 1995. *A Dictionary of Hawaiian Legal Land Terms*. Honolulu: Native Hawaiian Legal Corporation.

McGregor, Daviana P. 2007. *Nā Kua'āina: Living Hawaiian Culture*. Honolulu: University of Hawai'i Press.

Nelson, Melissa K., ed. 2008. *Original Instructions: Indigenous Teachings for a Sustainable Future*. Rochester, VT: Bear & Company.

Oliveira, Katrina-Ann R., and Kapā'anaokalāokealoa Nākoa. 2014. *Ancestral Places: Understanding Kanaka Geographies*. Corvallis: Oregon State University Press.

Perkins, Mark Umi. 2013. "Kuleana: A Genealogy of Native Tenant Rights." PhD diss., University of Hawai'i at Mānoa.

Preza, Donovan C. 2010. "The Empirical Writes Back: Re-Examining Hawaiian Dispossession Resulting from the Mahele of 1848." MA thesis, University of Hawai'i at Mānoa.
Pukui, Mary Kawena. 1983. *Ōlelo No'eau: Hawaiian Proverbs and Poetical Sayings*. Honolulu: Bishop Museum Press.
Rhodes, Frank H. T. 2012. *Earth: A Tenant's Manual*. New York: Cornell University Press.
Simpson, Leanne. 2011. *Dancing On Our Turtle's Back: Stories of Nishnaabeg Re-Creation, Resurgence, and a New Emergence*. Winnipeg: Arbeiter Ring Publishing.

Farmer Typology in South Kona, Hawai'i: Who's Farming, How, and Why?

Noa Kekuewa Lincoln and Nicole Ardoin

Abstract

Agricultural systems are increasingly being recognized as producing a wide range of benefits and impacts on society, and the potential of small-scale farmers in particular has been highlighted. Recognition of farmers' varying drivers and priorities is important for developing appropriate policies and engagement strategies to foster multifunctional agricultural practices that generate multiple social benefits from agricultural lands. The use of typologies to classify the diversity of farmers and their respective farming priorities is a practical way to understand important decision-making drivers and capture impacts. This article classifies 128 farmers in the South Kona region of Hawai'i by assessing their reasons for farming. The types of farmers are discussed regarding their environmental and sense of place values, and an MFA scorecard measuring farming practices in five categories: Environment, Economics, Education, Community, and Culture. Farmer types explained a significant amount of variation seen in each category, suggesting that reason for engaging in farming is an important driver in farming practices; however, significant nuanced variation on value expression in farming practices was apparent.

Introduction

Agricultural systems are increasingly being recognized as producing a wide range of benefits and impacts on society, including environmental, economic, and socio-cultural (Millennium Ecosystem Assessment [MEA] 2005). These impacts of farming have been forwarded in scientific and political debates under the concept of *multifunctional agriculture* (e.g. Renting et al. 2009). Small-scale farmers, in particular, have been highlighted as an essential element provider of such benefits (UNCTAD 2013). Although many stress the importance of multifunctional landscapes and communities (e.g. O'Farrell et al. 2010), the objectives of individual farmers may not align with these higher-level goals desired by communities, governments, or global organizations (Gilg 2009). For example, technological or programmatic incentives to improve agricultural practices often exist but are not adopted by farmers (e.g. Ahnstrom et al. 2008; Reimer et al. 2012), while conversely other farmers engage in environmentally or socially beneficial practices even at personal cost (e.g. Kabii and Horwitz, 2006; Ryan et al. 2010). Recognition of the different drivers and priorities of farmers is important for developing appropriate policies and engagement strategies to foster development of multifunctional agricultural practices and the multiple benefits resulting to society from agricultural lands.

The use of *typologies* to classify the diversity of farmers is a practical way to capture important drivers in their decision-making process and their impacts (Darnhofer et al. 2005). Such groupings may help us to understand and anticipate responses to programmatic incentives, particularly as certain typologies become more or less dominant in certain regions over time (Valbuena et al. 2008; Carmona et al. 2010; Van de Steeg et al., 2010). Farmer types are often used to distinguish between groups that, even under similar conditions, do not necessarily make similar choices (Darnhofer and Walder 2013). Researchers typically use typologies to address specific research questions with most applications using the production system to define related groups (e.g. Duvernoy 2000; Köbrich et al., 2003; Carmona et al. 2010; Nainggolan et al. 2013); fewer studies have used this technique to examine value-based or other underlying drivers (e.g. Darnhofer et al. 2005; Greiner et al. 2009).

Some underlying drivers shown to influence farmers' practices include economics (e.g. Maybery et al. 2005), social pressure (e.g. Michel-Guillou and Moser 2006), personal values (e.g. Schoon and Te Grotenhuis 2000), environmental awareness (e.g. McCann et al. 1997), environmental knowledge (e.g. Fairhead and Scoones 2005), motivation and risk perception (e.g. Greiner et al. 2009) and sense of place (e.g. Ryan et al. 2010), among others. These and other studies strongly suggest that value-based drives may be translated into reasons and motivations for farming and specific actions at the farm level (e.g. Lincoln and Ardoin 2015, Schoon and Te Grotsenhuis 2000). This approach, encompassing individual drivers and farm-level analyses, falls into the "actor-oriented approaches," as opposed to the "market regulation," "land-use," or "public regulation" approaches as defined by Renting et al. (2009). According to a review by Pannell et al. (2006), the adoption of innovations, such as conservation practices, is principally influenced by the character and circumstance of the farmer.

Building upon the statement by Pannell et al. (2006), we develop a farmer typology defined by character and circumstance for the agricultural community of Kona, Hawai'i to explore the impact on agricultural practices and the nuanced interactions between agricultural practices and values. This region has undergone, and continues to undergo, a massive shift in agricultural focus and demographics; using typologies, we aim to understand how these shifts have and will continue to affect agricultural sustainability. In essence, we are interested in delving into the relationship between values and practices. Utilizing surveys, we examine motivations and values at the farm level to develop a typology based on *why* individuals are using agricultural lands, which is then used as a lens through which we examine *who* is using the agricultural landscape in terms of basic demographics, and environmental and place-based values. Finally, how the individual farmer is farming is discussed as a function of the farmer types. Through this process, we examine priorities and outcomes among groups of farmers, and how these outcomes impact the broader landscape and community. We conclude by using our results to interpret current trends in the farming landscape and how certain interventions may help meet stated agricultural goals regarding local food production and multifunctional agriculture.

Site History

Our study site was the South Kona region, located on the leeward side of Hawai'i Island, Hawai'i. Before European contact, Kona supported a vast network of agricultural developments, covering sixty square miles in intensive agriculture and another sixty square miles in sparser, informal agriculture (Newman 1971; Ladefoged et al. 2009; Lincoln and Ladefoged 2014; Lincoln et al. 2014). This extensive agricultural landscape supported a burgeoning population, elite class, complex political hierarchy, and robust supply of luxury goods (Kirch 2010). Complex systems of land tenure and resource management supported populations that in most locales were similar or greater than that which exists today (Dye 1994). The extent and productivity of Hawaiian agriculture is unparalleled in the pre-industrial tropics, and the mechanisms of its operation are still poorly understood.

Following the arrival of Capt. James Cook in 1778, Kona agriculture evolved to include new plants and economies, but remained highly productive and essential to the sustenance of the people. Until 1845, lands were primarily worked as small plots that represented family-tenured parcels. After land privatization in 1848, large-scale, organized plantation agriculture and ranching grew rapidly. Coffee production, in particular, thrived in Kona and grew substantially from 1850 through the 1880s. In the 1890s, the coffee industry experienced difficulties; many plantations were divided into small lots (three to twenty acres) and by 1915 tenant farmers were cultivating most of the coffee in Kona. Large landowners—who owned the infrastructure, goods, and markets—controlled the aggregation of coffee through lease contracts, competition, and the control of food and retail distribution. The Great Depression caused a mass exodus from Kona, which finally broke the plantations' hold; large mills closed and gave way to farmers' cooperatives, and lessee farmers gained more opportunities to buy their own farmland. Since the late 1940s, there has been a continued revival of coffee in Kona. Through rigorous community organizing to develop and preserve the branding of Kona Coffee, local producers have been able to obtain a sale price that is substantially above the industry average since 1994 (Page et al. 2007). Despite some market declines, the South Kona region is still the core of Hawai'i's coffee industry today.

Beginning in the early 1970s, Hawai'i's agriculture has shifted in important ways, driven by the closure of plantations (primarily sugarcane and pineapple) across Hawai'i. These closures simultaneously created more farms and farmers while significantly decreasing the total land farmed. Hawai'i, and Kona specifically, has seen a revitalization of diversified agriculture in the wake of the plantations (Page et al. 2007). This growth has intensified over the past decade with an increased statewide focus on food security, as well as broader national and global food movements focused on local production and self-sufficiency. Unfortunately, Hawai'i still performs poorly in terms of food self-sufficiency. Despite having over 1,000,000 acres of active agricultural lands, Hawai'i produces a mere 15 percent of its food locally (KS-LAD 2009). Some of the most fertile and potentially productive soils in the state are utilized for low-yielding activities such as pasture and timber, or are even left fallow.

Contemporarily, Kona is a patchwork of agricultural development. There is still a strong presence of coffee on the landscape, but it is variable. There are well-maintained coffee farms of original plantings, poorly maintained "wild" coffee farms, farms that grow other crops alongside remnant coffee, and newly bulldozed farms planted with fresh coffee. Macadamia nuts are also prevalent, with the same mix of plantings and maintenance. At the same time, there is a range of diversified agriculture with various levels of success. For instance, several apiaries exist in Kona, including the world's largest exporter of queen bees. There are some small pockets of traditional Hawaiian agriculture, and a range of diversified fruit and vegetable growers. To support these various endeavors, many cooperative organizations exist that that facilitate joint marketing, advocacy, and processing. In addition to agricultural production, some operations have added alternative activities and revenue streams, such as agricultural education and agricultural tourism. Vacation or long-term rentals constitute a significant portion of total farm income for many agricultural lands.

The social makeup of Hawai'i and Kona has also changed dramatically. Hawai'i has seen a considerable turnover of population over the last several decades. As indicated by the American Community Survey conducted by the Census Bureau, new out-of-state immigrants constitute over 5 percent of Hawai'i's population each year (US Census 2012). While many of these immigrants leave again, this is nonetheless indicative of a rapidly changing demographic. This considerable and consistent shift in the local population can be expected to change the "local" values and norms associated with individual communities.

Methods

Surveys and organization

This study was conducted in the South Kona region on Hawai'i Island, Hawai'i, in the communities of Hōnaunau, Captain Cook, Kealakekua, and Hōlualoa. The area was chosen for its primary designation as agriculturally zoned lands, its relatively small farm sizes, and its highly diverse population in regards to cultural background, length of residency, and socio-economic status. Between June 2010 and February 2011, we conducted on-site oral surveys,[1] ranging from 45 to 210 minutes, and farm inspections with 128 farmers (Figure 1). Respondents consisted of 82 males and 46 females, ranging in age from 31 to 78. The most common educational attainment was a bachelor's degree and the most common household income range was $30,000–45,000/year. With regard to ethnic background, 25 percent of respondents were of Asian descent, 16 percent were of Native Hawaiian decent, 82 percent were of European descent, and 13 percent reported other ethnicity.[2] The average duration of residence in Kona was 18.3 years. These figures for income and race generally align with overall statistics describing the South Kona population (US Census 2010).

In this article, we focus on four principal areas of the survey: motivations for farming, environmental and place-based values, farming practices, and demographics (age, education, income, race/ethnicity, farm size, time as a farmer, length of residence, and time period of immigration). We use typologies to delve further into the relationships seen in a previous study between both environmental values and sense of place with farming practices (Lincoln and Ardoin 2016) by examining how values and farming practices differ among groups of farmers.

Analysis Tools and Development of a Multifunctional Agriculture (MFA) Scorecard

Environmental values were measured with the New Ecological Paradigm, using all fifteen items from Dunlap et al. (2000). Sense of place was measured using the nineteen items from Ardoin et al. (2012). A multifunctional agricultural (MFA) scorecard measuring farming practices was developed[1] to represent local goals regarding agricultural sustainability in five categories: Community, Environment, Economics, Education, and Culture. Between eight and 12 individual items were used to score each category. Items measuring practices were adopted from several sources in the literature, and selected based on stated goals in multiple local agricultural development plans at the organizational, community, county, and state levels.

Survey items were used to create scales of environmental values, sense of place, and farming practices in each of the five categories, which were amalgamated to create an overall measurement of MFA that includes social, economic and environmental impacts; this MFA scorecard occurs on a scale of 0–5 and represents the agricultural "scores" reported throughout the paper and figures.

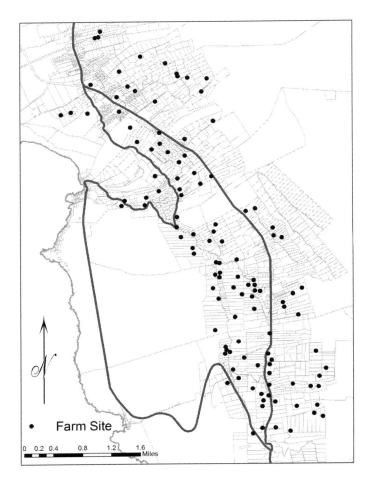

Fig. 1: Location of farms surveyed in South Kona, Hawai'i Island, Hawai'i.

The Cronbach's alpha (Mallery and George 2010) of these scales indicates their reasonable usage as coherent scale items (Table 2). We used SPSS 20.0™ (IBM Corp., Armonk, NY) for analysis of survey items. We transcribed open-ended questions using a combination of a priori and open coding and processed the transcriptions data both qualitatively and quantitatively, preserving intact thoughts and using qualitative analysis. Data management and coding for open-ended data was conducted using NVivo 10™ (QSR Int., Burlington, MA).

A typology of farmers was developed to examine previously recognized relationships between environmental values, sense of place, and demographic items as they pertain to agricultural practices (see Lincoln and Ardoin 2016). We distill the survey results and organize them through the lens of farmer type, presenting both statistical results and supporting qualitative statements. These results are then discussed in a synthesis that pulls on the researchers' broader experience within the community.

Development of farmer typology

We utilize local knowledge and grounded theory as a lens through which to examine the results. During the survey process, we noted the recurring theme from participants suggesting distinct groups of farmers in the region; we therefore developed a typology based on survey responses to reflect the local perception. We follow the general method for developing typologies presented by Escobar and Berdegue (1990) and Valbuena et al. (2008), slightly modified, to conduct: (1) selection of framework, (2) selection of criteria, (3) collection of data, (4) parameterization, (5) allocation, and (6) validation. We perceived that the typological division should relate primarily to the purpose of individuals occupying agricultural lands and what they did with their agricultural goods. We then selected a number of survey items addressing concepts, such as, "How important is it to profit from your farm activities?"; "In managing your farm, how important is it to have a beautiful property?"; and "In managing your farm, how considerate are you of meeting state agricultural requirements?" All survey items were standardized. In the case of highly correlated variable ($r^2 \geq 0.90$), variables were averaged to create a single item.

Principal Component Analysis (PCA) and Cluster Analysis (CA) were conducted in SPSS (Carmona et al. 2010). PCA condenses the selected variables into a smaller number of discrete non-correlated components, and CA is used to classify the observations by computing the similarity between any pair of observations (Köbrich et al., 2003). A Kaiser–Maier–Olkin (KMO) test and Bartlett's test of sphericity were used to check the suitability of the variables for PCA; KMO value was > 0.8 and Bartlett's test was significant ($p < 0.01$), indicating suitability (Field 2009). We retained components with eigenvalues > 1 (Kaiser's criterion). Following the selection of components, we characterized different types of farmers using a CA. Survey participants indicated at least three and up to six farmer types. We, therefore, ran multiple CAs, forcing the amount of groups to three, four, five, and six; the CA with the highest measure of cohesion and separation was retained.

Finally, each group was "identified" based on respondents' descriptions of farmer types. A simple validation was conducted by examining the coded results of two open-ended questions, "What are the three most important reasons for you engaging in agriculture?" and "What are the three most important reasons for you choosing this parcel of property?"

Results

Farmer typology

A consistent theme of farmer types emerged naturally in response to an open-ended survey question that asked respondents to, "Describe the farming community in South Kona." Of the 128 responses, sixty-two (48 percent) described the farming community by types of farmers. These groupings ranged from very specific to very broad descriptions. For example, one of the broadest descriptions loosely grouped farmers as:

> ... those that have to farm, those that want to farm, and those that don't really farm.

Another interviewee proposed a more detailed grouping:

> There are the coffee farmers, obviously. Most of them do it because that's what they grew up with. Or they bought an established farm. And there's the Hawaiians and the other old timers who still grow just to feed the family. They still trade a lot. Smoked meat for kalo (taro), or whatever you get. Some of the hippies who have moved here do the same thing amongst themselves. The big one now is all the retirees. They like it because the weather is nice and the land is nice. And it's cheap! Or it was before they came and drove up the price. Some of them actually do a good job farming. They don't got anything else to do. But others are just here for the view.

We developed a five-class farmer typology: Classic Farmers, Hobby Farmers, Leisure Farmers, Progressive Farmers, and Subsistence Farmers (Table 1).[3] Here we briefly describe each type based on descriptions from respondents and observations of the farms:

- *Classic Farmers'* primary employment and income is farming, growing one or more of the well-known regional cash-crops, namely coffee or macadamia nuts, selling through classic economic pathways, and engaging in some level of processing. A single crop dominates these farmers' land, typically in a mono-crop style of agriculture.
- For *Hobby Farmers*, agriculture is not a livelihood, or even necessarily a priority. They were alternatively described as "retiree farmers," "backyard farmers," or "the gardeners." They engage in farming but are not focused on production, although many see production as a side-benefit. These farmers spend less than full time on farm activities, generate the majority of their income from non-farming sources, and typically only sell what is convenient.
- *Leisure Farmers* were also referred to as "gentleman farmers" and "non-farmers." Their primary reasons for occupying agricultural lands relate to land benefits, such as property size, tax and water rates, semi-remote location, and the ability to write off farm expenses. Leisure Farmers typically engage in minimal agricultural activities in order to maintain their occupation.
- *Progressive Farmers* rely on agriculture as their livelihood and produce atypical goods such as honey, fish, vegetables, tropical fruit, flowers, or other crops. Other descriptions of this category included "innovative

THE FOODWAYS OF HAWAI'I

Table 1. Items used for typology classification, indicating high (+), moderate (+/–), and low (–) results for each item by farmer type.

Item description	Farmer type				
	Classic	Hobby	Leisure	Progressive	Subsistence
Importance to profit from property	+	+/–	–	+	–
Importance to feed others	–	+/–	–	–	+
Importance to satisfy state or lesser requirements	–	–	+	–	–
Importance of beautiful property	–	+	+	–	+/–
Percentage of goods sold	+	+/–	–	+	–
Percentage of cash crops	+	+/–	–	–	–
Labor hours	+	–	–	+	+

farmers," "alternative farmers," the "farmers with all the technology," and "the ones growing all the new-kind stuff." These farmers often use informational and mechanical technology to expand the farm's capabilities, such as through aquaculture or processed products (e.g. essential oils or processed foods).

- *Subsistence Farmers*, also described as "traditional farmers" or "hippy farmers," prioritize growing food to feed themselves, their family and friends, and the community. These farmers consume, trade, or give away the majority of their agricultural goods. They tend not to engage much in classic economic pathways and also tend to need outside income to support their farming lifestyle.

General validation of this classification examined the responses from two open-ended questions probing (1) the reasons for engaging in agriculture and (2) the reasons for occupying their particular parcel of land (Table 2). This simple validation showed differences in the coded responses that generally reflect the values associated with each farmer type. For us, this confirmed that the typology was accurately grouping farmers by their value-based drivers.

FOOD,
CULTURE &
SOCIETY

Using the typology, we examined the distribution of the survey results within each category of farmer we defined (Table 3); ANOVA showed that farmer types differed significantly by environmental values (r^2 0.31, $p < 0.001$), sense of place (r^2 0.48, $p < 0.001$), income (r^2 0.34, $p < 0.001$), ancestral or personal immigration (r^2 0.20, $p < 0.001$), length of residency (r^2 0.19, $p < 0.001$), and

Table 2. Grouped response to open-ended questions: (1) Please explain your top three reasons for engaging in agriculture, and (2) Please explain your top three reasons for obtaining this particular property.

Type	n	Reason for agriculture	Percent	Reason for property	Percent
Classic	37	Economic opportunity	84	Affordable	78
		Rural lifestyle	57	Proximity to infrastructure	57
		Legacy	46	Land attributes	57
Hobby	31	Work outdoors	77	Affordable	94
		Community dynamic	58	Existing agriculture	81
		Environment/nature	58	Climate	77
Leisure	11	Open space	73	Affordable	64
		Low/lower taxes	64	Scenery	64
				Taxes	55
Progressive	32	Economic opportunity	88	Affordable	78
		Rural lifestyle	56	Agricultural opportunity	66
		Environment/nature	45	Proximity to infrastructure	66
Subsistence	17	Rural lifestyle	88	Affordable	82
		Community dynamic	76	Community/neighbors	76
		Environment/nature	59	Spiritual connection	53

farming practices (r^2 0.54, $p < 0.001$). No significant differences existed between farmer typology for age, education, or size of farm. We partitioned the responses into three categories: (1) demographics including income, length of residency in Hawai'i, and era of personal or ancestral immigration, (2) environmental values and sense of place, and (3) farming practices including the five categories of farm performance and an overall MFA score.

Farmer types and trends

Most farmer typologies utilize aspects of the farming system to define the farmer types. Our typology, however, focused on people's motivations for using agricultural lands as the defining variable, with only a single item relating to farm practices (the percentage of property planted with coffee or macadamia nuts). By largely removing the farming system from our typology definition, the results suggest how people's motivations for farming may translate into practices and, consequently, into impacts on the landscape, community and broader society. We present the following narratives to critically unravel the multifaceted and interactive relationships between farmers' values, demographics, and farming practices. Included are the interviewees' observations about Kona's changing community and farming landscape, and our analysis of how these patterns may be interpreted to inform current and future trends.

Farmer typology and multifunctional agriculture (MFA) practices—pathways to practice. Farmer types showed significant and substantial differences in their farming practice scores within each of the categories, and as an amalgamated MFA score (see Table 3). Since the groups were identified based on motivational and value-based differences, this finding speaks to the importance of individual actors in the expression or implementation of MFA practices. In this narrative, we delve further into the distinctions between the groups to better understand the pathways through which values manifest as farming practices.

Interestingly, the two groups with the highest (and statistically indistinguishable) MFA scores were those that might be perceived as being extremely different from each other: Subsistence Farmers and Progressive Farmers. Subsistence Farmers tended to avoid economic markets, grew highly diversified crops, and used few inputs or technology. In contrast, Progressive Farmers typically sold most of their goods, focused on one or two crops, and depended heavily on technology or inputs. The differences between these two farmer types could be seen in the results of individual survey items, as well as in field notes and qualitative interviewee statements. As one example, Subsistence Farmers scored higher in enhancing natural soil fertility and the non-use of chemicals, while Progressive Farmers scored higher in incorporating natural areas and enhancing wildlife. This implies that Progressive Farmers had less land devoted to agriculture, thereby enhancing the landscape, whereas Subsistence Farmers cared for their agricultural land better and thus also enhanced the landscape. The end results is that both farmer types scored well in the "Environmental" category, but through entirely different pathways.

From this, we interpret that Progressive Farmers excelled because of the high-value efficiency of time and land. As one case illuminated, an intensive aquaculture development utilized less than an acre of land and 25 hours per week, leaving four acres of land and many hours a week to devote to other activities, such as the cultivation of natural areas and educational or community engagement. In this sense, MFA and specific farm activities are related but do not necessarily overlap; the way Progressive Farmers operate their farms provides freedom to pursue other benefits. Subsistence Farmers, on the other hand, scored well because of the way they grew and distributed their crops. From our on-farm observations, we note that their farms were typically the most diverse, the most meticulously cared for, and often incorporated aspects of education or community engagement into their farming operations. For

FOOD,
CULTURE&
SOCIETY

Table 3. Mean values (and standard deviation) of key items and scales from survey by farmer typology.

Demo-graphics	Leisure	Hobby	Subsist-ence	Progres-sive	Classic	Total
n	11	31	31	18	37	128
Income	110,000 (14,000)	47,000 (36,000)	30,500 (18,000)	62,000 (28,000)	38,500 (22,500)	48,000 (33,500)
Residency	10.8 (7.3)	15.9 (14.3)	36.2 (21.2)	20.3 (17.3)	26.3 (18.2)	24.0 (19.0)
Immigration	1.3 (0.5)	2.0 (1.5)	3.8 (1.8)	3.2 (1.7)	3.0 (1.9)	1.8 (1.8)
Values						
Environ-mental values	2.93 (0.61)	3.79 (0.59)	4.25 (0.42)	4.09 (0.60)	3.91 (0.48)	4.20 (0.52)
Sense of place	3.25 (0.31)	4.03 (0.39)	4.56 (0.34)	4.47 (0.30)	4.18 (0.44)	3.90 (0.62)
Farming practices						
Community	2.17 (0.49)	3.15 (0.81)	3.39 (0.75)	3.11 (0.86)	3.08 (0.54)	3.08 (0.76)
Culture	1.70 (0.27)	2.40 (0.59)	2.81 (0.66)	2.75 (0.48)	2.18 (0.50)	2.42 (0.63)
Economics	2.22 (0.27)	2.95 (0.70)	2.88 (0.42)	3.40 (0.25)	3.66 (0.37)	3.19 (0.62)
Education	1.75 (0.41)	2.71 (0.78)	3.04 (0.67)	2.97 (0.55)	2.56 (0.48)	2.69 (0.70)
Environ-ment	2.24 (0.28)	2.96 (0.74)	3.58 (0.53)	3.34 (0.51)	2.83 (0.35)	3.04 (0.63)
Total	2.01 (0.20)	2.84 (0.34)	3.14 (0.30)	3.11 (0.30)	2.86 (0.24)	2.88 (0.40)

Subsistence Farmers, the positive impacts were integrated into every aspect of farming practices, with environmental and community values expressed directly through the agricultural activities.

This presents opposing arguments for optimal agricultural development. One type exemplifies the benefits of high input–high output agriculture while the other demonstrates the benefits of holistic, integrated agriculture. One allows the time and resources to pursue external benefits, while the other integrates benefits into the farming process. From our analysis, both pathways have strong merit, and each tends to excel in slightly different areas. Despite their differences, notes from the interviews and on-site inspections indicated that these two groups represented the most passionate farmers—those who loved farming and wanted to do it well—even though the pathways they perceived as "doing agriculture well" may have differed substantially.

At the other end of the spectrum, Leisure Farmers had, by far, the lowest MFA score. This is not unexpected, since the survey itself was targeted towards farming practices and, in many ways, Leisure Farmers are not farmers. The occupation of agricultural lands by these users shows strong contradiction to expressed agricultural goals.

Farmer types, values, and value expression. Farmer types differed significantly in their scores for environmental values and sense of place (see Table 3). This appears to suggest either that environmental values and sense of place are influential in determining the type of farmer, or that the different types of farmers are inclined to develop different environmental and place values. We are inclined towards the former, but it is equally likely that feedback exists. For instance, coffee farming in the region appears to be socially reinforced, through historic trajectories, high engagement with cooperatives, and extensive educational opportunities. This form of social normative behavior was noted often within the open-ended responses. In discussion of farming practices, we often heard different forms of the same three responses: "That's the way it's always been done," "That's the way everybody does it," and "The extension guys said that's the best thing to do." Classic Farmers farm, more or less, the same way, which we argue is at least partially because of normative reinforcement. Over time, this may influence their perception of values regarding, for instance, good environmental practices in agriculture.

Using the entire data set, we previously reported that environmental and place values each independently correlate to MFA practices (Lincoln and Ardoin 2016). Furthermore, environmental values and sense of place each showed relative strengths in the different categories of MFA. Using our new lens, farmer type plays a significant role in our previously reported correlations between values and agriculture practices (Fig. 2). The Leisure Farmers have a particularly strong influence over the previously reported relationships, dominating the lower-left portion of either correlation: Leisure Farmers scored the lowest in sense of place, environmental values, and all categories of farming practices.

While we previously observed a linear correlation across all farmers between sense of place or environmental values and farming practices, these correlations were weaker, and in many cases not significant at all, when examined by farmer type. Although the sample size for each farmer type is small, these results suggest to us that environmental and place values may play a different role among the different farmer types. Classic Farmers, for instance, were relatively homogeneous (as indicated by the lowest coefficient of variation) in their farming practices, despite considerable variation in their environmental and place-based values. Conversely, within Hobby Farmers, both environmental and place-based values showed significant correlation to the broad range of farming practices observed. We perceive that the opportunity to express one's

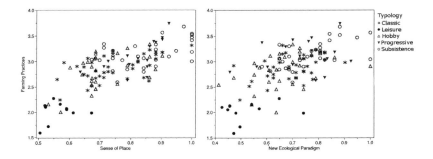

Fig. 2: Correlation of the New Ecological Paradigm and Sense of Place scales to the MFA scale by farmer type. New Ecological Paradigm and Sense of Place scales have a potential range of 0–1, MFA practices have a potential range of 0–5.

values is limited in the case of Classic Farmers, because they are bound economically to their style of agriculture and because their farming style is socially reinforced. Conversely, Hobby Farmers may express their values more freely, as they are not bound to farm income or any single crop or farming style. The potential for environmental or place-based values to be expressed in farming practices may be higher for farmers with fewer economic or social pressures.

Income—stifling values and empowering options. Although not a focus of our study, a multivariate fit model shows income—more than any other demographic—to have the strongest correlation to farmer type. Based on our data and observations, we believe the causality here to be bi-directional; the strength and direction of influence is dependent on the farmer type. Leisure Farmers (who have the highest income) appear to be defined by their pre-existing wealth, which allows them to acquire and manage their lands without generating any direct agricultural benefits. In this case, it seems reasonable to assume that income is driving the use of the land rather than the other way round. Individual survey items provide further evidence for this; all Leisure Farmers responded that their farms incurred losses and that virtually all of their income came from off-farm sources. Leisure Farmers even indicated in open-ended questions that farm losses were good for them, because farm-related losses are tax deductible. Conversely, Classic Farmers are highly reliant on farm income. Here, the land use clearly drives the farmers' income.

Progressive Farmers seem to encompass both directions of influence. Progressive Farmers indicated that they rely primarily on the farm income (74 percent), linking their relatively high, variable income to farming profits. However, many Progressive Farmers had high initial infrastructure costs, which suggests that being previously wealthy, or at least financially secure, played a role in developing their high-profit agriculture. So, while "reliant" on farming income, Progressive Farmers do have, or had, other significant sources of income as well. One Progressive Farmer described the situation as follows:

> Many people say that farming is really hard work, but it all depends how you farm. We grow hydroponics in those four greenhouses. It's all on timers, so we don't have to worry about irrigation. There is no weeds, so there is no weeding or spraying. And it's all sterile and clean, so we don't have to clean the produce before sending it out. All we really have to do is plant and harvest, and clean out the system every once in a while. It cost us a good chunk to get it all set up, but it was certainly worth it.

Conversely, some Progressive Farmers established their products with low infrastructure costs, but have still profited from their efforts, increasing their income based on farm products.

> About ten years ago we decided to start getting out of coffee.... We had just gone to [name omitted]'s course on how to grow cacao and make chocolate, and we thought, well, cacao seems like it could be something that could work. So we started planting within the coffee and a few short years later started getting our first pods. We ferment them in that simple rig ... my husband built out of an old rain barrel, and then we dry them on tables under the tent that's right there. It's all really simply and cheap, but the secret it is the timing.... And it's worked out for us financially—way better than coffee ever did.

As exemplified in the above quotes, in some cases it appears that financial security allowed the profitable farming practices in the first place, but in other cases it appears that the higher farm revenues are the main influence on the farmers' income level.

Subsistence Farmers had the lowest reported incomes ($30,500), are highly reliant on off-farm income, and their farm products typically provide non-economic benefits. Subsistence Farmers indicated that their farms generally broke even, but many expressed that they had difficulty with the question since the value of their farm products was generally not monetarily equated. Concurrently, while not explicitly asked, Subsistence Farmers expressed that the vast majority of their food consumption was achieved through harvest and trade. One Subsistence Farmer said, for example:

> We don't sell, but we get everything we need from the land—all our fruits and vegetables, all our starches. We get so much, we give away to all our 'ohana (extended family and close friends), and then they give back. We get fish and eggs and meat. We never go supermarket. Our supermarket is the 'āina (land).

Residency and trends in farmer types. Farmer types differed significantly by residency and immigration; the patterns seen are indicative of the changing population of the region, and, consequently, changing uses of the land. Residency (measured by how many years one had lived in Hawai'i) correlated very strongly ($r^2 = 0.92$) to immigration (measured by which era one's ancestry in Hawai'i dated to). We interpreted these results to mean that residency was the true representation of habitation length, rather than simply representing different age groups or other confounding correlations. Indeed, no significant relationship existed between age and length of residency. Length of residency correlated strongly with an individual's sense of place, which may be a process of developing and deepening place connection over time, or, conversely, a process of emigration of those with low levels of place connection—perhaps more generally.

Overall trends in residency by farmer type tell a story of a changing farming population in the region. Subsistence Farmers was the group with the longest residency, followed closely by Classic Farmers. The residency histogram for both groups showed a distinctive double peak, indicating two primary populations in this group. One population tended to be descendants of immigrants from the plantation era who had maintained the farms in the family for multiple generations, while the other tended to have immigrated within the last twenty years. This became evident in the interviews, where different versions of the same two tales were often related, such as these two examples:

> My grandfather worked the old coffee plantation. He worked hard, every day. And so did we. Get up, help pick, go to school, come home, help with the farm again. After ... my father was able to get his own farm. Now we still work hard, but we work for ourselves.

> I had always kinda wanted to be a farmer, to get away from the hustle, y'know? So I saved up enough money and started looking. When I found this land it seemed too good to be true.... But now I understand why they [previous owners] wanted to get out. Even with everything all set up it is still a lot of hard work. But even though [it is hard work], I still think it's worth it.

The histogram trends appear to indicate that there is a succession of these two farmer types, as indicated by the double peak in the population figures. However, this succession does not appear adequate to replace the aging, long-term population—suggesting that these two farmer types may be slowly dying out of the region.

At the other end of the spectrum, Leisure Farmers have the lowest time of residency, followed by Hobby Farmers. We do not find it coincidental that these two more casual farming types showed the lowest residency figures. We perceive that these two groups are more motivated by a desire to have land in Hawai'i than they are to engage in agriculture. For instance, Leisure Farmers accounted for only 8.5 percent of respondents but represented 45 percent of the part-time residents. These groups are more concerned with the non-agricultural attributes of the land than they are with the productive potential. The many auxiliary benefits of agricultural lands—such as lower tax rates, reduced water costs, large property size, and desirable locations—attract retirees or wealthy second landowners. Our survey respondents in this category were not shy to discuss their motivations and priorities. In the words of one respondent:

> I had wanted a second home in Hawai'i for a long time because my wife and I would come here several times a year.... I was worried that it was going to be a big pain to deal with the requirements [for agricultural lands], but it turns out that it was pretty simple. I had a consultant to develop an agricultural plan, had a few fruit trees planted, and here I am with my own slice of heaven. Pretty damn good deal if you ask me. I got a bigger house, more acreage, and a better view than if I had bought in town.

Although agricultural lands are zoned as such in order to promote and maintain local agricultural production, the requirements and enforcement regarding the land's proper usage are typically poor. Results of this poor enforcement can be seen in many areas in Hawai'i where high-end agricultural community developments cater to wealthy landowners. In these communities, it is not uncommon to have dwellings of several thousand square feet, while a handful of fruit trees, horses, or simply an agricultural plan are sufficient to qualify for the agricultural designation. While currently this phenomenon is less prevalent in Kona than other areas of the state, likely due to the high density of lease lands rather than fee simple parcels, small pockets of leisure farms do exist in the region.

As suggested by the low length of residency of Leisure and Hobby Farmers, these groups are largely composed of immigrants to Hawai'i. As immigration continues, it may be expected that these forms of casual farming will increase. Coupled with results regarding income, we also suggest that wealthier individuals are encroaching on desirable agricultural lands. This presents a danger of displacing farmers committed to agricultural production. The results of this trend are evidenced by the high cost of agricultural lease transfers in the area. For instance, it is common for a five-acre lease to be sold, with as little as ten years left on the agreement, for over $200,000. This high cost of obtaining leases from other tenants (for which a yearly rate is then charged by the landowner) is often described as a major barrier to those who want to farm as an occupation, while it is not a barrier to wealthier individuals who simply want to occupy agricultural lands.

The Progressive Farmers appear to be a special case. Statistically speaking, they showed the largest coefficient of variation and a well-distribute residency histogram; this suggests that Progressive Farmers were represented by newcomers, long-term residents, and others in between. We observed that the Progressive Farmers did not seem to fit any particular mold. Some Progressive Farmers even related how they had changed farming techniques over their tenure, and may have previously been Classic or Subsistence Farmers as they described themselves. Our interpretation is that these changes are reflective of larger social transformations, which is, in part, why they appear to affect all parts of the demographic. Therefore, while the shift from Classic/Subsistence Farmers to Hobby/Leisure Farmers is a manifestation of a changing demographic of the region, the shift to more Progressive Farmers represents larger shifts in knowledge and social norms regarding food and food systems.

Summary of results

This research emphasizes that is it important to consider *who* is farming, and that typologies may be an effective way to target specific groups of farmers and their motivations. *Who* is farming in our study relates very strongly to *how* they are farming. By defining individuals by their motivations, we see strong partitioning of their practices. Finally, we see that *why* individuals farm in these ways is not only a function of who they are, but of their situation, community and social norms, and their relationship to the place.

Overall, the typification of farmers by value-based drivers was an effective method for grouping. Farmer type played a significant role in the agricultural practices as measured by a multifunctional agricultural (MFA) scorecard. The variation in MFA scores across groups appears to be largely driven by people's underlying values and reasons for occupying agricultural lands. The expression of these values is influenced by social normative behaviors and income, which can stifle or empower value expression. A high reliance on farm income can stifle values, while greater wealth allows for value expression. The role of values is therefore not equal across farmer groups; while values play a key role in determining practices, some groups have a greater ability to express their values through practice than others. Length of residency correlated strongly with sense of place values, and ultimately to MFA scores. In the case of Kona, the large turnover and low habitation length among residents indicates a trend toward farmer groups that, in general, perform lower on our MFA scale.

Groups with similar values and agricultural practices express those values through very different pathways, as in the case of the Subsistence and Progressive Farmers. Similar scores in the MFA categories did not necessarily capture the variation seen in individual survey items. Furthermore, the specific pathways of how benefits were generated differed strongly, and were only illuminated through a detailed look at the individual practices. Generalizations represented by the typology go only so far; within each type, nuanced understandings of farmer practices are important for understanding the function and impact of each farm. No farm performed extremely well across every category of MFA, much less across all items; instead, each farm expressed particular strengths and weaknesses. Tradeoffs must be made regarding farming practices—there is only so much time and land within which an individual can work, and within the current support structure of our study area no farm can excel in all aspects of farming, land management, and social/community development. It may, therefore, be best for a farming region to have a mix of different farm types that can excel in different aspects and support a vibrant agricultural landscape overall.

Conclusion

This study suggests a changing farmer population that will correspondingly result in changing values and practices relating to agricultural lands in South Kona. We show that motivations and desires of these individuals are highly diverse and multifaceted. Because of the diverse interests and population of the Kona region, *who* is farming (or occupying agricultural lands) appears to be very important in moving towards self-sufficiency and multifunctional agriculture. Here we highlight some key actions based on this research that might facilitate a more sustainable food future for the islands.

- *Leisure Farmers* have a marginalizing place within the farming landscape, lacking a substantial contribution to sustainability or production of agricultural goods. They discuss manipulating the agricultural zoning regulations as an opportunity to lower their tax rate, while simultaneously increasing the competition and price for agricultural lands for individuals who actively farm. Thus, policy measures that more carefully enforce current agricultural zoning restrictions may prevent this unintended use (or non-use) of agricultural lands.
- *Hobby Farmers* constituted a large portion of the total farming population. Although they can and do contribute to MFA, food production and economics, they do so at a relatively small scale. Current demographic trends would suggest a continued increase in this farming group. Unlike Leisure Farmers, these farmers typically perform within the current agricultural zoning restrictions; therefore, to encourage Hobby Farmers to increase their productivity or to cede their land to more productive farmers would require more stringent agricultural land use restrictions.
- *Subsistence Farmers* are likely overlooked by "official" numbers regarding food production on the island because they do not engage in classic, accountable economic pathways. They are, however, substantial contributors to MFA in the region, being large producers of food and engaging heavily with the social aspects of the community. As such, many important agricultural reports such as Page et al. (2007), KS-LAD (2009), and the Kohala Center (2010) may systematically be underestimating food production, at least in the South Kona region.
- *Classic Farmers* engaging in cash crops for export do not contribute much to MFA, being relatively poor performers in environmental and social aspects. We add to this statement that they do not appear to be as successful economically as newer diversified agricultural producers, many of whom do contribute to local food production. Demographic trends indicate that this farming group is in decline, and supporting the transition to new diversified crops may help speed a shift to more beneficial forms of agriculture.

FOOD,
CULTURE &
SOCIETY

- *Progressive Farmers* are among the largest contributors to MFA, the agricultural economy and local food production, and often showed high returns for farmers. However, in general a higher level of expertise or startup capital is needed to engage in these types of endeavors. These types of farmers may be encouraged with better political or institutional support, such as education and training to develop expertise, or startup funds or loans to allow for their development.

If the farming population continues to shift towards a more casual farmer there may be social feedback as the dominant values and practices change. For example, the great increase in Leisure and Hobby farms makes a community of individuals who do not really care about agricultural issues. This would presumably result in less support for, and engagement with, farming cooperatives, extension services, etc. Subsequently, people who truly want to be good farmers may find it harder to find supporting resources because of the changing face of the community. Although people have conflicting ideas of how mobility and sense of place interact (Gustafson 2001), it does seem clear that high levels of immigration clearly change the cultural norms associated with a place, particularly when the immigration is so high as to make the local population a minority, as in the case of Kona (less than half the respondents were born in Hawai'i). To address such changes over time, tenant requirements of large private landowners and the state agricultural requirements should be adjusted and enforced to facilitate a population of farmers that provides the multiple benefits of agriculture society wants and needs for a sustainable future.

Acknowledgments

We would primarily like to acknowledge the many farmers who gave freely of their time to openly share their experiences.

Disclosure statement

No potential conflict of interest was reported by the authors.

THE FOODWAYS OF HAWAI'I

ORCiD

Nicole Ardoin http://orcid.org/0000-0002-3290-8211

Notes

1. Further details of the study methods are reported in Lincoln and Ardoin (2015), including development of the farming sustainability scale, along with a more extensive description of the research motivation and purpose.
2. Respondents were allowed to indicate multiple ethnicities if they identified as such.
3. Each of these terms was derived from an interviewee quote. We chose the terms we felt most adequately described each group of farmers.

References

Ahnström, J., J. Höckert, H. L. Bergeå, C. A. Francis, P. Skelton, and L. Hallgren. 2008. "Farmers and Nature Conservation: What is Known about Attitudes, Context Factors and Actions Affecting Conservation?" *Renewable Agriculture and Food Systems* 24 (1): 38–47.

Ardoin, N. M., J. S. Schuh, and R. K. Gould. 2012. "Exploring the Dimensions of Place: A Confirmatory Factor Analysis of Data From Three Ecoregional Sites." *Environmental Education Research* 18 (5): 583–607.

Carmona, A., L. Nahuelhual, C. Echeverria, and A. Baez. 2010. "Linking Farming Systems to Landscape Change: An Empirical and Spatially Explicit Study in Southern Chile." *Agriculture, Ecosystems and Environment* 139 (1–2): 40–50.

Darnhofer, I., W. Schneeberger, and B. Freyer. 2005. "Converting or not Converting to Organic Farming in Austria: Farmer Types and their Rationale." *Agriculture and Human Values* 22 (1): 39–52.

Darnhofer, I., and P. Walder. 2013. "Farmer Types and Motivation." In *Encyclopedia of Food and Environmental Ethics*. Dordrecht: Springer.

Dunlap, R. E., K. D. Van Liere, A. G. Mertig, and R. E. Jones. 2000. "Measuring Endorsement of the New Ecological Paradigm: A Revised NEP Scale." *Journal of Social Issues* 56 (3): 425–442.

Duvernoy, I. 2000. "Use of a Land Cover Model to Identify Farm Types in the Misiones Agrarian Frontier (Argentina)." *Agricultural Systems* 64 (3): 137–149.

Dye, T. 1994. "Population Trends in Hawai'i before 1778." *Hawaiian Journal of History* 28: 1–20.

Escobar, G., and J. Berdegue. 1990. "Conceptos y metodologías para la tipificación de sistemas de finca: la experiencia de RIMISP." In *Tipificación de Sistemas de Producción. RIMISP*, edited by G. Escobar and J. Berdegue, 13–43. Santiago de Chile: RIMISP.

Fairhead, J., and I. Scoones. 2005. "Local Knowledge and the Social Shaping of Soil Investments: Critical Perspectives on the Assessment of Soil Degradation in Africa." *Land Use Policy* 22: 33–41.

Field, A. P. 2009. *Discovering Statistics using SPSS (and Sex and Drugs and Rock 'n' Roll)*. 3rd ed. London: SAGE.

Gilg, A. 2009. "Perceptions about Land Use." *Land Use Policy* 26: S76–S82.

Greiner, R., L. Patterson, and O. Miller. 2009. "Motivations, Risk Perceptions and Adoption of Conservation Practices by Farmers." *Agricultural Systems* 99 (2): 86–104.

Gustafson, P. 2001. "Roots and Routes: Exploring the Relationship between Place Attachment and Mobility." *Environment and Behavior* 33 (5): 667–686.

Kabii, T., and P. Horwitz. 2006. "A review of Landholder Motivations and Determinants for Participation in Conservation Covenanting Programmes." *Environmental Conservation* 33 (1): 11.

KS-LAD (Kamehameha Schools Land Assets Division). 2009. *Strategic Agricultural Plan*. Honolulu: Kamehameha Schools Press.

Kirch, P. V. 2010. *How Chiefs Became Kings: Divine Kingship and the Rise of Archaic States in Ancient Hawai'i*. Oakland: University of California Press.

Köbrich, C., T. Rehman, and M. Khan. 2003. "Typification of Farming Systems for Constructing Representative Farm Models: Two Illustrations of the Application of Multi-variate Analyses in Chile and Pakistan." *Agricultural Systems* 76 (1): 141–157.

Ladefoged, T. N., P. V. Kirch, S. M. Gon, O. A. Chadwick, A. S. Hartshorn, and P. M. Vitousek. 2009. "Opportunities and Constraints for Intensive Agriculture in the Hawaiian Archipelago Prior to European Contact." *Journal of Archeological Science* 36: 2374–2383.

Lincoln, N. K., and N. M. Ardoin. 2016. "Cultivating Values: Environmental Values and Sense of Place as Correlates to Sustainble Agricultural Practices." *Agriculture and Human Values* 33 (2): 389–401.

Lincoln, N. K., O. Chadwick, and P. Vitousek. 2014. "Indicators of Soil Fertility and Opportunities for Precontact Agriculture in Kona, Hawai'i." *Ecosphere* 5 (April): 1–20.

Lincoln, N. K., and T. Ladefoged. 2014. "Agroecology of Pre-Contact Hawaiian Dryland Farming: The Spatial Extent, Yield and Social Impact of Hawaiian Breadfruit Groves in Kona, Hawai'i." *Journal of Archaeological Science* 49: 192–202.

Mallery, P., and D. George. 2010. *SPSS for Windows: Step by Step (17.0 update)*. Boston, MA: Allyn & Bacon.

Maybery, D., L. Crase, and C. Gullifer. 2005. "Categorizing Farming Values as Economic, Conservation and Lifestyle." *Journal of Economic Psychology* 26 (1): 59–72.

McCann, E., S. Sullivan, D. Erickson, and R. De Young. 1997. "Environmental Awareness, Economic Orientation, and Farming Practices: A Comparison of Organic and Conventional Farmers." *Environmental Management* 21 (5): 747–758.

Michel-Guillou, E., and G. Moser. 2006. "Commitment of Farmers to Environmental Protection: From Social Pressure to Environmental Conscience." *Journal of Environmental Psychology* 26 (3): 227–235.

Millennium Ecosystem Assessment. 2005. *Ecosystems and Human Well-Being: Scenarios*. Washington, DC: Island Press.

Nainggolan, D., M. Termansen, M. S. Reed, E. D. Cebollero, and K. Hubacek. 2013. "Farmer Typology, Future Scenarios and the Implications for Ecosystem Service Provision: A Case Study from South-eastern Spain." *Regional Environmental Change* 13 (3): 601–614.

Newman, T. S. 1971. "Hawaii Island Agricultural Zones, Circa A.D. 1823: An Ethnohistorical Study." *Ethnohistory* 18 (4): 335–351.

O'Farrell, P. J., B. Reyers, Le D. C. Maitre, S. J. Milton, B. Egoh, A. Maherry, C. Colvin, D. Atkinson, W. De Lange, J. N. Blignaut, and R. M. Cowling. 2010. "Multi-functional Landscapes in Semi Arid Environments: Implications for Biodiversity and Ecosystem Services." *Lands Ecol* 25 (8): 1231–1246.

Pannell, D. J., G. R. Marshall, N. Barr, A. Curtis, F. Vanclay, and R. Wilkinson. 2006. "Understanding and Promoting Adoption of Conservation Technologies by Rural Landholders." *Australian Journal of Experimental Agriculture* 46: 1407–1424.

Page, C., L. Bony, and L. Schewel. 2007. *Island of Hawaii Whole System Project Phase I Report*. Colorado: Rocky Mountain Institute.

Reimer, A. P., A. W. Thompson, and L. S. Prokopy. 2012. "The Multi-dimensional Nature of Environmental Attitudes among Farmers in Indiana: Implications for Conservation Adoption." *Agriculture and Human Values* 29 (1): 29–40.

Renting, H., W. A. H. Rossing, J. C. J. Groot, J. D. Van der Ploeg, C. Laurent, D. Perraud, D. J. Stobbelaar, and M. K. Van Ittersum. 2009. "Exploring Multifunctional Agriculture: A Review of Conceptual Approaches and Prospects for an Integrative Transitional Framework." *Journal of Environmental Management* 90: S112–S123.

Ryan, R. L., D. L. Erickson, and R. D. Young. 2010. "Farmers' Motivations for Adopting Conservation Practices along Riparian Zones in a Mid-Western Agricultural Watershed." *Journal of Environmental Planning and Management* 46 (1): 19–37.

Schoon, B. E. N., and R. Te Grotenhuis. 2000. "Values of Farmers, Sustainability and Agricultural Policy." *Journal of Agriculture and Environmental Ethics* 12: 17–27.

The Kohala Center. 2010. *The 2010 County of Hawai'i Agricultural Development Plan*. Kamuela, Hawaii: Research and Development Department.

UNCTAD (United Nations Conference on Trade and Development). 2013. *Trade and Environment Review 2013: Wake Up Before It's Too Late*. Geneva: UNCTAD.

US Census. 2010. Accessed August 21 2013. census.gov.

Valbuena, D., P. H. Verburg, and A. K. Bregt. 2008. "A Method to Define a Typology for Agent-Based Analysis in Regional Land-use Research." *Agriculture, Ecosystems and Environment* 128 (1): 27–36.

Valbuena, D., P. Verburg, A. Veldkamp, A. K. Bregt, and A. Ligtenberg. 2010. "Effects of Farmers' Decisions on the Landscape Structure of a Dutch Rural Region: An Agent-based Approach." *Landscape and Urban Planning* 97 (2): 98–110.

Van de Steeg, J. A., P. H. Verburg, I. Baltenweck, and S. J. Staal. 2010. "Characterization of the Spatial Distribution of Farming Systems in the Kenyan Highlands." *Applied Geography* 30 (2): 239–25.

FOOD,
CULTURE &
SOCIETY

From the Sugar Oligarchy to the Agrochemical Oligopoly: Situating Monsanto and Gang's Occupation of Hawai'i

Andrea Brower

Abstract

As the site of origin for nearly all herbicide-tolerant corn seed, and with more experimental field trials of genetically engineered crops than anywhere else in the United States, Hawai'i is placed at the epicenter of the agrochemical+seed+biotechnology industry's global chains of production. This paper offers a critical reading of why most genetically engineered corn seed sold globally can be traced back to the most isolated islands in the world. Contra dominant narratives, it is argued that it is more than sunshine that makes Hawai'i's soils ideal for growing patented seeds engineered to withstand pesticide. Ideas of naturalness and inevitability are interrogated for what they elide and sustain. It is suggested that true alternatives require attention especially to the things assumed most immutable.

Introduction

As the primary site for development of all herbicide-tolerant corn seed, and with more experimental field trials of genetically engineered crops than anywhere else in the world, Hawai'i is placed at the epicenter of the agrochemical+seed+biotechnology industry's global chains of production. Perusing the popular press, economic reports, and legal and State documents, it quickly establishes as common sense that the industry exists in the islands due simply to good weather and "natural competitive advantage." While not untrue—

Hawai'i's year-round growing season is certainly favorable for speeding up the development of herbicide-tolerant seeds and testing other agricultural technologies—this smooth narration obscures fundamental socio-political and historical context. Further, the oft-repeated assertion that industry "contributions … are at no cost to the State" (Loudat and Kasturi 2013, 4) neglects mention of dependence on wide-ranging government supports and subsidies, and to whom "contributions" and "costs" accrue. Such omissions are never politically neutral (Jones and Murtola 2012, 133).

In this paper I offer a critical reading of why the most geographically isolated islands in the world have become central to a global agrochemical+seed+biotechnology oligopoly's chains of production, and assert that the conditions of possibility for the industry's occupation of Hawai'i are not merely "natural," and, likewise, not inevitable. In other words, I argue that it is more than sunshine that makes Hawai'i's soils ideal for growing patented seeds engineered to withstand pesticides, and interrogate ideas of naturalness and inevitability for what they elide and sustain.

I begin by describing the agrochemical+seed+biotechnology oligopoly, and the arrangements of capital and imperial state power that facilitate its global accumulation processes. I then briefly sketch Hawai'i's plantation trajectory from sugar to Monsanto, colonial past to colonial present, all of which is conditioned upon original and ongoing dispossessions of land and political self-determination from indigenous Hawaiians. This is followed by a more detailed examination of local invitations of the agrochemical+seed+biotech industry as sugar was vacating the islands, which demonstrates much about the structural and ideological setting. I then move through specific local conditions that facilitate the industry's operations, reading these alongside those of a plantation sugar and oligarchy past. My aim is not to fully detail or compare each, but to note important continuities that tend to be taken for granted.

In endeavoring a critical overview of the agrochemical industry in Hawai'i that attends to root matters of capital, imperialism and power, I do not wish to introduce a sense of fatalism/idealism that implies "waiting for the revolution" before confronting the daily lived impacts of Monsanto and gang. To the contrary, I suggest in the final sections of this paper that opening for contestation core conditions of plantation occupations is what gives rise to truly alternative possibilities. While what is immediately possible in the social order is limited by conditions of the present, to pass through a situation requires attention especially to the things assumed most immutable. The concern for construction of social possibility that threads through this paper has resonance far beyond the specificities of Hawai'i's situation.

This paper comes out of my nearly decade-long involvement in agrifood issues in Hawai'i, especially on my home island of Kaua'i. More specifically, it is based on activist work related to the agrochemical industry since 2013, including thousands of hours of meetings, conversations, actions, media productions, and other organizing. As such, its primary methodology is one of participant ethnography, and especially engaged methods grounded in an "emancipatory ethos" that seeks not merely to describe the world, but to change it (Gordon 2008, 8; Freire 1982). Some formal interviews were also conducted, and much of the data that inform this paper are based on extensive examination of government, legal, industry, media, and public testimony texts. To be clear, then, I start from an explicit rejection of false ideas of neutrality, and here much of my critique is set against claims of objective natural "realities" in the social order that are the zenith of "profoundly ideological and political projects" (McCarthy and Prudham 2004, 276).

The Agrochemical+Seed+Biotechnology Oligopoly

In capitalism's unceasing drive to generate ever-new commodities, it has drawn seeds and genes into its circuits of accumulation. Until fairly recently, seeds and plant material were considered non-exclusive "commons," with decisions over seed saving and sharing made within the overarching social systems and norms of which they were a part (Kloppenburg 2010, 153). In recent decades, capitalist enclosure of genetic commons has taken place through intertwined legal (intellectual property rights) and technological (hybridization and genetic engineering) strategies (Howard 2009; Kloppenburg 2004). While commodification of seed began most notably in the 1930s with the development of hybrid varieties of corn, the full patenting of living organisms was only made legal in the 1980 landmark *Chakrabarty* v. *Diamond* US Supreme Court decision. Revolutions in law and simultaneous advances in biotechnology opened lucrative new opportunities that were swiftly seized by already dominant capitalist firms.

Following a decade of rapid mergers and acquisitions, and most remarkable maneuverings to stockpile intellectual property rights, a handful of giant companies branding themselves the "life-sciences" industry emerged as the major players in seeds, agrochemicals and agricultural biotechnology (Srinivasan 2003; Howard 2009). Today the industry is dominated by six transnational conglomerates—Monsanto, Dow, DuPont, Syngenta, BASF, and Bayer—that all boast long histories manufacturing war and chemical products. Together they control 75 percent of private sector plant breeding research, 60 percent of the commercial seed market, 76 percent of agrochemical sales, and virtually all commercialized transgenic traits (ETC Group 2013; Moss 2013).

Despite dominant narrative focus on drought-resistant, nutritionally enhanced, and other potentially useful crops, forty years into research and twenty years after their initial commercialization, over 99 percent of global acres planted in GE crops are either engineered for herbicide tolerance or to produce their own insecticide (James 2014). The first, and still top-selling GE crops offered were Monsanto's "Roundup-Ready"—coupling seeds with their blockbuster proprietary herbicide—a major breakthrough for the company as it faced a sunsetting patent on Roundup™, failure to bring new chemical products to market, and lawsuits and regulations over consequences of past products (Glover 2010). Seed+herbicide combos remain the dominant capital-generating technology pathway. This has deepened the pesticide treadmill as new crops engineered to withstand more toxic herbicides and combinations of multiple herbicides are developed, largely in an ecologically nonsensical response to evolution of Roundup-resistant weeds (Benbrook 2012; Mortensen et al. 2012; Dow 2014). The vast majority of these crops feed factory farms and fuel cars.

As perhaps the world's first truly "capitalist empire" (Wood 2003; Panitch and Gindin 2012), the American state has been essential in producing global conditions that the agrochemical+seed+biotechnology industry relies upon for expansive capital accumulation. With the United States playing the most active role in freeing capital movements around the world, recent decades have been defined by compulsive and coercive erosion of various social protections limiting capital, alongside the strengthening of states in facilitating property rights, markets, financialization, and "accumulation by dispossession" (Harvey 2003; Panitch and Gindin 2012). As Sam Gindin argues, "The crucial point about American empire is that unlike national empires of the past, which actually carved up the world, this empire is trying to create a global capitalism and is acting on behalf of global capital and penetrating through capitalist institutions," all with critical collaboration from, and to the benefit of, dominant classes globally (Gindin et al. 2011, 109).

The past decades of policy liberalizing capital have manifested a crippling of agricultural autonomy especially in subordinate countries, increasingly globalized and financialized food flows, and extreme concentration of corporate wealth and power from seed to shelf to speculator. One aspect of this has been the dismantling of state supports for rural development and agriculture, and farmers' increasing dependence on global markets for seeds, agrochemicals, and other inputs dominated by corporate agribusiness. Contra state versus market fiction, the transnational firms dominating these agricultural input markets are wholly dependent upon many nation-states acting internally to guarantee particular property and market arrangements, including through extensive bureaucracies and laws (Gindin et al. 2011). Central to the intensification of capitalist logic has been the advancement of strict intellectual property regimes, compelled initially through the World Trade Organization (WTO), and more recently through bilateral and regional trade and investment treaties, where there is a notable "ratchet" effect (Drahos 2002; Sell 2011).

US commitment to the spread and deepening of capitalist logic attends specifically and contradictorily to advancing the interests of dominant American and/or transnational capitals (often not clear to distinguish), with the agrochemical+seed+biotech industry being a notable priority and influence. The United States consistently champions the industry's interests globally, not only in regards to intellectual property, but also to aggressively open markets, promote its technologies, and weaken regulations that constrain its profits and consolidations. Every US diplomatic post worldwide is instructed to "pursue an active biotech agenda," typically alongside industry (Food and Water Watch (FWW) 2013, 3); paradoxically, the United States vigorously opposed international provisions for biotechnology transfer and benefit sharing with poorer countries (McAfee 2003). International trade rules have been used to attack national laws taking a precautionary approach to GE crops and foods, while the mere threat of trade restrictions has forced countries to adopt policies dictated by the United States (Newell and Glover 2003). Recent mega trade and investor treaty negotiations indicate a push also to erode national pesticide protection laws and strengthen companies' rights to block public access to information regarding pesticide ingredients and potential dangers (Smith, Azoulay and Tuncak 2015). Most directly, the United States intervenes in foreign countries' affairs on behalf of individual firms to negotiate seed royalty settlements, accelerate approval of their crops, and extend patent lengths (FWW 2013).

Colonial Plantations

Hawai'i has long been a space of exploit for extraction of wealth by American and other capitalist interests, as well as a hub for US imperial maneuverings. Today, capital and empire take shape around a dominant vertically integrated transnational corporate tourism economy, US military occupation of 25 percent of land mass on the main Hawaiian island and thousands of square miles of surrounding airspace and sea, and agriculture at the periphery. The formation of this socio-ecological landscape began and continues with the dispossession of land and political self-determination from indigenous Hawaiians, and the present trajectory is inseparable from the founding of capitalist agribusiness.

The establishment of a sugar plantation economy in Hawai'i in the 1800s was the colonial force that most fully pulled the islands into processes of global capital. The conditions for enclosure of the Hawaiian commons and subsequent development of "King Sugar" were laid by radical colonial disruptions to Hawaiian society, including: death and disease, extractive sandalwood and whaling industries, imposed debts to Euro-American merchants, establishment of settler colonialists, and foreign military incursions onto the islands' shores (Kameʻeleihiwa, 1992; Kent, 1993; Kelly 1994; Osorio 2002). New England missionaries and capitalist interests (often one and the same) advocated that land privatization would assist in gaining recognition from other nations, and melded morality with the logic of profit to argue that exclusive ownership would unshackle the innate human drive to acquisitive individualism, inspiring "indolent" Hawaiian commoners to work and restoring a population decimated by disease (Beechert 1985, 23). Decades of debate and missionary proselytizing preceded the institution of private property by the Hawaiian governing class (Osorio 2002), perhaps most finally compelled by both the increasing imperatives of capital accumulation, and seeking to secure recognition of Hawaiians' rights to their lands in the face of heightened imperial takeovers throughout the Pacific (Kameʻeleihiwa, 1992; Silva 2004; Banner 2005). While imagined and preached in the language of freedom, the codification of private property in western-style law abolished freedoms that had previously been institutionalized in communal modes of production based on managed sharing of the commons, and resulted in a massive transfer of land and political power away from Hawaiian commoners (Kameʻeleihiwa 1992; Osorio 2002; Andrade 2008).

The privatization of land was never separate from Euro-American visions of a capitalist economy and large-scale export agriculture in particular, advocated as the only way the nation could survive independently, trade and reduce debt to imperial powers. Following land privatization, the rhetoric of plantation agricultural wealth and the overall health of the nation increasingly became inextricably linked (MacLennan 2014). As the sophisticated agricultural production systems of Hawaiians were being systematically displaced and ideologically denigrated, the Pacific nation was transformed into an exporter of commodity crops and an importer of plantation field-workers and consumer goods. Haole (white) planters amassed incredible wealth and became deeply invested in the success of sugar, which was increasingly in direct contradiction with the interest of national sovereignty (Osorio 2002). Emboldened by and seeking to secure their rapidly accumulating wealth and power, in the last decade of the nineteenth century factions of the local white elite orchestrated the overthrow of the Hawaiian monarchy in tandem with US military interests, simultaneously seizing nearly 1.8 million acres of government and crown lands (Coffman 1998). While not without tremendous struggle by those dispossessed (Silva 2004)—as well as between different capitalists—political and economic power under American occupation consolidated in the missionary-descendant "Big Five" sugar corporations, who also controlled banking, utilities, shipping and imports (Kent, 1993; MacLennan 2014).

Following World War II, sugar production in the islands grew less profitable as labor successfully organized, new "third world" territories were opened for cheaper monocrop production, and overseas capitalists began investing in Hawai'i as a tourism destination. As the number of tourists arriving in Hawai'i went from 429,000 to 2.6 million in the decade beginning in 1963 (now up to 8 million), development boomed and land prices soared. In step with post-war changes in capitalism, the Big Five local sugar corporations multinationalized, expanding to new places and new industries, while also holding on to large tracts of land for more lucrative tourism-development endeavors (Kent, 1993).

A Democratic Party "revolution" of the 1950s challenged the white sugar elite, ushered in some progressive reforms, and is popularly celebrated as the end of a particular epoch. However, many have also identified the ways in which an only partly changed now multi-ethnic elite became invested in the transnational corporate tourism-development economy, as well as the general failure to dismantle structural characteristics of the oligarchical political economy (Cooper and Daws 1985; Kent, 1993). Historian Noel Kent's analysis thirty years ago still stands: "The political elite, now a privileged class, could not represent both the popular classes and the interests of local and transnational capital, and it inevitably adopted policies that turned the government apparatus into an instrument of capital accumulation by the international bourgeoisie" (1993, 163). While today dominant transnational capitals and empire function through multi-ethnic local collaborators, ethnicized inequalities and a sharply stratified class structure remain (Okamura 2008).

Hawai'i today is deeply entrenched in the mono-economies of tourism and military, supplying extensive natural resources and government funds in exchange for low-paying service-industry jobs, an inflated cost of living, and a tremendous burden on fragile island ecologies. At the edges of this economy and in the tracts of abandoned sugar and pineapple fields, the agrochemical+-seed+biotechnology industry has become the dominant agribusiness interest in the islands. The seed industry first arrived in Hawai'i in the 1960s, operating on the fringes of plantation lands and primarily involved in hybrid corn endeavors (Brewbaker 2003). During the 1990s "merger mania" (Hauter 2012, 236), these seed companies were either acquired by chemical-pharmaceutical corporations or went out of business, including: Corn States (Monsanto), Illinois Foundation Seeds (Dow), Trojan Seed Co. (Pfizer to Monsanto), Funk's G (Ciba to Cargill to Monsanto), Northrup-King (Syngenta), and Pioneer Hi-Bred (DuPont). At the same moment, some of the earliest agricultural biotechnology field trials were happening in Hawai'i. As agricultural biotechnology, agrochemicals, and seeds became a single consolidated global industry already with tentacles in Hawai'i, space was being made by vacating plantations for expansion onto larger tracts of prime land equipped with water infrastructure. Hawai'i quickly became an epicenter for the industry's GE parent corn seed production and its crop research.

In step with the rapid commercialization of herbicide-tolerant and insecticidal transgenic crops, now planted on over half of American farmland, parent seed corn has become Hawai'i's largest agricultural commodity. Around eight million pounds were exported in 2013–2014, primarily to North and South America (USDA (United States Department of Agriculture) 2015). Hawai'i has more GE crop field tests than anywhere else in the United States, carried out almost entirely by one of the Big Six agrochemical firms, with herbicide resistance by far the most frequently tested trait (Freese, Lukens, and Anjomshoaa 2015). In 2014, 164 different field tests were conducted at 1,141 sites (ISB (Information Systems for Biotechnology) 2015). Behind Hawai'i, the island colony of Puerto Rico, another place occupied by American regulatory regimes with a year-round growing season, has the next highest number of GE field test sites (ISB, 2015).

Though the industry operates globally and is headquartered in multiple countries, finding places to operate within United States' territory and regulatory regimes is essential. The United States provides stringent intellectual property, "trade secret," and other "monopoly capital" protections (Foster and McChesney 2012), as well as a Reagan–Bush inherited deregulatory approach to agricultural biotechnology (Jasanoff 2005). Working within the United States is also necessary to the fluidity of the industry's production lines, enabling easy transfer and orderly movement of products through phases of seed development and distribution, as well as between research and commercialization.

FOOD,
CULTURE&
SOCIETY

Hawai'i's place both "within" and outside of the United States is critical to agrochemical+seed+biotech companies' decisions to locate in the islands. Unlike the continental United States, Hawai'i offers a year-round growing season to quicken the development of seed lines. Furthermore, it is isolated from other agriculture that could contaminate or be contaminated by experimental operations. As explained by industry pioneer James Brewbaker: "If you're in the middle of Iowa and studying a new [biotech crop], you've got to be in absolute isolation. Here it is concentrated in a way so that you'd think about all of [their acres are] made available for genetically modified crops" (Voosen 2011, n.p.). This isolation also means that lucrative corn seed is less exposed to pests and diseases that plague intensive monocrop production in the Corn Belt, and can more easily relocate without being re-exposed when disease occurs.

Diversifying the Plantation

Transnational capitalist interests are not merely imposed on Hawai'i, but require extensive facilitation by local actors and apparatuses of the state. Here I examine original invitations of the agrochemical+seed+biotech industry, which demonstrate much about the local ideological and structural setting as it is embedded in global capitalist dynamics and logics.

In the 1980s and 1990s, as the number of sugar farms went from 285 to four, there was much public, state, and private landowner conversation about what was to become of abandoned fields and workers, and how to preserve agricultural lands from being cemented over by the compulsions of the now dominant development-tourism economy (Kanehe and Mardfin 1987; DBEDT (Department of Business Economic Development & Tourism) 2012). Many private landowners had no hesitation turning to "inevitable" subdivisions and resorts. As described by a senior economist at First Hawaiian Bank: "The plantation land on O'ahu will be developed inevitably over the next decade. Also inevitable is that most of the farm workers who will be unemployed are middle-aged and older and will have a hard time finding other jobs" (Sahagun 1994). In the first wave of 1970s plantation closings, the State and ILWU sugar-workers union went as far as exploring the possibility of state-owned enterprises and other options for maintaining sugar production. They were sharply rebuked by land-owning plantation corporations, who asserted that they would not be "told what to do" (MacLennon 2014, 277).

In the next decades, the State offered more studies, talked about better urban planning, and funded some retraining programs for cane workers focused on lower paying service-industry jobs, despite the fact that tourism was also at an all-time low (Kanehe and Mardfin 1987; de Lama 1994; Kent 1994; Sahagun 1994). Within the halls of policy-makers and powerful institutions, the dominant idea endured that any meaningfully scaled agricultural predecessor and alternative to urbanization would remain in the plantation mold. The State and industry placed hope in discovering substitutions like sugar for ethanol and developing niche export crops, and argued for increasing public subsidization of sugar and slashing public health regulations to lower "the cost of doing business" in Hawai'i (Kanehe and Mardfin 1987, 43; see also Plasch 1981; Seo 1986). It was reasoned that crisis would require sacrifice: "to minimize problems resulting from closing a sugar operation, high risk ventures may have to be attempted (and) the community may also become willing to accept activities which it would otherwise oppose because of their negative environmental and social impact" (Plasch 1981, 246). By 1989, some within the State were advocating away from a future in agriculture at all, and for a more "enlightened approach to planning" that would cease to treat agricultural land as a "valuable resource" (MacLennan 2014, 278).

Others, especially on the outsides of power, pressed for different types of transitions that they believed could contribute to a more equitable economy, including agricultural production for local consumption and worker-owned cooperatives (Rohter 1992; Bacon 1995). Authoritative institutions like the Hawaiian Sugar Planters Association dismissed such visions as a "self-sufficiency myth" that would not attract capital investment, could not compete with cheap imports, and would require only a very small fraction of agricultural lands to saturate the local market (de Lama, 1994; Sahagun 1994). The fact that theirs had been an industry profitable and attractive to capital investment only due to trade policy, price supports, and government subsidy, was neglected. The State did make minimal gestures supporting non-plantation food production programs for both local and export markets. Yet without more fundamental system changes and significant redirection of public resources and state supports, anything of meaningful breadth could remain only a myth. University of Hawai'i crop scientist Hector Valenzuela describes one example: "When the plantations closed, about 200 farmers were given two acres of land [each] to cultivate, but they weren't given full support. We didn't show them how to farm. So after a few years they gave up" (Mitra 2014). Likewise, worker-owned cooperative initiatives that sprang up could not wrestle from the State or banks the larger amounts of land and start-up funding required to realize inspired visions (Bacon 1995).

Plantation closures were also situated in a period of tourist industry stagnation, with virtually no growth between 1990 and 1995 due to economic slowdown in Japan and the United States (Kent 1994; Aoudé 2001). Calls for "economic diversification," and especially creation of a high-technology "New Economy" sector, were loud across the political spectrum and largely intertwined with neoliberal logic. The State government created, staffed and funded numerous programs and agencies to "pursue the potential high tech utopia" (Herbig and Kramer 1994, 58), though many commentators chided the State for spending "tens of millions" (ibid.), but "failing to attract even one sizable company" (Darby and Jussawalla 1993, 45). This led to various prescriptions by advocates, always including that the State should strive to be more "pro-business" and to replicate the purported successes of other "innovative hot spots" by keeping apace with deregulation and doing more to "woo" entrepreneurs and corporations (Darby and Jussawalla 1993; Herbig and Kramer 1994). In the 1990s the State boasted that it had taken "bold" policy steps to "diversify," "stabilize," and bring Hawai'i into the "New Economy," including: some of the biggest business tax cuts in the nation, tax incentives for research and technology companies, partnership between business and government for high-tech growth, and mechanisms encouraging the University of Hawai'i to pursue commercial endeavors (Aoudé 2001, xxi; see also Cayetano 2000). At the same time, record allocations of State funds were poured into tourism in

FOOD, CULTURE & SOCIETY

attempts to attract new investors and visitors (Kent 1994). These "pump the economy" (Petranek 2001, 1) measures were the other half of policy aimed at wage freezes, cuts in workers' compensation, erosion of collective bargaining rights, general slashes in social spending, and privatization of state services (Witeck 2001, 47; see also Kent 1994).

Though seeking to capture a piece in the "New Economy," and clearly located in "neo"-liberal ideology and policy, in many ways there was nothing particularly "new" about the prescriptions being ushered in during this period. As conversations about what would come to fill the social and physical space of sugar and pineapple continued, policy-makers in Hawai'i and Washington were pulled into optimistic, often grandiose, projections about the future of agricultural biotechnology. Governor Ben Cayetano declared in 1998 that Hawai'i was destined to become the "Silicon Valley of the plant and ocean world," while local newspapers reported forecasts of a soon-to-be $7 billion industry in: "Crispier and less oily French fries, sweeter fruit with fewer calories, pest- and virus-resistant plants, bigger crop yields and better antibiotics" (Altonn 1998). State departments produced reports predicting that biotechnology would deliver high-value products and high-paying jobs, while futurist consultants warned that the State must act quickly if it wanted to attract global commerce in biotechnology (Altonn 1998). Perhaps more adept and familiar with facilitating overseas corporate investment and activity than critics leveraged, the State offered substantial tax incentives to biotechnology operations while also moving public lands and waters into the hands of agrochemical+seed+biotech companies (Petranek 2001; Higa 2012; Kanehe, 2014). Though healthy French fries and a multi-billion dollar economy never materialized, the agrochemical industry did indeed root itself in Hawai'i's soils, acquiring a range of public supports and subsidies, and finding highly suitable still intact plantation infrastructures, social structures and ideologies. They offered back a relatively small number of fieldwork jobs for local folks, brought in most of their own scientists and managers (and often lower paid field workers), and filled the fiction of high-tech competitive small entrepreneurs in an "innovation hot spot" with five giant conglomerates that monopolize agricultural biotechnology.

Indigenous activist and Moloka'i farmer Walter Ritte reflects on the brief post-sugar glimpse at a potential shift, even if slight, in policy trajectory:

> Back then the University of Hawai'i's agricultural extension agents would come by and say that we were going into diversified ag and truck farming and that they were going to provide us with the training and support to make that transition. But that never happened... All of a sudden the best lands were being given to these big chemical companies and we were back to industrial ag again. (Mitra 2014, n.p.)

In official policy, "diversified agriculture" was defined as anything that is not sugar or pineapple, regardless of structure, form, ownership, or distribution of benefits (DBEDT 2012). And while embedded in ideas of reducing economic dependencies, "economic diversification" dominantly came to refer to incentivizing new private capitalist initiatives, typically assumed as led and dictated by transnational capital with the islands acting as host.

Today, while the agrochemical industry's reach across the landscape is not close to replacing sugar's, it is largely credited with keeping agriculture alive in the islands, creating "green" and "high-tech" jobs, and preserving rural lands and lifestyles (Loudat and Kasturi 2013). Dominant and enduring narratives are reflected in the *New York Times* and as stated by Mayor of Kaua'i Bernard Carvalho, respectively: "The firms have spared farmland that would otherwise be lost to development" (Voosen 2011), and this is the "kind of agriculture [that] really feeds our families" (Mitra 2014). Moreover, described as the "anchor" of any agricultural possibility in the islands (Misalucha 2015), the "big ag" of the agrochemical companies is said to sustain all other farming operations by maintaining infrastructure and markets, providing land subleases, financing farmer organizations, and keeping resources devoted to agriculture generally. In the words of the former president of the Hawai'i Farm Bureau, "Small Ag survives because of Big Ag" (Hervey 2012). Alternatives to corporate agribusiness are, at best, imagined as small niche capitalist markets that can, and must, coexist with the former. And while it is no longer in vogue to assert that remote islands importing 90 percent of their food should not aim for some increase in local food production, the possibility of a truly substantial local food economy based in democratized ownership is still treated as naive. Indeed, according to dominant institutions like the Farm Bureau, it is largely the graciousness of agrochemical companies that sustains any local food production in the islands (Hervey 2012).

Locally Subsidized Plantations

The prevailing idea that large capitalist agribusiness that exports its wealth from the islands is the only economic form that can "feed our families" and offer realistic diversification to tourism assumes and obscures numerous forms of public subsidization, particular arrangements of resource control and power, and government facilitation of not only private sector profits, but corporate monopolies and dominance. Of course, these conditions and compulsions are also (re)produced globally and especially imposed by American occupation, but much is also co-determined by local social relations and decisions. For capitalist plantation agriculture to establish and entrench itself in Hawai'i, it took both imperial nations enforcing their commercial demands on the islands and the backing of a local state. From privatization of land by the Kingdom mid-nineteenth century, to a twentieth-century American territorial government negotiated within the control of a small oligarchy, the various state formations in Hawai'i increasingly functioned to secure the interests of particular capitals above other capitals or social priorities and forms. Without favorable land, water, forest, labor, infrastructure, tax and trade policies, sugar could not have been competitive or profitable on the global market (MacLennan 2014). Agrochemical operations today are likewise conditioned upon a range of supports from both local and federal governments, as well as structural arrangements largely left by a plantation-oligarchy past. A brief review of primary factors from within the islands follows.

Land acquisition by agrochemical corporations is made possible by a continuing history of consolidated land control, including the State of Hawai'i's management of lands seized from the Hawaiian Kingdom in its overthrow by American agribusiness interests. Following the privatization of land, early acquisition of fee simple property by missionary families and other foreigners in the islands enabled some of the first commercial sugar plantations and contributed to a never-dismantled legacy of consolidated land ownership that advanced through the oligarchy period. In addition to ownership, planters progressively gained large, long-term land leases on government lands, most especially through policies they themselves enacted following the 1887 "Bayonet Constitution" and the subsequent overthrow of the Kingdom government (MacLennan 2014). Leased at rates like 2 cents an acre per year, and sizes such as Hawaiian Agricultural Co.'s 190,405 acres or Waiakea Mill Co.'s 95,000 acres, perhaps over half of all land in sugar production was leased "public" lands, an exceptional government subsidy to the profit rates of the industry (Kent, 1993; MacLennan 2014).

Like sugar, much of the acreage occupied by the agrochemical industry today is "State" lands from which Kānaka Maoli (Native Hawaiians) continue to be dispossessed. On the island of Kaua'i, thousands of acres have been made available through the Agribusiness Development Corporation (ADC), a public–private corporation formed during sugar's closures with the vision of converting agriculture into a "dynamic growth industry," and structured to bypass "bureaucratic red tape" (Maehara 2007, 27). The large majority of the lands that it controls, considered amongst the most fertile in the islands and equipped with valuable infrastructures, are leased to agrochemical companies. Leases include twenty- to thirty-five-year agreements, most for over 2000 acres, at rates as low as $50/acre/year for tillable acres and $1/acre/year for non-tillable acres (some smaller leases are substantially higher).

In total, the agrochemical companies occupy roughly 25,000 acres on the islands of Kaua'i, Moloka'i, Maui and O'ahu, 85 percent of which is leased (Freese, Lukens, and Anjomshoaa, 2015). In addition to the State, leases are all with Hawai'i's largest landowners, with holdings born from plantation days that are either still in original private trusts or have been bought and sold in concentrated estates. Notably, Kamehameha Schools, the largest private landowner in Hawai'i, leases over 1,000 acres to Monsanto, which originated as a lease to Holden's Foundation Seeds in 1999 and passed over to Monsanto when they acquired the company four years later. Kamehameha Schools is amongst the wealthiest charitable trusts in the world, established in 1884 by the will of Princess Bernice Pauahi Bishop for the purpose of educating and supporting Kānaka Maoli. Many Hawaiians have protested that the trust's mission runs contrary to its business partnership with Monsanto (Yap 2013).

THE FOODWAYS OF HAWAI'I

Both the State and private landholders consider large leases to well-endowed and reportedly "more stable" corporations preferable to more numerous small leases to local enterprises. There are reported instances of local ranchers being evicted from private leases to make way for higher paying agrochemical firms. Consolidated landholdings and inflated land values contribute significantly to the expense of smaller local operations and their difficulty getting long-term land leases; this is an important factor in establishing the dominant sense that capital-intensive large agribusiness is Hawai'i's only real option.

Essential to the agrochemical companies, large tracts of public and private agricultural lands include irrigation infrastructure from sugar days. Control over fresh water was fundamental to the expansion and profitability of sugar, which would have dried up without the government-enforced ability to divert massive amounts of water out of forested island interiors and away from other ecological and human communities (MacLennan 2014, 273). While Hawai'i's laws today guarantee water as a public trust resource, it has taken lengthy and expensive citizen-initiated litigation to implement the law in select places. Water generally continues to flow towards Hawai'i's most powerful business and landowning interests (Sproat 2010).

A legal petition by the public interest group Earthjustice alleges that where the State leases thousands of acres to agrochemical companies on West Kaua'i, both entities "are committing unlawful waste, including outright dumping of diverted river water" (Henkin and Moriwake 2013, vii). The irrigation systems used by the agrochemical firms in this case were constructed by Kekaha Sugar plantation in the early 1900s, after it impaired its groundwater wells from overuse (ibid., 14). As is most typical, the State's Water Commission "merely rubber-stamped" historical diversions of the former sugar plantations when management transferred to the Agribusiness Development Corporation (ibid., vii). Earthjustice and residents, including Native Hawaiian right-holders, maintain that both streams and other users are being denied rightful water allocation, with testimonies of all-time lows in river water. Moreover, the State's Agribusiness Development Corporation has facilitated companies' exemption from the Federal Clean Water Act, including requirements for reporting and monitoring of pollutants in water. The exemption was advised by the State because discharge criteria for pesticides and other pollutants would be "extremely difficult to meet" (JFFSG (Joint Fact Finding Study Group), 2016, 48).

FOOD, CULTURE & SOCIETY

In addition to public resources, agrochemical companies are directly subsidized through property tax breaks, high-technology tax credits, investment capital, and loss of general excise tax revenue (Kanehe 2014; Bynum 2013). Hawai'i is noted by the subsidy tracking research center Good Jobs First (2015) for its "lavish tax credit programs," including high-technology tax credits enacted in 1999 that cost the State an estimated one billion dollars in lost tax revenue before they sunset in 2010. These credits were far above the level offered in any other state; for the majority of the time they were in place there was no public disclosure of who was receiving them (Higa 2012). Unlike other forms of agricultural production in the islands, the seed development conducted by agrochemical companies does not generate a product that is then sold, so excludes payment of general excise taxes. Similarly, companies take advantage of agricultural property tax and utility subsidies through land use agricultural dedication policy, originally designed to incentivize agricultural production in the islands (Kaua'i County Council Bill 2546). Adding to these various forms of subsidy, council members on the island of Kaua'i allege that numerous violations of County law by companies and the landowners who lease to them have resulted in millions of dollars in unpaid liabilities (D'Angelo 2014). While the various forms of subsidization covered here are proportionately much smaller than those that financed sugar's dominance over the landscape, the point is that plantation agriculture has always been, and continues to be, underwritten by public funds and resources.

Also of significance in regards to public supports is the role of research and education institutions and funds, and especially the University of Hawai'i's land grant College of Tropical Agriculture and Human Resources (CTAHR). Most generally, both public and private research institutions that originally serviced sugar today devote significant research to crop genetic engineering (Caron 2015). The critique here is not of agricultural biotechnology research in its own right, but the wider drives of academic capitalism and neoliberal science as they embed public universities and research funding in private commercial demands. Like other universities, the University of Hawai'i is today expected to function as a business, and be responsive first and foremost to market logic, including fostering "a culture of entrepreneurship pervasive throughout the university and a push for commercialization" (Enay 2011, n.p.). The mission of CTAHR to "support tropical agricultural systems" is thus carried out partly by "help(ing) all of our *clients* ..." (emphasis added, CTAHR 2015), with land grant mandates interpreted as fulfillable through patents, commodifiable products, and public science that generates private wealth. More broadly and outside of Hawai'i, agricultural biotechnology's profitability to the agrochemical industry is entirely built upon unpaid-for science developed in the public sector (Mazzucato 2013).

Alongside its research and education, CTAHR plays a critical role in shaping public discourse and opinion around agricultural biotechnology in ways that conveniently erase the role of the agrochemical oligopoly. Partly funded by Monsanto, its extensive outreach programs focus on feeding the world through largely unrealized imaginations of future technological possibilities, and occlude discussion of actual current control and use of biotechnology.

As with sugar, public supports for the agrochemical industry extend beyond resource use, direct financing, and institutional subsidies, and also include policy regimes that facilitate and exacerbate capitalism's privatization of benefits and socialization of costs. Most lasting and significant are impacts on human health and the environment, especially of intensive pesticide use (Freese, Lukens, and Anjomshoaa, 2015). The chemical legacies of sugar and pineapple are still marked by Superfund sites, contaminated drinking water systems, and overall "unusually widespread occupational and general population exposures" to pesticides (Allen et al. 1997, 679). Along with hundreds of toxic military sites (Ramones 2014), these chemical burdens continue to accumulate from today's pesticide-intensive GE seed and experimental operations, carried out by some of the same companies that manufactured the now banned chemicals used by pineapple and sugar (Freese, Lukens, and Anjomshoaa, 2015).

According to voluntary reporting, 36,240 pounds of total formulation restricted-use pesticides were used just on the island of Kaua'i by Syngenta, DuPont, Dow, BASF and Kaua'i Coffee in the 20-month period from December 2013 to July 2015. Restricted-use pesticides are those deemed by the Environmental Protection Agency to need a special permit and protective equipment for application due to their known harmful impacts. Based on these company-reported data, the Hawai'i Center for Food Safety estimates that Kaua'i's seed corn fields receive seventeen times more restricted-use insecticides than corn grown in the continental United States (Freese, Lukens, and Anjomshoaa, 2015). Other comparative estimates are lower; these are imprecise given incomplete data, especially concerning acreage use (JFFSG 2016). From a class-action lawsuit on Kaua'i, it was divulged that when general-use pesticides (such as glyphosate and 2,4-D) are accounted for, at least ninety pesticide formulations with sixty-three different active ingredients were used by DuPont between 2007 and 2012, and that pesticides were applied 250–300 days per year, at an average of ten to sixteen applications per day (Jervis and Smith 2013). Voluntary pesticide reporting for 2014–2015 indicates that other companies use a higher volume pesticides than DuPont, with particularly high usage of the neurotoxin organophosphate *chlorpyrifos*.

Many agrochemical+seed+biotechnology operations are located near schools, homes, hospitals, parks and waterways. Numerous local doctors have submitted official statements expressing concern that they may be witnessing effects of pesticide exposure in communities around fields, potentially including higher than average rates of rare birth defects, miscarriages, unusual cancers, respiratory and hormonal problems, and recurring dermatitis and nose-bleeds (public testimony for Kaua'i County Council Bill 2491).

The policy regimes that facilitate the "externalization" of burdens of pesticide use onto the public are multi-faceted, including local, federal and increasingly international layers. While a detailed examination is outside the scope of this paper, a few points illustrate the policy landscape that makes the islands most suitable to the agrochemical industry's operations. Unlike many other countries that adhere to a more precautionary approach, the Environmental Protection Agency (EPA) regulates pesticides according to a risk–benefit standard that weighs economic benefits against proven or potential harms. The biases of the US federal regulatory system are highlighted by the fact that non-American corporations Syngenta and BASF use pesticides like atrazine, alachlor and permethrin in Hawai'i that are banned in their home countries. The EPA delegates its pesticide monitoring duties to the Hawai'i State Department of Agriculture, which investigated seven of seventy-two possible pesticide violations on one island alone during 2011 and 2012 (Cocke 2013). According to the employee assigned to review violations, there has been "little if any action against pesticide misuse" (ibid.). There is no program in place for regular testing of pesticide contamination in the soil, air, or water.

GE crop experimentation and seed cultivation in Hawai'i falls under the US "coordinated framework for the regulation of biotechnology." The framework functions on the deregulatory principle that biotechnology products "should not be treated any differently for regulatory purposes from similar products manufactured by biological or chemical processes that did not involve gene manipulation" (Jasanoff 2005, 52). One percent of all field trials are required to go through a permitting process; the remaining 99 percent go through a notification process where risks such as harms to human health or the environment are not considered, and companies perform their own risk evaluations (Gibson 2014). The last full environmental assessment of a field trial in Hawai'i was conducted in 1994 (ISB 2015). Companies are able to protect information about field trials as "trade secrets," restricting the public and State government from accessing basic facts about the nature and location of trials, including about pesticide use.

The State of Hawai'i's own policies and *modus operandi* related to pesticide use and large agribusiness is largely left over from and reminiscent of sugar days. Recent attempts to regulate agrochemical industry operations within three of four counties have all been at least temporarily preempted by the State's (non)regulation. In ruling a County of Kaua'i pesticide disclosure and buffer zone bill invalid, a US District Court judge issued the opinion: "the State of Hawai'i has established a comprehensive framework for addressing the application of restricted use pesticides and the planting of GE crops, which presently precludes local regulation by the County" (Hofschneider 2014). That "comprehensive framework" includes none of the basic pesticide protection laws that have been enacted in many other states, such as no-spray zones around vulnerable population areas, poisoning surveillance programs, and notification requirements for pesticide applications (Freese, Lukens, and Anjomshoaa, 2015).

Over the past decades hundreds of pesticide bills have been introduced at the State legislature, though most are never scheduled for a first hearing. Only one (Act 105) was passed in an "extremely watered down" version of the original bill, ending as a law for making public highly generalized information about total annual pesticide sales. The law was not implemented for over two years due to alleged concern over industry lawsuits (Hofschneider 2015). While refusing or neglecting to pass new, or even enforce some existing health and environmental regulations, various State agencies have at the same time worked to facilitate agrochemical companies' exemptions from federal laws (Hooser 2015; Pala 2015).

The Plantation Landscape: Bosses and Workers, Benefits and Burdens

As examination of local subsidies and facilitations of agrochemical operations in the islands indicates, the industry relies significantly on local collaborations to materialize its interests. While today's agrochemical bosses and most privileged beneficiaries belong to the "global ruling class" (Robinson and Harris 2000), alliances with local elite are critical for shaping policy, insuring access to resources and infrastructures, and influencing public opinion. This should not suggest some conspiracy of local power, homogeneity of interests, or that all who collude with industry are merely maximizing their own interests. However, as has been frequently identified by scholars and commentators, concentration of political and economic power in the islands remains remarkable, operating especially through interlocked networks and institutions, and significantly tied to land control (Cooper and Daws 1985; Kent, 1993). This concentration of power, and corresponding normalization of tight webs of political elite relationship, has been essential to the ease with which the agrochemical industry spread its roots in the islands.

A review of the multitudinous spaces in which allegiances are made apparent is beyond the scope of this paper, but a few examples provide a representative description. Virtually all proposed legislation affecting the agrochemical industry receives strikingly consistent lobbying positions from industry, State departments, large landowners, dominant institutions (including the Farm Bureau, Hawai'i Cattlemen's Council, and Chamber of Commerce), and often from County government administrations. Chairs of the Hawai'i Department of Agriculture routinely harmonize their positions on issues with the industry, reciting identical talking points to the media and working directly with companies on strategies to assuage public resistance. The industry's extensive "community outreach" personnel are all affiliated with the islands' most powerful institutions, and frequently hired directly from within government. The functioning of industry power is also plainly evident in the apparatuses of media and idea dissemination that have mobilized to vindicate its pesticide practices and marginalize dissent. Industry presence in and influence over a wide range of organizations, from neighborhood associations, to hospital boards, to charities, to public schools, is revealing of the outsized political-financial influence it has brought to bear upon Hawai'i and its local "ruling circles" (Aoude 2001, xx).

Differentiation in allotment of the burdens and access to the benefits of agrochemical occupations are marked by ethnicity, race, class, gender and nationality. When the agrochemical+seed+biotech industry expanded its operations in the islands, the former sugar and pineapple lands that it occupied surrounded communities created and subsequently abandoned by the plantations. Many of these communities are isolated from tourist centers, located in places where lost jobs, housing and medical benefits were not easily replaced (Bacon 1995). While new agricultural jobs in the seed industry were initially welcomed, in recent years residents have also grown increasingly concerned about exposure to pesticides, dust, pollution and diversion of waterways, and other environmental impacts. These communities are predominantly working class, with higher concentration of Hawai'i's most marginalized ethnic groups. The structural inequalities that they face, including narrow employment options and spatial and socio-cultural separation from centers of political power, are continuations of plantation and colonial histories and hierarchies (Okamura 2008). Environmental injustices are multi-layered and cumulative. The westside of Kaua`i for example, where thousands of acres of agrochemical operations surround residents, is also host to the island's landfill, several highly contaminated toxic waste sites left by sugar, and the world's largest missile testing range.

Ethnicized plantation hierarchies are largely transposed onto today's fields, with many field workers and managers having transferred directly from sugar or pineapple. As one person dealing closely with the industry put it: "same bodies, different boss companies." While local people are hired for certain managerial roles (such as field supervision and public relations), most senior management positions are filled by internationally mobile white men (Shaw 2016a, 3). Nearly all field workers are either from Hawai'i's most marginalized ethnic groups, including Filipina/o and Native Hawaiians, or (temporary and more permanent) migrants from Southeast Asia, the Pacific Islands and Latin America (Shaw 2016b). Women appear over-represented in certain fieldwork tasks such as soy pollination, which is feminized as requiring patience, meticulousness, and "nimble fingers" (ibid.).

Given Hawai'i's occupational inequalities, the wages received in agrochemical fieldwork are likely higher than what would be earned at the bottom rung of the service industry (Okamura 2008; Loudat and Kasturi 2013). However, according to the industry, nearly half of the around 1400 jobs offered are part-time (Loudat and Kasturi 2013). Private conversations suggest that the proportion of seasonal work may actually be higher, and that third-party contractors typically bring in work crews during busier winter and summer harvest months.

While the industry represents job creation as its primary contribution to Hawai'i, it also speaks about the need for migrant labor because "local people don't want these jobs," and pursues international labor recruitment reminiscent of sugar days (labor recruiter, personal communication). An astounding lack of public information and regulatory oversight exists regarding the conditions of migrant workers arriving through the Compact of Free Association or temporary guest-worker schemes, which by their very structure tend to deprive and undermine basic labor and human rights and suppress worker organizing (Southern Poverty Law Center 2013). Migrant contract workers have reportedly been sent back to their countries of origin after suffering acute pesticide poisonings. Many migrants laboring for farms and agrochemical operations throughout Hawai'i were agricultural producers in their home countries, displaced by the compulsions of globalized and financialized capitalist agribusiness. As Shaw (2016b) argues, the incorporation of new migrant groups into agrochemical plantations is also a direct result of US imperialism. Micronesian migration to Hawai'i, for example, is largely a consequence of the United States detonating the equivalent of over 7,200 Hiroshima-sized bombs in the Marshal Islands (Letman 2013).

The Fortress of Necessity and Inevitability

The local networks, institutions, and actors that facilitate agrochemical industry occupation of the islands should not suggest a monolithic and uncontested power block or even uniformity of interests, but instead demonstrate the entrenchment of institutional designs, pathways and mentalities that are also shaped by structural power and wealth. Alliances, allegiances, and general resignation are crafted within the ideological contours of Hawai'i's political-economic history and wider capitalist norms, including real material constraints that cannot be imagined otherwise.

Most broadly, a sense of non-opportunity beyond the new Monsanto plantations is manufactured within the past decades' ideological reduction of social possibility to that of "global monopoly-finance capitalism" (Foster, McChesney and Jonna 2011; Fisher 2009), while Hawai'i's continuing past gives ideological and material truth to a perception of pathway dependence and lock-in. When sugar baron Samuel Castle responded to critics of the "close to slavery" contract labor system as "striking a serious blow at every interest in the country" (quoted in Osorio 2002, 176), he gave clear illustration of mechanisms by which injustice is constructed as inevitable. Indeed, by certain indicators it was true, as a 1905 study remarked, that "directly or indirectly, all individuals in the Territory of Hawai'i are ultimately dependent upon the sugar industry" (quoted in Kent, 1993, 74). The fundamental question too often unasked, and always easier to ask of the past than of the present, is the means by which dependence on not only the plantation economy, but also on the plantation oligarchy, was manufactured, sustained, and tangled up in ways that gave the appearance of indistinguishability between common goods and select private interests. Of course, there is also nothing unique about this problem in a capitalist society, where all are dependent on successful capitalist accumulation and growth: capital can "rely on his [the worker's] dependence on capital, which springs from the conditions of production themselves, and is guaranteed in perpetuity by them" (Marx 1992, 899).

FOOD, CULTURE & SOCIETY

Today, most people living in Hawai'i, from the lowest paid hotel cleaners to oligarch-descendant landowners, are entirely reliant on the steady flow of millions of visitors annually. At the same time, it is well understood that Hawai'i's model of transnational corporate tourism creates incredible vulnerabilities, and that an economy that offers low-paying jobs but drives up the cost of living has resulted in high rates of poverty, homelessness, and displacement from the islands. The compulsions of endless development and rural gentrification, and the huge sacrifices made to the environment and valued "island lifestyles," are widely lamented facts even amongst those who benefit financially. In a severely narrowed discourse of social possibility, the solutions to such systemic problems are most typically presented as better planning and creation of niche tourism markets, while the search for "economic diversification" remains ongoing, dominantly defined as piling new forms of wealth-extracting overseas-based capital (CEDS 2010). From within this extremely limited horizon of possibility, agrochemical operations appear a welcome "diversification," a tradeoff worth making in lieu of the only alternatives on offer—hotels, exclusive gated communities, and military bases. As previous head of the State Department of Agriculture Russel Kokubun put it, the plantations left a huge void to which the seed industry provided an alternative: "It's created an opportunity to view agriculture as a viable industry" (Voosen 2011, n.p.).

The dominant narrative that agrochemical companies have spared farmland and livelihoods assumes as immutable the social arrangements that give shape to Hawai'i's monoeconomy and make transnational corporate agribusiness the most viable addition. Beyond more universal relations of capital and empire, such arrangements include numerous forms of local public subsidy that exacerbate and extend capitalism's general privatization of benefits, and socialization of costs. The local and global conditions that give rise to the agrochemical industry and its occupation of Hawai'i are invisibilized or taken for granted. As arrangements (at all scales) that could be different are obfuscated, what corporate agribusiness systematically supplants and precludes is clouded or naturalized, most typically as the force of "the market." Moreover, in today's tales of a plantation past as evidence of the need for "big ag," a selective history neglects the direct marginalization and often violent displacement of alternatives, including the near entire devotion of natural resources and government treasury to particular business interests.

As this history repeats in corporate tourism and chemical companies, desires for something "other" are treated as naive misunderstanding of constraints. Material limitations from within the conditions of the present are taken to represent the entirety of possibility, guarded as evidence of the immutability of the situation. An endless list of realisms—state tax dependencies, a shortage of public funds, a population lacking the skills for preferred economies—all come to stand in for the whole, and draw attention away from the active reproduction of the very structural limitations that give testimony to non-possibility. In a "discourse of disconnection," issues are fragmented and treated as isolated dilemmas, narrowing collective capacity to perceive and respond to structurally and ideologically inseparable socio-economic-cultural problems (Giroux 2014, 65). In this regard, dominant ideas of necessity and inevitability are accurate—it is true that only very particular forms of capitalist agribusiness can outcompete other capitalist agribusiness within particular market arrangements, and it *becomes* true that only this form will sustain livelihoods, infrastructures and agricultural lands when treated as a single issue detached from other systemic features that must also be changed.

What also requires briefly extricating from constructions of inevitability is the global context by which consolidated corporate agribusiness and its attendant capitalist processes are continually re-formulated as imperative to feeding the world and making modern society possible. There is a sense that one does not have to "like" the consequences of a corporate capitalist food system, but society cannot live without it (Fisher 2009). Fundamental to such logic are ideologies of agricultural productivity and social progress, originating especially in the justification of enclosure of common lands across England as a transformation of "waste" into "improved" land. As Wood (2002) points out, to "improve" literally meant to do something for monetary profit; the "improvement" literature that emerged in the seventeenth century focused especially on peasant evictions and the commercialization of agriculture as necessary to the process of modernization and increasing grain yields, thus purportedly contributing to the common good (Ross 1998). Such rationality vindicated colonial endeavors, and persisted in Hawai'i's plantation development and capitalist enclosures 150 years ago. Only slightly repackaged today, the restructuring of the food system towards increased financialization, privatization, corporatization and industrialization takes place within a moral discourse of increasing grain yields to "feed the world," while neoliberalism has made synonymous "social progress" and private sector technological change (Newfield 2008).

The agricultural biotechnology project is wholly immersed in such constructions of solving hunger through capitalist markets, innovations and technologies. As a space central to development of such technologies, Hawai'i is imagined as playing a virtuous role in feeding the world. The invocation of morality works to silence debate, while the ideological hegemony of a particular capitalist trajectory of progress and productivity makes it "difficult to muster the discursive resources to challenge them" (McAfee 2003, 215). The critique here is not of productivity or technological innovation in their own rights, but what is justified or neglected by such logic as it operates in regards to capital. As an extensive literature has shown, many of the very projects purportedly aiming to increase agricultural productivity and innovation—from land grabs, to "free trade," to seed patents—are directly implicated in the causes of global hunger, and are more fundamentally about privatization, commodification, and capital accumulation (Magdoff et al. 2000; De Schutter 2011; Holt-Gimenez and Patel 2012).

Concluding Thought: The Possibility of Something(s) Different

As capital incessantly restructures food production systems to meet its commodification and accumulation imperatives, Hawai'i has changed from a landscape consumed by tropical monocrops, to one of agrochemical+seed+biotech product development on the peripheries of a tourism–military economy. Though significantly different in the transnational capitalist class now ruling operations and the intensification of capitalist dependencies and compulsions, in many ways, today's plantations by Monsanto and Dow also do not stray far from those of the sugar oligarchy. Much of sugar's infrastructures, institutions and ideas have been directly inherited, while agrochemical occupations similarly operate locally by way of concentrated resource control and power, undergirded by American imperial interests. As with plantation sugar, benefits are privatized and costs are socialized, with disproportionate impacts across race, class, and gender. While for decades virtually every local politician has dutifully spoken to the need for "economic diversification" from single plantation-economy dependencies, this has largely been a "politics of irrelevance" (Kent 1993, 160) that negates structural inequalities and what it would mean to actually democratize and more fairly distribute Hawai'i's abundant wealth.

Critiques of today's agrochemical+seed+biotech industry occupations must reach deeper and wider than the particularities of Monsanto, DuPont, Dow, Syngenta, or BASF. Structural injustice and inequity do not stem solely from isolated capitalist firms, or from a particular technology, and they cannot be addressed merely with straightforward substitutions of "local" for "global." Indeed, some of the greatest abuses of workers and violations of pesticide laws take place on locally owned farms producing local food in Hawai'i (David 2010). Today's most popular binaries—agriculture versus development, self-sufficiency versus export, modern high-tech versus traditional, etc.—tend to miss fundamental questions and reduce the scope of public consideration and debate. Rather, to consider actual alternatives is to look to the very root conditions that continue to facilitate plantations, oligarchies and oligopolies. It is to seek not a mere "diversification" of Hawai'i's highly unequal and anti-democratic mono-economy—from a little less Hilton-Hotel tourism to a little more Monsanto agriculture—but to disrupt the very systems and powers that preclude truly alternative possibilities. Without doubt, material and ideological conditions of the present—not the least being compulsions emanating from beyond the islands' shores—restrict what can be thought and done. But in opposition to the alibis of injustice and the incessant realisms that assert the current order as inevitable, justice demands claiming those very material limitations as precisely the indicators that deep systemic change is most necessary, and must be fought for.

In Hawai'i, recent waves of intertwined decolonial, environmental, democratic, and social justice struggle give hope, practicality and "realism" to the fact that things could be very different from the way they are (Brower 2016). These contemporary struggles are seeded in soils laid by prior generations, including powerful anti-colonial, radical labor, and racial justice movements, as well as Kānaka Maoli epistemologies and practices that have long refused erasure by colonial-capitalist rationalities and intrusions (Silva 2004; Horne 2011; Goodyear-Ka'ōpua, Hussey and Wright 2014). As much as plantations and oligarchies define Hawai'i, so do these glimmers of other possible worlds.

THE FOODWAYS OF HAWAI'I

Disclosure statement

No potential conflict of interest was reported by the author.

References

Allen, R., M. Gottlieb, E. Clute, M. Pongsiri, J. Sherman, and G. Obrams. 1997. "Breast Cancer and Pesticides in Hawaii: The Need for Further Study." *Environmental Health Perspectives* 105 (3): 679–683.

Altonn, H. 1998. "Biotechnology: Our Next Industry?" *Star Bulletin*, February 26. Accessed 19 September 2015. http://archives.starbulletin.com/98/02/26/news/story5.html.

Andrade, C. 2008. *Hā'ena: Through the Eyes of the Ancestors*. Honolulu: University of Hawai'i Press.

Aoudé, I. 2001. "Policy of Globalization and Globalization of Policy." *Social Process in Hawaii* 40: xi–xxvii.

Bacon, D. 1995. "Trouble in Paradise: Hawaii's Sugar Workers Fight for a New Life," September 24. Accessed 19 September 2015. http://dbacon.igc.org/Work/01Sugar.html.

Banner, S. 2005. "Preparing to Be Colonized: Land Tenure and Legal Strategy in Nineteenth-Century Hawaii." *Law & Society Review* 39 (2): 273–314.

Beechert, E. 1985. *Working in Hawaii: A Labor History*. Honolulu: University of Hawai'i Press.

Benbrook, C. 2012. "Impacts of Genetically Engineered Crops on Pesticide Use in the U.S.—The First Sixteen Years." *Environmental Sciences Europe* 24 (24): 1–13.

Brewbaker J. 2003. *Corn Production in the Tropics: The Hawai'i Experience*. Honolulu: University of Hawai'i Manoa, College of Tropical Agriculture and Human Resources.

Brower, A. 2016. "Hawai`i: 'GMO Ground Zero'." *Capitalism Nature Socialism* 27 (1): 68–86.

Bynum, T. 2013. "2491 A Chance to Control Destiny." *The Garden Island*, September 29. Accessed 20 September 2015. http://thegardenisland.com/news/opinion/guest/a-chance-to-control-destiny/article_1f3a3742-28d4-11e3-960c-0019bb2963f4.html.

Caron, W. 2015. "UHM Faculty Condemn Academic Freedom Violations." *Hawaii Independent*, July 21. Accessed 30 July 2015. http://hawaiiindependent.net/story/uhm-faculty-rally-condemn-academic-freedom-violations.

Cayetano, B. 2000. *State of the State Address*. 24 January. Accessed 20 June 2014. http://archives.starbulletin.com/2000/01/24/news/story1a.html.

CEDS. 2010. *Hawaii Statewide Comprehensive Economic Development Strategy (CEDS)*. Prepared by the State of Hawaii, Office of Planning of Department of Business Economic Development & Tourism. Accessed 20 September 2015. http://files.hawaii.gov/dbedt/op/spb/Final_CEDS_2010.pdf.

Cocke, S. 2013. "Does Hawai'i's Failure to Enforce Pesticide Use Justify Action By Kauai?" *Civil Beat*, October 5. Accessed 11 March 2015. http://www.civilbeat.com/2013/10/20066-does-hawaiis-failure-to-enforce-pesticide-use-justify-kauais-action/.

Coffman, T. 1998. *Nation Within: The Story of America's Annexation of the Nation of Hawai'i*. Washington, D.C.: Epicenter.

College of Tropical Agriculture and Human Resources (CTAHR). 2015. "Biotechnology and Agriculture Education Program." University of Hawaii, College of Tropical Agriculture and Human Resources. Accessed 20 September 2015. http://www.ctahr.hawaii.edu/biotech/CTAHR_Research.html#.

Cooper, G., and G. Daws. 1985. *Land and Power in Hawaii: The Democratic Years*. Honolulu: University of Hawai'i Press.

D'Angelo, C. 2014. "The Tip of the Iceberg." *The Garden Island*, October 7. Accessed 20 September 2015. http://thegardenisland.com/news/local/the-tip-of-the-iceberg/article_2ede7b44-4deb-11e4-8cb7-e33aa52f0a8c.html.

Darby, G., and M. Jussawalla. 1993. "Telecommunications." In *The Price of Paradise*. vol. II, edited by R. Roth, 45–50. Honolulu: Mutual Publishing.

David, M. 2010. "Honolulu FBI Crack Alleged 'Modern-Day Slavery' Case." *Hawaii News Now*, September 3. Accessed 20 September 2015. http://www.hawaiinewsnow.com/story/13095215/honolulu-fbi-crack-alleged-modern-day-slavery-case.

De Lama, G. 1994. "Sugar King No More in Hawaii." *Chicago Tribune*, June 19. Accessed 19 September 2015. http://articles.chicagotribune.com/1994-06-19/business/9406190289_1_sugar-mill-sugar-planters-sugar-workers.

De Schutter, O. 2011. "How Not to Think of Land-Grabbing: Three Critiques of Large-Scale Investments in Farmland." *Journal of Peasant Studies* 38 (2): 249–279.

Department of Business Economic Development & Tourism (DBEDT). 2012. *Increased Food Security and Food Self-Sufficiency Strategy, Vol. II: A History of Agriculture In Hawaii and Technical Reference Document*. Prepared by the State of Hawaii, Office of Planning of Department of Business Economic Development & Tourism, in cooperation with the Department of Agriculture. Honolulu.

Dow. 2014. "Enlist Duo Herbicide Moves Forward in Regulatory Process." Press Release, April 30. Accessed 30 June 2015. http://www.dow.com/news/press-releases/article/?id=6497.

Drahos, P. 2002. "Developing Countries and International Intellectual Property Standard-Setting." *Journal of World Intellectual Property* 5 (5): 765–789.

Enay, S. 2011. "Hawaii's Tech Industry After Act 221." *Hawaii Business*, January 2011. Accessed 20 September 2015. http://www.hawaiibusiness.com/hawaiis-tech-industry-after-act-221/.

ETC Group. 2013. *Putting the Cartel Before the Horse … and Farm, Seeds, Soil, Peasants, etc*. Communiqué No. 111. Ottowa: ETC Group.

Fisher, M. 2009. *Capitalist Realism: Is There No Alternative?* Ropley: Zero Books.

Food and Water Watch (FWW). 2013. *Biotech Ambassadors: How the US State Department Promotes the Seed Industry's Global Agenda*. Washington, D.C.: FWW.

Foster, J., and R. McChesney. 2012. *The Endless Crisis: How Monopoly-Finance Capital Produces Stagnation and Upheaval from the USA to China*. New York: Monthly Review Press.

Foster, J., R. McChesney, and R. Jonna. 2011. "Monopoly and Competition in Twenty-First Century Capitalism." *Monthly Review* 62 (11): 1–39.

Freese, B., A. Lukens, and A. Anjomshoaa. 2015. *Pesticides in Paradise: Hawai'i's Health and Environment at Risk*. Hawaii Center for Food Safety. Accessed 20 September 2015. www.centerforfoodsafety.org/reports.

Freire, P. 1982. "Creating Alternative Research Methods: Learning To Do It By Doing It." In *Creating Knowledge: A Monopoly*, edited by B. Hall, A. Gillette and R. Tandon, 29–37. New Delhi: Society for Participatory Research in Asia.

Gibson, D. 2014. "Remembering the 'Big Five': Hawai'i's Constitutional Obligation to Regulate the Genetic Engineering Industry." *Asian-Pacific Law & Policy Journal* 15: 213–283.

Gindin, S., G. Albso, L. Panitch, and S. Lilley. 2011. "Capitalist Crisis and Radical Renewal." In *Capital and Its Discontents: Conversations with Radical Thinkers in a Time of Tumult*, edited by S. Lilley, 105–122. Oakland: PM Press.

Giroux, H. 2014. *The Violence of Organized Forgetting: Thinking Beyond America's Disimagination Machine*. San Francisco: City Lights Books.

Glover, D. 2010. "The Corporate Shaping of GM Crops as a Technology for the Poor." *Journal of Peasant Studies* 37 (1): 67–90.

Good Jobs First. 2015. "Accountable USA—Hawaii." Accessed 20 September 2015. http://www.goodjobsfirst.org/states/hawaii.

Goodyear-Ka'ōpua, N, I. Hussey, and E. Wright, eds. 2014. *A Nation Rising: Hawaiian Movements for Life, Land, and Sovereignty*. Durham, NC: Duke University Press.

Gordon, U. 2008. *Anarchy Alive!: Anti-authoritarian Politics from Practice to Theory*. London: Pluto Press.

Harvey, D. 2003. *The New Imperialism*. Oxford: Oxford University Press.

Hauter, W. 2012. *Foodopoly: The Battle Over the Future of Food and Farming in America*. New York: The New Press.

Henkin, D., and I. Moriwake. 2013. "Petition Regarding Waimea River. Before the Hawaii State Commission on Water Resources." Accessed 19 September 2015. http://earthjustice.org/sites/default/files/files/WaimeaRiverFlowPetition.pdf.

Herbig, P., and H. Kramer. 1994. "The Potential for High Tech in Hawai'i." *Social Process in Hawai'i* 35: 58–70.

Hervey, T. 2012. "Boss GMO." *Honolulu Weekly*, January 4. Accessed 18 April 2015. http://honoluluweekly.com/cover/2012/01/boss-gmo/.

Higa, M. 2012. "Audit of the Department of Taxation's Administrative Oversight of High-Technology Business Investment and Research Activities Tax Credits." Report No. 12-05. Honolulu: State of Hawaii Office of the Auditor.

Hofschneider, A. 2014. "Federal Judge Invalidates Kauai's Anti-GMO Law." *Civil Beat*, August 25. Accessed 20 September 2015. http://www.civilbeat.com/2014/08/court-declares-invalid-kauai-ordinance-regulating-gmos-pesticides/.

Hofschneider, A. 2015. "After 2 Years, Hawaii Still Won't Enforce Pesticide Disclosure Law." *Civil Beat*, March 23. Accessed 20 September 2015. http://www.civilbeat.com/2015/03/after-2-years-hawaii-still-wont-enforce-pesticide-disclosure-law/?utm_medium=email&utm_source=users&utm_campaign=morning_beat.

Holt-Gimenez, E., and R. Patel, eds. 2012. *Food Rebellions: Crisis and the Hunger for Justice*. Oakland: Food First Books.

Hooser, G. 2015. "Trick or Treat? The Good Neighbor Program—A Masquerade of Disclosure." *GaryHooser's Blog*, October 9. Accessed 1 November 2015. https://garyhooser.wordpress.com/2015/10/09/trick-or-treat-the-good-neighbor-program-a-masquerade-of-disclosure/.

Horne, G. 2011. *Fighting in Paradise: Labor Unions, Racism, and Communists in the making of Modern Hawai'i*. Honolulu: University of Hawai'i Press.

Howard, P. 2009. "Visualizing Consolidation in the Global Seed Industry: 1996–2008." *Sustainability* 1 (4): 1266–1287.

ISB (Information Systems for Biotechnology). 2015. "Sponsored by the USDA." Accessed 15 August 2015. http://www.nbiap.vt.edu/.

James, C. 2014. *Global Status of Commercialized Biotech/GM Crops: 2014*. ISAAA Brief No. 49. Ithaca, NY: ISAAA.

Jasanoff, S. 2005. *Designs on Nature*. Princeton, NJ: Princeton University Press.

Jervis, G., and K. Smith. 2013. "Presentation by Plaintiffs' Attorneys in Lawsuit by Waimea, Kaua'i Residents Against Pioneer, DuPont." July 13. Accessed 11 March 2015. http://vimeo.com/70580803.

JFFSG (Joint Fact Finding Study Group). 2016. *Pesticide Use by Large Agribusiness On Kaua'i*. Prepared by Accord 3.0 Network. Accessed 1 June 2016. http://www.accord3.com/pg1000.cfm.

Jones, C., and A. M. Murtola. 2012. "Entrepreneurship, Crisis, Critique." In *Handbook on Organization and Entrepreneurship*, edited by D. Hjorth, 116–133. Cheltenham: Edward Elgar.

Kameʻeleihiwa, L. 1992. *Native Land and Foreign Desires*. Honolulu: Bishop Museum Press.

Kanehe, L. 2014. "Kūʻē Mana Māhele: The Hawaiian Movement to Resist Biocolonialism". In *A Nation Rising: Hawaiian Movements for Life, Land, and Sovereignty*, edited by N. Goodyear-Kaʻōpua, I. Hussey and E. Wright, 331–353. North Carolina: Duke University Press.

Kanehe, J., and J. Mardfin. 1987. *The Sugar Industry in Hawaii: An Action Plan*. Report No. 9. Honolulu: State of Hawaii Legislative Reference Bureau.

Kauai County Council Bill 2546. Relating to Real Property Taxes. Introduced May 28, 2014. Lihue, Hawaii.

Kent, N. 1993. *Hawai'i: Islands Under the Influence*. Honolulu: University of Hawai'i Press.

Kent, N. 1994. "The End of the American Age of Abundance: Whither Hawai'i?" *Social Process in Hawai'i* 35: 179–194.

Kloppenburg, J. 2004. *First The Seed: The Political Economy of Plant Biotechnology*. Madison, WI: University of Wisconsin Press.

Kloppenburg, J. 2010. "Seed Sovereignty: The Promise of Open Source Biology." In *Food Sovereignty: Reconnecting Food, Nature and Community*, edited by A. Desmarais, H. Wittman and N. Wiebe, 152–167. Nova Scotia: Fernwood Publishing.

Letman, J. 2013. "Micronesians in Hawaii Face Uncertain Future." *Aljazeera*, October 3. Accessed 11 March 2015. http://www.aljazeera.com/humanrights/2013/10/micronesians-hawaii-face-uncertain-future-201310191535637288.html.

Loudat, T., and P. Kasturi. 2013. *Hawai'i's Seed Crop Industry: Current and Potential Economic and Fiscal Contributions*. Sponsored by Hawaii Crop Improvement Association and Hawaii Farm Bureau Federation. Accessed 11March 2015. http://www.hciaonline.com/hawaiis-seed-crop-industry-current-and-potential-economic-and-fiscal-contributions/.

MacLennan, C. 2014. *Sovereign Sugar: Industry and Environment in Hawai'i*. Honolulu: University of Hawai'i Press.

Machara, E. 2007. *Agribusiness Development Corporation: Revisited*. Report No. 3. Honolulu: State of Hawaii Legislative Reference Bureau.

Magdoff, F., J. Foster, and F. Buttel, eds. 2000. *Hungry for Profit: The Agribusiness Threat to Farmers, Food, and the Environment*. New York: NYU Press.

Marx, K. 1992. *Capital*. Vol. 1. London: Penguin Classics.

Mazzucato, M. 2013. *The Entrepreneurial State: Debunking Public Vs. Private Sector Myths*. London: Anthem Press.

McAfee, K. 2003. "Neoliberalism on the Molecular Scale: Economic and Genetic Reductionism in Biotechnology Battles." *Geoforum* 34 (2): 203–219.

McCarthy, J., and S. Prudham. 2004. "Neoliberal Nature and the Nature of Neoliberalism." *Geoforum* 35 (3): 275–283.

Misalucha, B. 2015. "Pesticides Have Wide-Ranging Benefits." *Star Advertiser*, February 22. Accessed 12 March 2015. http://www.staradvertiser.com/s?action=login&f=y.

Mitra, M. 2014. "Could Small, Biodiverse Farms Help Hawaii Grow Enough Food to Feed Itself?" *Grist*, June 19. Accessed 20 September 2015. http://grist.org/food/could-small-biodiverse-farms-help-hawaii-grow-enough-food-to-feed-itself/.

Mortensen, D., F. Egan, B. Maxwell, M. Ryan, and R. Smith. 2012. "Navigating a Critical Juncture for Sustainable Weed Management." *BioScience* 62 (1): 75–84.

Moss, D. 2013. "Competition, Intellectual Property Rights, and Transgenic Seed." *South Dakota Law Review* 58: 543–559.

Newell, P., and D. Glover. 2003. "Business and Biotechnology: Regulation and the Politics of Influence." In *Agribusiness and Society: Corporate Responses to Environmentalism, Market Opportunities and Public Regulation*, edited by K. Jansen and S. Vellema, 200–231. London: Zed Books.

Newfield, C. 2008. *Unmaking the Public University: The Forty-Year Assault on the Middle Class*. Cambridge, MA: Harvard University Press.

Okamura, J. 2008. *Ethnicity and Inequality in Hawai'i*. Philadelphia: Temple University Press.

Ordinance 960. Kaua'i County Code 1987, Chapter 22, Article 23. Accessed 2 February 2014. http://qcode.us/codes/kauaicounty/revisions/960.pdf.

Osorio, J. 2002. *Dismembering Lāhui: A History of the Hawaiian Nation to 1887*. Honolulu: University of Hawai'i Press.

Pala, C. 2015. "Pesticides in Paradise: Hawaii's Spike in Birth Defects Puts Focus on GM Crops." *The Guardian*, August 23. Accessed 20 September 2015. http://www.theguardian.com/us-news/2015/aug/23/hawaii-birth-defects-pesticides-gmo.

Panitch, L., and S. Gindin. 2012. *The Making of Global Capitalism*. London: Verso Books.

Petranek, L. 2001. "Will the Task Masters of the New Economy Please Stand Up!." *Social Process in Hawaii* 40: 1–35.

Plasch, B. 1981. *Hawaii's Sugar Industry: Problems, Outlook, and Urban Growth Issues*. Honolulu: Hawaii State Department of Planning and Economic Development.

Ramones, I. 2014. "The True Cost of Hawaii's Military." *Hawaii Independent*, September 11. Accessed 20 September 2015. http://hawaiiindependent.net/story/the-true-cost-of-hawaiis-militarization.

Robinson, W., and J. Harris. 2000. "Towards a Global Ruling Class? Globalization and the Transnational Capitalist Class." *Science & Society* 64 (1): 11–54.

Rohter, I. 1992. *A Green Hawaii: Sourcebook for Development Alternatives*. Honolulu: Nā Kāne o ka Malo Press.

Ross, E. 1998. *The Malthus Factor: Poverty, Politics and Population in Capitalist Development*. London: Zed Books.

Sahagun, L. 1994. "Bitter End to Hawaii's 'Sugar Life.'" *Los Angeles Times*, March 19. Accessed 11 March 2015. http://articles.latimes.com/1994-03-19/news/mn-35842_1_cane-fields.

Sell, S. 2011. "TRIPS was Never Enough: Vertical Forum Shifting, FTAS, ACTA, and TPP." *Journal of Intellectual Property Law* 18: 447–478.

Seo, K. 1986. *A Study of the Economic Viability of Alternative Uses for Bagasse, Agricultural Land, and Sugar in Hawaii*. Honolulu: Hawaii Sugar Planters Association.

Shaw, A. 2016a. "Gendering in Seed-Agrichemical Companies: Workforce Composition, Divisions of Labour and Corporate Policies". PhD thesis, London School of Economics.

Shaw, A. 2016b. "*TechnoPlantations: Gender, Race and Labour in Hawai'i's Seed Production Economies*". Unpublished paper, London School of Economics.

Silva, N. 2004. *Aloha Betrayed: Native Hawaiian Resistance to American Colonialism*. Durham, NC: Duke University Press.

Smith, E., D. Azoulay, and B. Tuncak. 2015. *Lowest Common Denominator: How the Proposed EU–US Trade Deal Threatens to Lower Standards of Protection from Toxic Pesticides*. Washington, D.C.: Center for International Environmental Law.

Southern Poverty Law Center. 2013. *Close to Slavery: Guestworker Programs in the United States*. 2013 ed. Accessed 11 March 2015. http://www.splcenter.org/get-informed/publications/close-to-slavery-guestworker-programs-in-the-united-states.

Sproat, D. 2010. "Where Justice Flows Like Water: The Moon Court's Role in Illuminating Hawai'i Water Law." *University of Hawai'i Law Review* 33: 537–579.

Srinivasan, C. 2003. "Concentration in Ownership of Plant Variety Rights: Some Implications for Developing Countries." *Food Policy* 28 (5): 519–546.

USDA (United States Department of Agriculture). 2015. "Pacific Region—Hawaii Seed Crops." National Agricultural Statistics Service, released May 5.

Voosen, P. 2011. "King Corn Takes Root in Hawaii." *New York Times*, August 22. Accessed 19 September 2015. http://www.nytimes.com/gwire/2011/08/22/22greenwire-king-corn-takes-root-in-hawaii-28466.html?pagewanted=all.

Witeck, J. 2001. "Public Policy in Hawaii: Globalism's Neoliberal Embrace." *Social Process in Hawaii* 40: 36–68.

Wood, E. 2002. *The Origin of Capitalism: A Longer View*. London: Verso.

Wood, E. 2003. *Empire of Capital*. London: Verso.

Yap, B. 2013. "Against the Grain?" *Mana Magazine*, July/August. Accessed 2 February 2014. http://www.welivemana.com/articles/against-grain.

Index

Abbott, Isabella 19
abstention from alcohol 36–7, 45–6
abuse of ice 44
access analysis 104–6
access theory 104–5
accumulation by dispossession 164
ADC *see* Agribusiness Development Corporation
affluent habitus of whiteness 60–61
aftermath of US annexation 97–8
age of ice importation 35–57
agrarian imaginaries 60, 62–3, 72, 77–8, 83
Agribusiness Development Corporation 172–3
agrochemical oligopoly 161–88; +seed+biotechnology oligopoly 163–5; colonial plantations 165–8; conclusion 181–2; diversifying the plantation 168–71; fortress of necessity 179–81; introduction 161–3; locally subsidized plantations 171–6; plantation landscape 177–9
ahupua'a system 2, 63–4, 95–6, 115
'āina 3–4
"aloha spirit" 13
American Community Survey 140
American processed food 26
American settlement 1–4, 11–12, 18, 75; *see also* annexation
analysis tools 141–3
ancestral cuisines 21–4
ancestral immigration 146
ancestral practices 93, 105–6, 114
Anderson, E.N. 16
Annales School 16
annexation 1–4, 11–12, 18, 28, 37–8, 75, 93–8; treaty of 37–8
Annual Report of the Chief Justice 44–5

anthrax 67
anti-farmer protests 77–8
anti-liquor associations 46
Ardoin, N.M. 141
aristocratic Hawaiian cuisine 23
Armelagos, George 21
Atlantic Slave Trade 20
authenticity 17

"bad" milk 67–8
Bartlett, Virginia 17
Bartlett's test of sphericity 143
BASF 163, 175, 182
Bayer 163
"Bayonet Constitution" 1887 172
Bazore, Katherine 26
Beamer, Kamanamaikalani 115
Beeton, Isabella Mary 43–4
Beeton's Book of Household Management 43–4
benefits of farming 137–9
benefits privatization 172–4, 180
benefits vs. burdens 177–9
Bentley, Amy 2–3
Bentley, Jeremy 20
Berdegue, J. 143
Berkes, Fikret 119
"Big Five" sugar corporations 166
Big Island 62, 75, 77–8, 81–3; protests 77–8
Big Island Dairy 71, 77, 79
biomass depletion 93, 106
biophysical environment 92–3
biotechnology 77–8
Bishop, Bernice Pauahi 116, 172
Blue Hawaii 27
bootlegging 41–2, 44, 47
bosses vs. workers 177–9
bounty of *terroir* 16–17
Brachiaria mutica (California grass) 117–18

INDEX

Brewbaker, James 167–8
Brown, Marilyn 45–6
Bush, George 167
Buy Local, It Matters branding program 72

California grass 117–18, 120–23; clearing 120–23
The Californian 37
"canoe foods" 28
carbon footprints 60
caring for the land 3–4
Carvalho, Bernard 80, 171
Castle, Samuel 179
Catholic cuisine 22
cattle production 66–70
Cayetano, Ben 170
CBSF *see* community-based subsistence fishing
CEDS *see* Comprehensive Economic Development Strategy
centralization 94, 100, 119
Chakrabarty v. *Diamond* 163
Chang, K.C. 16
changes in farming practice 155–6; classic farmers 155; hobby farmers 155; leisure farmers 155; progressive farmers 156; subsistence farmers 155
changes in land tenure 93, 96–7
changing farmer population 155–6
Chinese planters 116–17
Choy, Sam 28
classic farmer type 144, 149–50, 152, 154–5
clearing California grass 120–23
clearing space 120–24
climate change 71–2, 92–3, 106
Clinton, Bill 28
closures 140, 168
Cloverleaf Dairy 71
coastal fisheries *see* customary access; near shore fisheries
cocktails 35–8, 46–7; *see also* ice importation
coffee production 139–40
cohesion 105
"cold water hymns" 37
College of Tropical Agriculture and Human Resources 174–5
collusion 177
colonial gaze 69
colonial plantations 165–8
colonialism 96–7, 131–2
Columbian Exchange 20
commercialization 174

commodification of seed 163–5
communication breakdown 130–31
community outreach 177
community-based subsistence fishing 105–6
community-supported agriculture 60, 71–2
Compact of Free Association 178
Comprehensive Economic Development Strategy 72
contextualizing "local" 1–9
control of fresh water 94
controlling food locally 91–112
controversy over dairy 78–81
Cook, James 23–4, 63–4, 139
coral bleaching 106
coral reef fisheries 93–4; *see also* customary access
Corntassel, Jeff 119
corporate "local washing" 61
cosmopolitanism 44
cost of living 2, 13, 166–7, 179
creating local food 13–19
Creole 2, 12, 14, 16–19
Cronbach's alpha 142
Crosby, Alfred 20
Crosby, Patricia 19
Cross-Cultural Trade on World History 20
CSA *see* community-supported agriculture
CTAHR *see* College of Tropical Agriculture and Human Resources
cuisine and empire 22–7
Cuising and Empire 12, 21–2
culinary cosmos theory 21, 23
culinary dissemination 21
culinary evolution 12
culinary future of Hawai'i 27–9
cultural bequest values 105
cultural construct of kalo 131
cultural ecosystem services 105
cultural survival 2
cultural ties: perpetuation 100–104
cultural traditions 113–35; ahupua'a system 115; clearing space, growing kalo 120–24; conclusion 131–2; embodying the Hāloa triad 117–19; grinding/milling kalo 127–9; He'e'ia Uli transformed 115–17; introduction 114; Mahuahua 'Ai o Hoi management strategies 129–31; preparing kalo for poi 124–7; theory and methods 119–20
Curtin, Philip 20

INDEX

customary access 91–112; history of near shore fisheries governance 95–8; implications for accessing near shore fisheries 104–6; introduction 91–5; perpetuating social/cultural ties 100–104; study site 98–100
Cutrell, Peck 38, 42, 44, 46

Daily Bulletin 69
dairy protests 77–8
dairy's decline 59–90
Dancing on Our Turtle's Back 124
DAR *see* Division of Aquatic Resources
Datta, As 79
David, Elizabeth 16
Davidson, Alan 16, 18–19
Daws, Gavan 41, 45
decline of dairy 59–90; conclusion 81–3; explaining preferences for local food 71–6; historical shifts in food production 63–6; history of dairy 66–71; introduction 59–63; value of local milk 76–81
Democratic Party "revolution" 166
demographic change in Halele'a moku 99–100
Department of Agriculture 72, 77–8, 177, 180
Department of Land and Natural Resources 97
dependent economy 2, 61, 63–5, 71–2, 74–5, 79
deregulatory approaches 167
description of surround net fishing 99
development of farmer typology 143
development of multifunctional agriculture scorecard 141–3
disconnect 129–30
disruptions to food supply lines 71–2
dissent 36
diversified agriculture 170–71
diversifying the plantation 168–71
diversity 94–5
Division of Aquatic Resources 98, 102–4
"doing agriculture well" 149
Dow 163, 167, 175, 181–2
drought resistance 163
drunkenness 44–5
Dunlap, R.E. 141
DuPont 163, 167, 175, 183
dynamics of production intensification 114

Earthjustice 173
eating "local" 1–9
economic change in Halele'a moku 99–100
economic diversification 168, 170–71, 179–80
"Elite Ice Cream Parlors" 69
elitism 2
emancipatory ethos 162–3
embodying Hāloa triad 117–19
Emmert, Paul 42
empowerment options 150–51
environmental awareness 138
environmental degradation 59–60, 79–80
environmental friendliness 75, 77
Environmental Protection Agency 175
environmental resilience 131–2
environmental significance 79
EPA *see* Environmental Protection Agency
Escobar, G. 143
ethnic cuisine 26
ethnic hierarchies 2–3
ethnicized plantation hierarchies 178
explaining preferences for local food 71–6
expression of values 149–50
extraction of raw materials 63–4

Farb, Peter 21
farmer typology 137–59; conclusion 155–6; introduction 137–9; methods 141–3; results 143–55; site history 139–40
Federal Clean Water Act 172
Ferdandez, Doreen 18–19
First Hawaiian Bank 168
fisheries tenure 95
fishing rights 91–8
fluid milk 66–71, 79
Food of China 16
Food in Chinese Culture 16
Food Commission 67–8
food culture 16
Food, Culture and Society 19
Food and Foodways 19–20
food importation 2, 71–2, 75, 91–5
Food of Paradise 4–5, 12, 18–19
food politics 59–63
food processing 15, 20–21, 91–5
food security 91–5, 104–6
food system control mechanisms 106
fortress of necessity 179–81
Fortunio 39

INDEX

free trade 181
"Fresh Moloka'i Butter" 67
fresh water 18, 94, 106, 114, 124, 129–30, 173–5
funding 129–31

Garden Isle 78–81
GE *see* genetic engineering
gender divisions in cuisines 23
gendered ideologies 42–4
genetic engineering 5–6, 28, 74–5, 77–8, 82, 163–7, 174–6
gentrification 179
geographic isolation 75, 93
Gindin, Sam 164
global capitalism 2, 65–6
global culinary change model 19–22
"global ruling class" 177
Global South 63
globalization 77
Godey's Lady's Book 43
Good Jobs First research center 173
Goodyear-Ka'ōpua, Noelani 63, 75–6
Gourmet magazine 19
governance of near shore fisheries 95–8
Great Depression 97, 139–40
great flood 1969 115–16
Great Mahele 96–7, 102–3, 115–16
Greenwell, H.N. 66
grinding kalo 127–9
growing kalo 120–24
Guthman, Julie 60

Hackfeld, Henry 49
Halele'a, Kaua'i 98–100; economic/demographic change 99–100; surround net fishing 99
Hāloa triad 5, 117–19
Hamilton, Bill 19
haoles 14, 24–5
Harriet T. Bartlett 40
Hart-Cellar Immigration and Nationality Act 1965 17
harvesting rights 93–7, 99, 102–3
Hau'ofa, Epeli 63
Hawaii 5-0 27
Hawai'i Community Development Authority 117, 119–20
Hawai'i Dairy Farms 79–81
Hawai'i as epicenter of GE crops 161–88
Hawai'i Farm Bureau 171, 177
Hawai'i Green Growth Initiative 72
Hawai'i State Plan 72
Hawaiian Gazette 35

Hawaiian Kingdom 95; land tenure 95–6; near shore fisheries tenure 96
Hawaiian Milk Act 70–71
Hawaiian and Pacific Foods 26
Hawaiian Star 67–8
Hawaiian Sugar Planters' Association 168
Hawai'i's place in food history 11–33
HCDA *see* Hawai'i Community Development Authority
HDF *see* Hawai'i Dairy Farms
health inequities 59–60
healthy French fries 170
He'e'ia Wetlands 113–35
Heeren, Edward 40
hierarchical cuisines 22–3
historical shifts in food production 63–6
historical significance 79
history of dairy 66–71
history of food in Hawai'i 11–33
history of near shore fisheries governance 95–8; changes following US annexation 97–8; changes in land tenure 96–7; land tenure 95; near shore fisheries tenure 96
hobby farmer type 144, 149–50, 152–5
hō'ihi 91–5, 100–101
homegrown cuisine 11–33; creating local food 13–19; culinary future 27–9; introduction 11–12; model for global culinary change 19–22; rethinking Hawai'i's culinary history 22–7
homegrown theory 12, 17
Honolulu 35–57; ice importation 35–57
Honolulu Advertiser 18–19
Honolulu Dairymen's Association 68
Honolulu Sailor's Home Society 46
Honolulu Temperance League 46
hukilau 91–5, 99; *see also* surround net fishing
humeral theory 21
hunger 2–3, 14, 59–60

ice importation 35–57
ice-cream 42–4, 50–51, 68–9
"if the barge doesn't come" mentality 75–6
immaterial benefits 105
immigration 2–3, 12–17, 26, 96–7, 146, 152–4; in farming populations 152–4

INDEX

impacts of farming 137–9
imperialism 178–9, 181–2
implications for access in near shore fisheries 104–6; access, planning, policy change 105–6; access theory 104–5; local control of food systems 106
importance of ancestral practices 106
importing ice 35–57
income from farming 150–51
indigenous displacement 3–4
indigenous planting 131–2
indigenous rights movement 28
industrialization 2, 181
inevitability 179–81
intellectual property 167
intensity of production 80–81
introduction of cattle 66
investment capitalism 78–81
inviting ability 101–2
irrigation 23, 65–6, 101, 114–16, 120–21, 173
Islamic cuisine 22
Island Fresh branding program 72

Jaffee, Kelila 3
James Beard award 4
Jones, Cyrus W. 42
Journal of Food and Society 19
Journal of World History 20
Judd, Gerrit P. 46
Judd, Sybil Augusta 46
just compensation 97

Ka Hae Hawai'i 50
Kaiser–Maier–Olkin test 143
Kalākaua, David 51
kalo 120–29; grinding/milling 127–9; growing 120–24; preparing for poi 124–7
kamaainas 18, 24–7
Kamehamehas 23–4
Kānaka Maoli 3, 41, 44–6, 48–50, 63, 76, 113–35
Kaplan, Steve 19
Kaua'i 81–3, 91–112; local control of food on 91–112
Kaua'i Farm Bureau 80–81
Kawailoa Development 80
Kekeha Sugar 173
Kelly, Marion 114
Kent, N.J. 65–6, 166
King David Kalakaua 23–5
King Kamehameha I 66
King Kamehameha III 36–8, 42, 44, 50–51, 96–7

"King Sugar" 165
KMO test *see* Kaiser–Maier–Olkin test
Knudsen, Valdemar 66
Kohala Center 155
Kokobun, Russell 77, 180
Kona Coffee 139–40
konohiki 91–105, 116
Ko'olaupoko Hawaiian Civic Club 117
kuleana 64, 91–5, 100–105
kūpuna 95, 103, 115–17, 129–30
Kuykendall, Ralph 38

LA Times 19
labor mobilization 101–2, 104–5
lack of funding 129–31
land dispossession 82–3
land privatization 116, 139–40, 165–6
land tenure 95, 139–40
landscape of plantations 177–9
leisure farmer type 144, 149–50, 152–5
Lewers, C.H. 39, 48–50
Lingle, Linda 28
"local but not in my backyard" 78–81
local control of fishing 91–112
local control of food systems 106
"Local Food" 11–33; *see also* homegrown cuisine
"local" milk politics 59–90
"local washing" 61
local-level access management 105–6
locally subsidized plantations 171–6
"locavore" movement 61
luau cuisine 25–6
Lucas, Paul F. Nahoa 115
Lukens, Ashley 3
luxury items 35–6, 47–8, 50

MacFarlane, Henry 39
McGregor, Davianna Pōmaika'i 116
McNeill, William 20
Māhuahua 'Ai o Hoi project 118–32; management strategies 129–31
maintaining values 100–106; inviting ability 101–2; respectful reciprocity 100–101; responsibility 102–4
maintenance of nets 102–4
management strategies for Māhuahua 'Ai o Hoi 129–31
market regulation 138
Maui Home Demonstration Council 15
MEA *see* Millennium Economic Assessment

INDEX

mechanisms of access 94–5
"melting pot" 2, 17
Merchants' Exchange 37–8, 42, 46–7
"merger mania" 167
Meyers' Dairy 67
MFA *see* multifunctional agriculture
military incursions 165
milk consumption 66–7; *see also* decline of dairy
milk importation 61–2
Millennium Economic Assessment 137–8
milling kalo 127–9
Mintz, Sidney 42
missionary proselytizing 165, 172
model for global culinary change 19–22
moderation 44
modern cuisines 21–4
modernization 181
monitoring pollutants 173
monocropping 4, 75, 166, 168, 181–2
monopoly capital 167
Monsanto occupation of Hawai'i 78, 161–88
morality 43
motivations for farming 147–9, 154–5
Mountain Apple brand 76
multi-ethnic society 2–4, 11–12, 16, 116, 166
multifunctional agriculture 137–8, 141–3, 147–9, 154–6; practices 147–9; scorecard 141–3, 154–5

national dairy intensification 71
natural competitive advantage 161–3
natural disasters 93
naturalized cuisine 11–33
Nature Conservancy of Hawai'i 117
near shore fisheries 95–100, 104–6; governance 95–8; implications for access 104–6
necessity 179–81
neoliberalism 181
New Day Plan 72
New Ecological Paradigm 141, 150
New Economy 168–70
New York Times 171
New Zealand-based pastoral model 79
NIMBYism 78–81
non-native plant proliferation 117
nutrition 64

Obama, Michelle 59–60
observing change 11–12
ocean acidification 106
O'Connor, Kaori 3
Office of Hawaiian Affairs 28
'ohana 63–4, 100–104
Okinawan andagi 13
Old World Encounters 20
oligarchic control 65
oligopoly of agrochemical+seed+biotechnology 163–5; *see also* agrochemical oligopoly
Oliveira, Katrina-Ann 114, 123–4
Olney, Richard 16
O'Meara, James 37–8, 50–51
Omidyar, Pierre 79, 81
On Persephone's Isle 17
oppression 2
options for empowerment 150–51
oral histories 95
Organic Act 1900 97
organization of research 141
Ornellas, Jerry 80
Ottoman Empire 24
overfishing 93
owner-occupation 99–100
Oxford Symposium on Food and Cookery 16–17

Pacific Commercial Advertiser 44, 67
Page, C.L. 155
Pākī, Abner Kahoʻoheiheipahu 116
Pannell, D.J. 138–9
Paradise Hawaiian Style 27
pasteurization 76
pathways to MFA practice 147–9
Paty, John 47
Pearl, Eden 77
Peluso, N.L. 95
Penal Code of the Hawaiian Islands 44
perpetuating ties through surround net fishing 100–104
personal values 138
Petits Propos Culinaires 16
Pfluger, J. Charles 49
Pickles and Pretzels 17
pidgin *see* Creole
place of Hawai'i in food history 11–33
placemaking 2
Plagues and People 20
planning 105–6
plantation diversification 168–71
plantation economy 115–17
plantation landscape 177–9

INDEX

"plate lunches" 14–15, 17, 29
poi production 23–5, 113–35
policy change 105–6
politics of irrelevance 182
politics of "local" milk 59–90
Polynesian Voyaging Society 28
The Polynesian 38–41, 48, 67
possibility of something different 181–2
powdered milk 71
pre-contact Hawai'i 63–4, 71, 93–4, 96–7, 114, 139–40, 162–3
preferences for local food 71–6
preparing kalo for poi 124–7
preservation efforts 81
Presley, Elvis 27
privatization of benefits 172–4, 180
privatization of land 116, 139–40, 165–6
production of poi 113–35
progressive farmer type 144–5, 147, 150–51, 153–6
prohibition 36–7, 44–6
propagated management 119–20
property rights 104
public food 11–33; *see also* homegrown cuisine
public health 2–3
Pursuit of Power 20

racial divisions 41–5, 47–50, 60
re-localization 59–63, 71, 75–6, 81–3
re-planting 119, 131
Reagan, Ronald 167
reciprocity 105
reflections from the field 120–29; clearing space, growing kalo 120–24; grinding/milling kalo 127–9; preparing kalo for poi 124–7
regenerative powers 118–19, 131
religions of salvation 22
research theory 119–20
residency 152–4
resilience 131–2
resistance 2, 119, 131–2
respectful reciprocity 100–101
responsibility 102–4
restoration of kalo farming 119–20, 129–32
restructuring food production systems 181–2
results of survey 143–55; farmer types and trends 146–54; farmer typology 143–6; summary of results 154–5

resurgence 119, 124–5
rethinking culinary history 22–7
rhetoric of local food 82, 166
Ribot, J.C. 95
"right to farm" argument 81
risk perception 138
Ritte, Walter 170
"rock fever" 13
Roundup™ 163–4
Rozin, Elizabeth 21
runoff 79–80
Russian American Commercial Ice Company 40

sacrificial cuisines 21–4
Safeway 71
sandalwood trade 64
Sato, Charlene 18
Saturday Press 49
Savoring the Past 16
Sea Bird 37–8
seasonal work 177–8
seeds of discontent 77–8
self-interest 80
self-reliance 71
self-sufficiency 4–5, 28, 61–5, 71–8, 82, 105–6, 140, 155–6
"sense ability" 124
sense of place 138, 141–2, 145–50
settler colonialism 4, 63–4
"shave ice" 36
Shaw, A. 178–9
shifts in food production 63–6
Simpson, Leanne 124
Smith, Randall 46–7
snowy mountaineers 35–57
social cohesion 105
social good 81–3
social justice 60–61
social pressures 138
social relationships 103–5
social ties: perpetuation 100–104
sociocultural relationships 105
soda waters 35–57
soft power 24
something different 181–2
South Kona 137–40
sovereignty 75–6
soy pollination 178
SPAM musubi 4, 14, 17, 27
spawning times 94
spiritual nourishment 115–16
Stainbeck Wilson, Jonathan 43
standard of living 63–4
State Constitution 1978 65
stifling values 150–51

INDEX

study methods 141–3; analysis tools 141–3; development of farmer typology 143; surveys/organization 141
subsistence farmer type 145, 147–8, 151–2, 154–5
sugar oligarchy 161–88
Sunday Advertiser 67
Superfund sites 174–5
Surfrider Foundation 79
surround net fishing 91–5, 99–104; perpetuating ties 100–104
surveys 141
sustainability 3–4, 59–60, 74–9
sustaining local control 91–112
Swan & Clifford 39–42, 48
Syngenta 163, 167, 175, 182

"talk stories" 120
taste for ice 35–6; *see also* ice importation
tax credit systems 173–4
Taylor Simeti, Mary 17
teetotalism 36–7, 45–6
tension within local food paradigm 77–8
Territorial Planning Board 66
Thanksgiving 21
themes of farmer typology 143–6; classic farmers 144; hobby farmers 144; leisure farmers 144; progressive farmers 144–5; subsistence farmers 145
theocratic cuisines 21–4
Thompson, Fred W. 40
Thrum's Hawaiian Annual 39
Thurston, Lorrin 45
tobacco farming 124–5
tourism 28, 75, 168–9, 179–82
"trade secrets" 167, 176
Trader Vic's 27
traditional farmer type 145, 155
Traditions and Encounters 20
traditions with food 113–35
transformation of He'e'ia uli 115–17

transgressive space 43
trends in farming 146–54; farmer values 149–50; income 150–51; pathways to practice 147–9; residency 152–4
Tudor, Frederic 39–40
types of farming 137–59
types of value 149–50
typology of Hawai'ian farmers 137–59

Ulupono Initiative 78–81
University of Hawaii Press 19–20
urbanization 93
US annexation 97–8
US intervention 163–6

Valbuena, D. 143
Valenzuela, Hector 168
value of local milk 76–81; NIMBYism 78–81; seeds of discontent 77–8
values 149–50
Vancouver, George 66
voluntary pesticide reporting 175–6
vulnerability 2, 71–2, 75, 93, 179

well-being 72
whaling 37, 41, 64, 165
Wheaton, Barbara 16
Whitesides Dairy 77
why farmers are farming 137–59
Wiley, Iris 19
Wong, Alan 28
Wong, Lori 28
Wood, E. 181
World Trade Organization 164
World War II 27, 67, 69, 97, 166
A World History 20
WTO *see* World Trade Organization

Yamaguchi, Roy 28–9

Zeldin, Theodore 16
Zemon Davis, Natalie 16
Zip Pac 14